# THE GOOD, THE BAD, AND THE UGLY
# PHILADELPHIA FLYERS

# THE GOOD, THE BAD, AND THE UGLY
# PHILADELPHIA FLYERS

## HEART-POUNDING, JAW-DROPPING, AND GUT-WRENCHING
## MOMENTS IN PHILADELPHIA FLYERS HISTORY

Adam Kimelman

TRIUMPH
BOOKS

Library of Congress Cataloging-in-Publication Data
Kimelman, Adam, 1975–
    The good, the bad, and the ugly Philadelphia Flyers: heart-pounding, jaw-dropping, and gut-wrenching moments in Philadelphia Flyers history / Adam Kimelman.
        p. cm.
    ISBN-13: 978-1-60078-021-9
    ISBN-10: 1-60078-021-0
    1. Philadelphia Flyers (Hockey team)—History. I. Title.
    GV848.P48K56 2006
    796.962'640974811—dc22

                                    2008029116

This book is available in quantity at special discounts for your group or organization. For further information, contact:

**Triumph Books**
542 South Dearborn Street
Suite 750
Chicago, Illinois 60605
(312) 939–3330
Fax (312) 663–3557

Printed in U.S.A.
ISBN: 978-1-60078-021-9
Design by Patricia Frey
Editorial production by Prologue Publishing Services, LLC
All photos courtesy Getty Images unless otherwise noted

# CONTENTS

# FOREWORD

The good, the bad, and the ugly. Why would I be asked to write the foreword for such an important book chronicling the history of one of professional hockey's most storied franchises? I suppose if one were to assimilate my career with the Flyers as an analogy, I have been involved with all three.

By no means is that to suggest my career as a Flyer was of greater importance than anyone else who ever wore the orange and black, but I can attest to the importance and value placed on pulling on that sweater. I always felt, even before I arrived here—and certainly after I arrived—as though the Flyers organization should have been an Original Six franchise because of its rich tradition.

I also know why the Philadelphia Flyers are such a revered franchise, and as a player, why so many athletes want to play in this city, for this organization, and more importantly this ownership. Mr. Snider is the epitome of class, professionalism, philanthropy, and most importantly, leadership. Therein lies the secret to why Philadelphia is such a desired destination for free agents and players in general league-wide. Mr. Snider cares about this city (look at the facilities), the people of this city (just ask the kids involved in the Ed Snider Youth Hockey Foundation), and his players (just ask Joe Watson, Dave Schultz, Bob Kelly, Bernie Parent, Bob Clarke, and anybody else who ever played here). In a business that says owners owe the players nothing but a paycheck, those same people don't know Mr. Snider and his moral convictions.

So what is the good, the bad, and the ugly? Well, I will let the stories you will read here satisfy your fascination for the bad and the ugly; I will touch on only the good.

For me, the good is the people of Philadelphia. Some may believe I overstate my affection for Flyers fans, but I am very sincere when I say the people here salvaged my career. The joy of playing professional hockey climaxed for me in Philadelphia— always there for games and always there when the community asked for generous support of whatever the cause may be. There was and still is no other place I wanted to play than right here in front of the greatest fans in the world.

So please enjoy the following stories, insights, and memories as much as I enjoyed being a part of your history.

—Keith Primeau

# ACKNOWLEDGMENTS

The book you hold in your hands today wouldn't exist without the help and support of some very important people.

I came to the Flyers, and hockey in general, fairly late. I was in Hebrew school at M'Kor Shalom synagogue, and one of my classmates, Scott Fleishman, would bring to class a dozen and a half bagels from his father's store, The Bagel Shop, on Chapel Avenue in Cherry Hill. He also would bring in his tiny Sony Watchman, and an entire class, including our teacher, Mr. Pont, would gather around the five-inch screen to watch Flyers playoff games against the Penguins and Canadiens in 1989. I quickly was hooked by the speed and passion of players like Dave Poulin, Ron Sutter, Mark Howe, and Rick Tocchet, plus the seemingly psychotic netminder, Ron Hextall.

From there, I began watching more and playing with friends, and now I've moved on to writing about hockey for a living. And I consider it a life very well lived.

Thanks go to Michael Emmerich and the folks at Triumph Books for believing that I could pull off this project. There were many times I wasn't so sure myself. Prior to this book, the longest story I had ever written was a 35-page honors thesis my senior year of college. Hopefully this is a little more interesting.

I owe a tremendous debt of gratitude to all the people who gave their time to speak with me for the book: Ed Snider, Peter Luukko, Bob Clarke, Paul Holmgren, John Stevens, Terry Murray,

Kjell Samuelsson, Daniel Briere, Sami Kapanen, Simon Gagne, Tony Voce, Keith Primeau, Keith Jones, Gary Dornhoefer, Bernie Parent, Joe Watson, Bill Barber, Bob Kelly, Dave Poulin, Mark Howe, Tim Kerr, Ron Hextall, Dave Brown, Brian Propp, Brian Boucher, Russ Farwell, Al Morganti, Howard Eskin, Chuck Gormley, Rick Curran, John LeClair, Rod Brind'Amour, Jody Clarke, Lauren Hart, Brian Hart, Ken Hitchcock. Talking with all of them reinforced something I already knew—hockey people are the best people in sports, and sometimes just in general.

A number of research materials were hugely important to putting this book together, most notably Jay Greenberg's *Full Spectrum*, and *Walking Together Forever* by Jim Jackson, the current—and outstanding—voice of the Flyers.

Credit also goes to the Flyers' senior director of communications Zack Hill, who helped me jump through a month's worth of hoops to get that first interview with Mr. Snider (I blame Allen Iverson). Zack also was indispensable in helping me track down a few other Flyers of the past.

Peter Anson's outstanding website, FlyersHistory.net, provided box scores from every game in club history and also made for an invaluable resource.

Most of all, I have to thank my wife, Sheryl, who for more than a year put up with my writing this book while we both worked full-time and played parents to our beautiful daughter, Breanna. During the process, we also added a son, Logan.

I also have to thank you, the reader, for taking the time to pick through this tome. I hope you're entertained and educated, and if you like it, please encourage as many of your friends and family members to pick up a copy. My kids will need to go to college someday.

To quote the immortal Gene Hart: "Good night, and good hockey."

# THE BEGINNING

## BOBBY ORR AND THE NEW YORK RANGERS

Why would a book about the Philadelphia Flyers start with a reference to the Boston Bruins legend and arguably the Flyers' biggest rival?

Because if it weren't for the happy confluence of the Hall of Fame defenseman and two Rangers—goalie Gump Worsley and president Bill Jennings—just over 40 years ago, there might not be a hockey team in the City of Brotherly Love.

In the early 1960s Ed Snider wasn't the multimillionaire sports and entertainment mogul he is today.

Snider was living in Washington, D.C., where he co-owned a record company. In New York on business, Snider met up with a friend, Juggy Gayles, presumably to go out to dinner. Gayles had a different idea.

Recalls Snider, "He had seats at the old [Madison Square] Garden, and he said, 'Come on, my buddies and I are going to the game, and I'll take you.' I said, 'What game?' He said, 'Rangers and Montreal.' I said, 'What are you talking about?' That's how little I knew."

For Ed Snider, hockey was love at first sight. Actually, it was love for Worsley.

Growing up in Washington, Snider followed the Washington Redskins, and as a kid enjoyed the old Washington Senators, but he had never seen anything like pint-sized Gumper the goalie.

"Maybe it was the fact that he didn't look like an athlete or that he wasn't wearing a mask, I'm not sure," Snider said in *Full Spectrum*. "But I know I was fascinated with Worsley. I thought, 'This is the greatest spectator sport I've ever seen.'"

Not long after that, Snider's record company hit a bad patch, and he and his partner sold out.

In 1964 Snider, along with his brother-in-law, Earl Foreman, and one of Foreman's young law clients, developer Jerry Wolman, purchased the Philadelphia Eagles. Snider, who owned a 7 percent stake in the team, moved to Philadelphia to become the team's treasurer.

That winter Snider was in Boston on business when he went with friends to a Celtics-76ers NBA game. Who won was irrelevant; in the end, it was the city of Philadelphia that came out on top.

As Snider's group was leaving Boston Garden, Snider noticed a line at the ticket window. It was a remarkably long line for a late Sunday afternoon.

Recalls Snider, "I asked my friend, 'What is that line for?' And he said, 'It's for the hockey game tomorrow.' I said, 'Are they in the playoffs? Big rivalry?' He said no,they put a thousand seats on sale for every game, and people line up the night before to buy them. They're in last place, but it doesn't matter, the fans here just love hockey."

By 1965 Snider's main task was financing Wolman's dream home of a multipurpose stadium that could house his Eagles and the Philadelphia Phillies (Wolman also owned their home Connie Mack Stadium). The building was going to be erected on the south end of Broad Street, near the Philadelphia Navy Yard.

During a meeting with Bill Putnam, an executive with Morgan Guaranty Trust Company in New York—Putnam had helped set up the loan that allowed Wolman's group to buy the Eagles—Putnam told Snider he was leaving Morgan to move to Los Angeles and run Jack Kent Cooke's sports properties. Cooke was a minority owner of the Redskins and also owned the Los Angeles Lakers. He was planning on building a new home for his basketball team in suburban Inglewood, California. For a second tenant

# NEAR-SALE

The evolution of the Philadelphia Flyers slowly was proceeding when it nearly stopped cold. A pair of outside investors had approached Jerry Wolman and offered him $1 million for the franchise, with the money being split equally among the four prospective owners.

Jerry Schiff, Ed Snider's brother-in-law, agreed with Wolman to sell. But Snider and Bill Putnam said no sale, killing the deal.

"He [Wolman] thought hockey was going to fail, and he wanted to sell the franchise before we got started," recalls Snider. "I said no, so he got angry. He wanted to sell the franchise to people who wanted to move it to somewhere in New York."

Snider believes that decision led to Wolman firing him from the Eagles the night of the Flyers' home opener.

in his Fabulous Forum, Cooke had applied for a National Hockey League expansion franchise.

Snider was shocked. "I said, 'Wait, what did you say? They're expanding in the National Hockey League?' There was nothing in the papers here—the only story had been a six-paragraph blurb buried in the *Philadelphia Daily News*. Nobody knew anything. He said the National Hockey League is going to double in size, and he named a bunch of cities. I asked about Philadelphia, and he said, 'I'm sure Philadelphia would be one they would consider, but there's no arena, there's no anything.'"

While Putnam was explaining the NHL's grand plan to add six new teams, an earlier meeting with Philadelphia 76ers owner Ike Richman rebounded into Snider's mind. Richman had approached Snider about convincing Wolman to build a new home for his basketball team. The 76ers had been playing at Convention Hall, but he wanted a new, modern building. At the time, Snider had told Richman that the Eagles weren't in the arena-construction business.

Suddenly pieces of a puzzle were coming together in Snider's mind—the NHL's expansion, the growing population of

Philadelphia, the rapidly developing New Jersey suburbs, and an NBA team looking for a new building.

Snider was sure hockey would work in Philadelphia. He knew the passion of Philadelphia sports fans, how they lived and died with the local teams. If Boston fans would stand in the cold to buy tickets for a last-place hockey team, he knew Philadelphia fans would love the NHL just as much if they were exposed to it.

What Snider didn't know was the ignominious history of hockey in Philadelphia. Most fans don't know the Flyers were not Philadelphia's first NHL team.

In the 1920s former light-heavyweight boxing champion Benny Leonard owned the Pittsburgh Pirates, but the team needed a new arena, and a request was made to move the team temporarily to Philadelphia; Leonard renamed the team the Quakers.

The Philadelphia Quakers' one season of existence, the 1930–1931 season, was historical for one reason: sheer ineptitude. In 44 games, the team went 4–36–4. The four wins are the fewest ever posted by an NHL team, and the .136 winning percentage remains the second-lowest in league history. After the season,

## GIRARD BANK

After raising barely enough money to buy the team, Ed Snider had debts to repay, including a $500,000 load from ARA's Bill Fishman.

Snider and partner Joe Scott went bank shopping for a loan.

Recalls Snider, "I went to banks...and they said, 'What's a hockey puck?' One guy thought it was soccer. Another banker fell asleep while we were talking to him."

Their seventh stop was Girard Bank, which was placed down the list due to its conservative reputation. Snider didn't know Girard president Steve Gardner had grown up in Boston as a hockey fan, as had vice president Bill Baer, who also was a Philadelphian.

Girard gave the Flyers $1.5 million, and Snider was able to make good on all his debts.

Leonard folded the franchise. He lost so much money on the team he was forced to return to prizefighting.

There also were a number of failed minor-league hockey experiments in town.

The Philadelphia Arrows of the Canadian-American Hockey League played at the Philadelphia Arena on Market Street from 1927 to 1935; the team later became a minor-league affiliate of the New York Rangers and was renamed the Ramblers. The Ramblers played until 1941, when they were renamed the Rockets, then folded in 1942.

The Philadelphia Comets of the Tri-State Hockey League blinked in and out of existence in four months, just in time to lose all 16 games they played in the 1932–1933 season.

The Philadelphia Falcons played in the Eastern Amateur Hockey League from 1942 to 1946, but ceased play until the 1951–1952 season. The second version of the Falcons, though, didn't make it to the 1952 part of their schedule, as the team was disbanded in December 1951 due to poor attendance.

According to Philadelphia hockey historian Bruce Cooper, hockey's death knell in the city could best be summarized in a quote from Peter A. Tyrell, president and general manager of the Philadelphia Arena, when he announced the Falcons' folding: "The attendance this season to date has proven that there are not enough Philadelphians interested in hockey to warrant its continuance."

The Philadelphia Rockets of the American Hockey League gave the town another shot, playing from 1946 to 1949. They barely lasted the first season, though, as the Rockets went 5–52–7, for a winning percentage of .133, an all-level record of futility that remains today.

The Philadelphia Ramblers of the Eastern Hockey League played decent but undistinguished hockey from 1955 to 1964 before moving to Cherry Hill, New Jersey, and becoming the Jersey Devils.

Snider knew nothing of this inglorious hockey history; for today's Flyers fans, his ignorance is their bliss.

"I was young and full of enthusiasm," Snider said in the Flyers video, *Twenty-Five Years of Pride and Tradition.* "I had seen hockey and loved it. I had seen its success in the six cities that had it. But I didn't realize the history of hockey in Philadelphia or in other places. Maybe if I had, I wouldn't have gone through with it."

Snider went to Wolman and suggested they should build an arena—the parking lot of the previously planned stadium was a desired location—and apply for an NHL franchise. Wolman thought it would be a good idea, and they planned to move forward.

First for Snider was a visit to Jennings, the head of the expansion committee.

A number of cities already had put in bids, like Pittsburgh, Buffalo, Los Angeles, Baltimore, and Vancouver, but Snider said Jennings was ecstatic when the idea of a team in Philadelphia was brought up.

"He was just glad I showed up," says Snider. "It's a great metropolitan area, a great rivalry for New York. He was great to me from the day I met him."

Jennings gave Snider the rundown on what he had to do. First, there was a $10,000 application fee. Also, there needed to be an arena with a seating capacity of at least 12,500. All the applicants would have to make presentations before the NHL Board of Governors, outlining why the NHL would work in their area. And there was a $2 million franchise fee.

Snider was on board, and said his only request was that his bid be kept secret so it would be the only one coming out of Philadelphia. Jennings agreed.

Snider took his arena plan to Philadelphia city councilman Paul D'Ortona and Mayor James Tate. The mayor especially was pleased that a 15,000-seat, privately financed arena could be built in the parking lot of what would eventually become Veterans Stadium, and fast-tracked the project.

Now all Snider had to do was prepare the franchise presentation.

First he enlisted Putnam, who decided working for the demanding Cooke was not the job for him. He joined Snider, Wolman, and Jerry Schiff, Snider's brother-in-law, as the nascent club owners. It was agreed Putnam would own 25 percent and hold the title of team president. Schiff, Wolman, and Snider

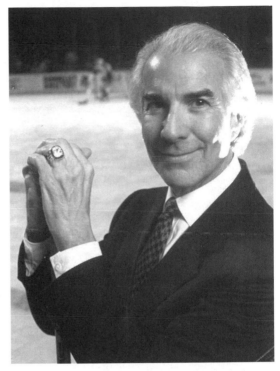

When he founded the
Flyers in the 1960s, Ed
Snider wasn't the sports
powerbroker he is today,
but it was his passion
for hockey that drove
him to bring an NHL
team back to
Philadelphia.

would own 22 percent each. The remaining 9 percent was purchased by friends of Wolman and Snider.

A five-page brochure was printed to explain to NHL owners
that, with a population base of 5.5 million and three established
professional sports franchises, the hockey team could join the
Phillies, Eagles, and 76ers in the pantheon of Philadelphia sports.

On February 8, 1966, at the St. Regis Hotel in New York,
Wolman and Putnam met with the NHL board of governors and
made their pitch.

The next day, the phone rang in Putnam's hotel room. It was
Jennings. "You're in," was all he said.

Snider, who had stayed behind in Philadelphia, joined Mayor
Tate at City Hall to announce plans for the new arena. Not long
after, office space was rented on the ground floor of the Life of
Pennsylvania Building, at 15th and Locust Street. Bud Poile, the 42-
year-old general manager of the San Francisco Seals of the Western
Hockey League, was hired as the club's first general manager. The

# COLOR SCHEME

Ever wonder why the Flyers look like they skated out of a Halloween catalogue? There are two reasons.

"The hot colors are always more attractive from a marketing standpoint," founding team president Bill Putnam said in *Full Spectrum*. "Since Detroit and Montreal already used red in their color schemes, the closest the Flyers could get was orange."

The other reason?

"The fact that I graduated from the University of Texas, where the colors are orange and white, might have had something to do with the choice."

After adding black to complete the scheme, Putnam was told the NHL logo also was orange and black. Putnam offered to use just orange and white, but league president Clarence Campbell gave his okay, and black stayed.

first coach was 43-year-old Keith Allen, then the coach/GM of the Western League's Seattle Totems.

Team colors of orange, black, and white were chosen, and uniforms and a logo—a winged *P* with an orange puck in the center—were unveiled, as was the name—the Philadelphia Flyers, a suggestion first made by Phyllis Foreman, Snider's sister.

The foundation was set, but one item still remained—raising the $2 million franchise fee.

Snider thought he'd get half that amount from Wolman, but when Wolman tried to sell the team out from under him, Snider decided to trade his 40 percent stake in the arena for Wolman's 22 percent share of the franchise. Snider also bought out Schiff, becoming majority owner of the club.

With Wolman out of the picture, Snider was in a difficult spot. "I had never wanted to own more than 22 percent of the team," he recalled in *Full Spectrum*. "I didn't think I could afford it."

In fact, he couldn't. Snider remortgaged his home and started borrowing money from banks: $25,000 from one, $50,000 from another.

Despite not being part of the ownership group, Snider still thought Wolman would make good on his promise to foot half the expansion fee. But with the June 5, 1967, deadline fast approaching and Wolman having financial difficulties, Snider knew something was wrong.

"To my recollections," Snider said in *Full Spectrum*, "It was seven to 10 days before the money was due that Jerry told me he didn't have it."

Snider previously had lined up a $1 million loan from Fidelity Bank. Now he needed to scramble to replace Wolman's money.

The team's television rights for the first three years were sold to Kaiser Broadcasting, which owned Channel 48, for $350,000. Snider also took out a $150,000 loan independently.

Still a half-million dollars short, Snider went to Bill Fishman, president and founder of ARA Services (today known as ARAMARK), which already had invested $2 million to provide food services at the planned arena. Snider asked Fishman for a loan, and Fishman was agreeable if a bank would take his personal ARA stock as collateral. Provident Bank said yes, and on deadline day, Fishman wrote a check to the Philadelphia Hockey Club.

Snider took the check, plus the other $1.5 million, to Fidelity Bank to make the wire transfer to Putnam, who had gone to Montreal for the expansion draft.

And then the lights went out.

## THE BIRTH OF THE LOGO

Mel Richman Inc., a Philadelphia advertising and graphic design company, was hired to design the Flyers' logo and uniforms.

Team president Bill Putnam suggested a winged skate for the logo, but artist Sam Ciccone drew a stylized *P* with four wings to connote speed. An orange dot was placed in the middle of the *P* to symbolize a hockey puck.

Simple and effective, it remains nearly unchanged 40-plus years later.

# WHAT'S IN A NAME?

A number of names were suggested for Philadelphia's expansion hockey team, from Lancers and Raiders to Ice-Picks, Acmes, and Scars and Stripes.

But it was Phyllis Foreman, Ed Snider's sister, who blurted out "Flyers."

"I was thinking of people skating and sliding around the ice," she said in *Full Spectrum*. "And 'Flyers' just popped into my head. Everybody thought it was great."

There was a name-the-team contest for fans run by Acme supermarkets, but the only vote that counted came from Ed Snider, who favored "Flyers."

Officially, Alec Stockard, a nine-year-old boy from Narberth, Pennsylvania, was named the winner, and took home the grand prize of a 21-inch color television, plus two inaugural season tickets.

Of note is the fact that Stockard spelled it "Fliers." No one is sure how the *i* became a *y*.

"There was a blackout in Philadelphia," says Snider. "Everything went dead. They couldn't wire [the money]. They're waiting in Montreal, and nothing's happening. We couldn't communicate by any way, phone or otherwise."

At approximately 10:23 AM, a power failure had shut down a 15,000-square mile area, ranging from New Jersey south to Maryland and west to Harrisburg.

The NHL needed confirmation of the Flyers' money by 2:00 PM, or all the hard work put in by Snider, Putnam, and others would go for naught.

At noon, the power came back on in Center City Philadelphia. Fidelity was able to establish a communication link with a bank in New York, which was able to wire the money to Royal Bank of Canada in Montreal. Putnam ran the $2 million check over to the Queen Elizabeth Hotel, saving the day—and the Flyers—for Philadelphia.

"How could something like that happen?" Snider asks now with a laugh that only 40-plus years of success can allow. "It happened. That's how we started."

# THE EXPANSION DRAFT

The first step in building the Flyers' inaugural roster was Snider's purchasing the Quebec Aces of the American Hockey League for $350,000. The move provided the club its first 16 players.

The roster would be filled out by the NHL's first-ever expansion draft, held June 6, 1967, in Montreal. No player with fewer than two years of professional experience (NHL or minor leagues) was eligible. The six established clubs were allowed to protect 11 skaters and one goalie. After a team lost a skater or a goalie, it could protect one more of the like. After it lost a second player, it could add one more to its protected list. After that, every remaining player was up for grabs.

The Flyers were to pick second among the six new clubs— California, Los Angeles, Pittsburgh, St. Louis, and Minnesota were the others—in the two-round goaltender portion of the draft, and fifth in the 18-round skater-selection process.

The Flyers, led by general manager Bud Poile and coach Keith Allen, were focused on young players.

"I think we reached a consensus almost from the start that we were going to think young," said Poile in *Full Spectrum*. "We didn't just want to have a team that could be competitive with the new clubs, but one that in a few years could compete with the old ones."

Allen, Poile, and top scout Marcel Pelletier had spent the 1966–1967 season scouring minor-league outposts throughout North America.

"We'd go on the road, usually alone, for as many as two weeks at a time," Pelletier recalled in *Full Spectrum*. "I'd played in St. Paul [in the Central League], so I had a real good idea of the players in that league. Bud and Keith had been in the Western League, so they knew that, too. We also scouted the American League heavily. The National League we did less. We knew what was there."

One of the players Pelletier, a former minor-league goalie, had seen was a Boston Bruins goaltending prospect toiling for the Oklahoma City Blazers of the Central Hockey League. After Los

The fledgling Flyers surprised the league when they plucked little-known goalie Bernie Parent from the Boston Bruins in the NHL's 1967 expansion draft.

Angeles took veteran goalie Terry Sawchuk with the first pick, the Flyers shocked the draft room by taking 22-year-old Bernard Parent.

In 36 games as a rookie in the 1965–1966 season, Parent had posted a 3.69 goals-against average for a last-place Bruins squad. He fared slightly better in his second campaign, in Oklahoma City, finishing with a 2.70 GAA and four shutouts in 14 games.

"He was supposed to be immature," recalled Pelletier in *Full Spectrum*. "And he probably was. But when I saw him play at Oklahoma City, I thought he looked like the perfect goalie."

Parent wasn't overjoyed at the thought of heading to an unknown hockey land.

"I was a little disappointed because I was leaving an original team for an expansion team," he says today. "Little did I know it would turn out real good."

After the Flyers picked Parent, they hoped to land a veteran with their next choice. The pickings were slim, though, when their next turn came up. With the 11$^{th}$ selection, the team opted for Parent's partner in Oklahoma City, Doug Favell.

With their first pick in the skater selection, the choice was 27-year-old Chicago Blackhawks blueliner Ed Van Impe. After five years in the minor leagues, Van Impe had just finished a distant second to Bobby Orr in rookie-of-the-year balloting.

Like Parent, Van Impe wasn't happy to land with an expansion team. He said in Jim Jackson's history of the Flyers' championship teams *Walking Together Forever*, "I had spent five years in the minors trying to work my way up to Chicago and finally accomplished that the season before expansion. We had an outstanding year, finishing in first place during the regular season. When I was picked by the Flyers, it was like starting all over again. The Stanley Cup was something I never even thought could happen in Philly. I can't even say I had mixed feelings. I was very, very disappointed."

Next for the Flyers was defenseman Joe Watson, Orr's 23-year-old road roommate.

"Talk about depression," Watson said in *Walking Together Forever* of getting picked by the Flyers. "A guy told me I just got drafted by the Philadelphia Flyers, and I said, 'Who? What are you talking about? What the hell is Philadelphia?' I knew nothing about it."

After Watson, the Flyers took 22-year-old center Brit Selby from Toronto. Selby had been NHL rookie of the year in 1966, but a broken leg the following season limited him to just six games, and the Leafs had given up on him.

Next was 29-year-old center Lou Angotti from Chicago, of whom Pelletier recalled, "We thought he'd be a character guy and a good two-way player." Angotti became the Flyers' first captain.

After Angotti, they selected 28-year-old right wing Leon Rochefort from Montreal, and then Chicago farmhand defenseman John Miszuk, 26, came aboard.

They next opted for 30-year-old Boston blueliner Dick Cherry, who was so happy at his selection he promptly retired to become a schoolteacher.

The Flyers then chose Montreal minor-league defenseman Jean Gauthier, left wing Don Blackburn from Toronto, center Garry Peters from Montreal, and center Jimmy Johnson from the Rangers.

They then went back to Boston for tall, skinny forward Gary Dornhoefer, 24. Dornhoefer had failed in three previous NHL tries with the Bruins, but unlike his draft brethren, he was ecstatic to be going to Philadelphia—or anywhere else, for that matter.

"I didn't know that much about Philadelphia, but it really didn't matter where I played, I just wanted to play in the National Hockey League," he says today. "I was thrilled about it."

Rounding out the Flyers' first 20 draft picks were veteran forwards Forbes Kennedy (Boston), Pat Hannigan (Chicago), Dwight Carruthers (Detroit), Bob Courcy (Montreal), Keith Wright (Boston), and defenseman Terry Ball (New York).

During and immediately after the draft, teams made substantial offers for Parent, Van Impe, and Watson, but Poile stood by his word of keeping young players rather than the veterans the established teams were trying to foist onto the new teams.

The new Flyers met for their first training camp, in Quebec City, on September 10, 1967. But there was discontent in the air, as Watson and Van Impe refused to show up and Parent nearly walked out of camp over a contract issue. Days before the regular season, Parent signed his $20,000-a-year contract; Van Impe signed a two-year, $45,000 deal; and Watson agreed to a two-year, $38,500 deal.

Those were the final additions to the opening day roster—Parent and Favell in goal; Watson, Van Impe, Gauthier, Miszuk, and Jim Morrison and John Hanna off the Quebec roster on defense; centers Angotti, Kennedy, Peters, and Ed Hoekstra from Quebec; left wings Selby, Blackburn, and Bill Sutherland from Quebec; and right wings Rochefort, Dornhoefer, Hannigan, and Quebec's Wayne Hicks.

The group finished the exhibition season in Providence, Rhode Island, then flew to Philadelphia, where the new Flyers got their first look at their new home.

It was far from love at first sight.

Watson's first image of the city came as the team's bus from the airport drove past the massive crushed-car graveyard next to the Penrose Avenue bridge.

"I looked over to the right and saw this big machine crushing cars," he said in *Walking Together Forever*. "I asked the driver about it, and he told me that the mafia ran the machine and that people were still in the cars as they were being crushed. I said to myself, 'What in the world am I doing in a city like this?'"

Van Impe shared Watson's opinion. He went to an Eagles game and saw planes toting banners that read "Joe Must Go," meaning coach Joe Kuharich. When the Eagles players were introduced, every one was booed. "One defensive back got especially bad treatment," Van Impe recalled in *Walking Together Forever*. "I found out he had a tough game the week before. I was wondering what kind of town was I in. What the hell was I doing there? It was an eye-opening experience."

## THE FIRST SEASON

The Flyers' inaugural season started October 11, 1967. They lost their first game 5–1 to the California Seals at the Oakland Coliseum. Bill Sutherland scored the Flyers' lone goal.

Three nights later, they played the Los Angeles Kings at the team's temporary home in Long Beach while the Fabulous Forum was being built in Inglewood. Despite Sutherland's second goal and a strong effort in net by Doug Favell, the Flyers fell 4–2.

With three days off before their next game, the Flyers flew home, where they were to be honored with a parade through Center City. When the team arrived at the airport, a rousing 35 fans greeted them. The next day, the team officially was welcomed to town at City Hall. Mayor James Tate sent his regards, but had other business to attend to. So did most of Philadelphia.

"We come to Philadelphia, they're having a parade down Broad Street to welcome us to the city," recalls Joe Watson, "and there's more people in the parade than watching it."

Bernie Parent has an idea why no one came. "That's because they advertised Joe Watson was going to be in the parade," he says with a laugh.

# FLYERS' FIRSTS

On October 11, 1967, at the Oakland Coliseum, the first Flyers made their NHL debut.

Coach Keith Allen's starting lineup had Lou Angotti, Brit Selby, and Wayne Hicks at forward, Jean Gauthier and John Miszuk on defense, and Bernie Parent in goal.

Angotti took the first-ever Flyers penalty—for interference—just 22 seconds into the game.

And at 10:07 of the second period, Bill Sutherland scored the first Flyers goal.

Watson wasn't laughing when he recalled the day in *Full Spectrum*: "About halfway down to the Spectrum, I swear to gosh, there was this guy there giving us the finger. He yelled, 'You'll be in Baltimore by December.' I'll bet there were 20 people, tops, all the way down Broad Street, who actually stood there to watch. All the rest were people on lunch hour wondering who the hell we were."

Parent, ever the optimist, wasn't upset about the low turnout.

"It's understandable because nobody knew about the Flyers," he said. "What they wanted to do was introduce the players to the city, but it was the first step toward a long journey. It wasn't an established team. It was something new in the city. I've always been the type of person, take one step at a time. That didn't bother me at all....In my mind, I was [more] preoccupied with performing well than with how many people we had at the parade."

Two days after the parade debacle, the Flyers hit the road again, this time in front of a sparse crowd of 5,234 in St. Louis. The Flyers trailed 2–0, but Lou Angotti scored with 35 seconds left in the second period to tie the game, and then Ed Hoekstra scored with 7:40 left in the third to give the Flyers their first-ever lead. Favell made it stand up, and the Flyers had their first victory.

On October 19 the Flyers hosted their first contest at the Spectrum, against the Pittsburgh Penguins, but only 7,812 took in the game. The ones who stayed away missed little, as the game's only goal came 2:59 into the third period, when Hoekstra knocked down a Pens clearing attempt, Sutherland shoved a Leon Rochefort rebound into the net, and the Flyers left with a 1–0 win.

With Gordie Howe in town a day early for a promotional press conference, the Flyers scored their first five-figure attendance mark—10,859—for their first game against an established team, a 3–1 loss to the Detroit Red Wings.

Slowly, though, things began to build as the Flyers began to win more. In early November the Flyers went to Montreal and returned home with a 4–1 victory. The next day, in front of 9,188 at the Spectrum, the Flyers played the famed Canadiens to a 1–1 tie. They beat the Bruins at Boston Garden and beat the New York Rangers 3–2; the 11,276 in attendance at the Spectrum gave the team a standing ovation.

The winning continued as the Flyers climbed over their expansion brethren to claim the top spot in the West Division, the exclusive home of the six new clubs.

In early February the Flyers drew their first set of consecutive sellouts, as scalpers were getting $10 for $3.25 tickets. The Flyers didn't let the fans down, beating Chicago and Toronto.

The sweet breeze of success, though, can change directions awfully fast. In fact, it changed to a gale-force gust that blew the roof off the Spectrum.

It's an exaggeration that the Spectrum became the world's first retractable-roof stadium on February 17, 1968. On a day when winds whipping off the Delaware reached nearly 50 mph, pieces of tar paper covering the roof were blown away, leaving a 100-foot-long-by-50-foot-wide spot of exposed sheet metal. There was no real hole, but light was visible through perforations in the sheet metal.

Mayor Tate agreed with a *Philadelphia Inquirer* editorial that said the building should be shuttered, but after meeting with Spectrum officials and representatives from McCloskey and Co., the architectural firm that built the Spectrum, the building stayed open but under the city's watchful eye. Days later, though, a city inspection called the damage "freakish," and the building was declared safe.

On March 1, with workers continuing to repair the arena's roof, more wind gusts tore off three layers of roofing paper and decking. This time there were three different holes, with the biggest 20 feet by 40 feet.

"This is a very windy area," Snider said of the South Philadelphia Sports Complex. "The architects had not done the wind tunnel studies that they should have done. The roof was made of this material [but] it wasn't a solid roof. You had the structure, but in between you had this material that wasn't solid. So some of it blew off and a little hole was seen up there. There was no structural damage, but it became a political football, and the goddamn mayor closed us down."

The team split its last seven "home" games between Madison Square Garden in New York, Maple Leaf Gardens in Toronto, and Le Colisee in Quebec City.

The Flyers may have been headed to the playoffs in their first season, but Snider had little opportunity to enjoy it. He was more worried with trying to keep the team in business for a second season.

"We're closed down for the last seven home games of the season," he said. "We had to refund the money, and I didn't have any money. We were mortgaged. We were getting the season-ticket money to pay the players. Everything was ahead of time. We had almost sold out all those games because we were headed to the playoffs, people were getting excited. I didn't know where the money was going to come from."

Girard Bank once again came to Snider's rescue. The bank had previously loaned the owner $1.5 million to pay off debts incurred in creating the team. Bill Baer, who was the bank's vice president, asked Snider what he needed. The owner said $1 million.

The money was in the team's account the next day.

"They saw our situation had been getting healthier and they wanted to protect their investment," Snider said in *Full Spectrum*. "I'm forever grateful. Without people like that, I never would have made it."

Despite their odd travel schedule, the team persevered and clinched the West Division title March 30, 1968, despite a 2–0 loss to the Pittsburgh Penguins. They received help from the re-named Oakland Seals, who got a late goal to tie the Los Angeles Kings and allow the Flyers to take the top spot by one point, despite finishing with a 31–32–11 record.

In goal, Parent and Favell each posted sub-2.50 goals-against averages, and each had four shutouts. Rochefort and Sutherland each scored 20-plus goals, and Angotti had team highs of 37 assists and 49 points.

Off the ice, the Flyers averaged 9,625 fans per game for their 30 home contests, including three sellouts.

The first round of the playoffs saw the Flyers face the St. Louis Blues, a team the Flyers had lost to just once in 10 regular-season meetings. GM Bud Poile predicted a four-game sweep. The Blues, though, took Game 1 at the reopened Spectrum, 1–0, on a third-period goal by Jimmy Roberts.

Rochefort broke a 3–3 tie early in the third period of Game 2 to earn a 4–3 series-tying win.

Game 3 in St. Louis was postponed for two days following the assassination of Rev. Dr. Martin Luther King Jr. When play resumed, the Flyers lost Gary Dornhoefer to a broken leg but were

## ED SNIDER FIRED

The Flyers' home opener, October 19, 1967, should have been the crowning moment of Ed Snider's life.

Instead, he lost a job and was forced to change careers.

While building the Flyers and the Spectrum, Snider maintained his job as treasurer of the Philadelphia Eagles. But his relationship with Eagles owner Jerry Wolman, who had helped Snider build the team and the arena, had fallen into disrepair. And after the Flyers' home opener, Wolman fired Snider from the Eagles.

While no real reason ever was given, today Snider says, "It was a blessing in disguise."

able to rally from a pair of one-goal deficits. They tied the game 2–2 when Joe Watson's shot bounced off the Blues' Gary Sabourin and into the net with 6:06 left in regulation.

Early in the second overtime, all three Flyers forwards were caught behind the net, leaving Larry Keenan unguarded on the post. He scored past a helpless Parent at 4:10 of the second extra session to put the Blues ahead two games to one.

Coach Keith Allen, switching goalies each game, went back to Favell for Game 4, but the Blues scored twice shorthanded to take a 5–2 victory and a commanding 3–1 series lead.

Parent made 30 saves in Game 5 at the Spectrum, and Rosie Paiement, just called up from Quebec City, had a hat trick as the Flyers routed the Blues 6–1.

Allen stuck with Parent for the crucial Game 6, and the net-minder made his coach look good, stopping 38 of 39 shots in regulation. But the Blues' Glenn Hall was just a little better, and as the final moments of the game approached, the Flyers trailed 1–0.

As the clock closed in on all zeroes, Allen pulled Parent for an extra attacker. The Flyers held the puck in the Blues' end, and when Hall slid out of position on Ed Van Impe's pass to Andre Lacroix, the diminutive French-Canadian scored into a gaping net to force overtime. Parent stopped Red Berenson on a two-on-one break in extra time, and once again the teams went to a second overtime. At 11:18 of the second extra session, Don Blackburn's backhand lob from the blue line went off a Blues player and past Hall for a 2–1 Flyers victory.

For Game 7 back at the Spectrum, Blues coach Scotty Bowman dug into his bag of tricks and pulled out 43-year-old defenseman Doug Harvey, who had been a player/coach for the Blues' AHL team in Kansas City.

With the future Hall of Famer controlling the action in the St. Louis end, the Flyers were limited to just 27 shots. The Blues scored first, but Sutherland tied the game when he tipped a Forbes Kennedy shot past Hall for a second-period power-play goal. The game turned, though, when defenseman Larry Zeidel accidentally tipped a puck into the Flyers' net to put St. Louis up, and Berenson hit an empty net late for a 3–1 Blues victory.

## HAROLD BALLARD

Harold Ballard's offer of Maple Leaf Gardens for the Flyers to use for a "home" game against the Boston Bruins while the Spectrum was out of commission in 1968 might sound like a magnanimous gesture, but it came with a price.

According to team president Bill Putnam, the Leafs kept 50 percent of the gate revenue for what was a "home" Flyers game.

"Then he kept our program money and sent us a bill for the ambulance service," he said in *Full Spectrum*.

The Flyers' first season might not have ended in Stanley Cup success, but not too many expansion teams can claim a division title in their first season. And it more than set the stage for the next 40-plus years, which featured many more great highs than lows.

# THE GOOD

## BUILDING THE BULLIES

The Flyers' first season ended in a seven-game first-round playoff loss to the St. Louis Blues. Their second season ended the same way, only it took the Blues just four games to dispatch the Flyers.

Snider still considered himself a newcomer to the game of hockey, but he was no dummy. He noticed what was happening on the ice and wasn't the least bit happy.

His Flyers were getting their asses kicked—literally and figuratively.

"We played St. Louis, and they had the Plager brothers [Barclay and Bob] and [Noel] Picard, and these guys were tough fighters," Snider said. "We had all these little French guys."

Those little French guys—Jean-Guy Gendron, Andre Lacroix, and Simon Nolet—had helped the Flyers win the West Division their first year and finish third the next.

"Teams had in those days what they called a policeman," said Snider. "When [Toronto's] John Ferguson takes on Simon Nolet, Simon Nolet didn't do bad in that fight, but he should have gotten the hell beat out of him. He was so scared. But when I see those kinds of things, I think, who said there can only be one policeman? We're not going to be intimidated."

Snider was determined to make his team bigger and tougher. He relayed the message to general manager Bud Poile and assistant GM Keith Allen.

"We might not be able to skate with these guys, we may not have the talent the Original 6 [teams] have, but we'll build our team with one thing, we can be as tough as anybody else," recalled Snider. "Let's just go out and get tough guys, and nobody is going to intimidate or beat up our players ever again."

That declaration by Snider started the ball rolling on the franchise's greatest success.

The transformation from victim to Bully began at the 1969 draft. The Flyers had the sixth overall pick, which Poile used on a center from the Cornwell (Ontario) Royals named Bob Currier, much to the displeasure of some at the Flyers' draft table.

The team's scouts, especially Jerry Melnyk, wanted a smallish kid from Flin Flon, Manitoba, who had some skill, but was a diabetic. After hearing Poile tab Currier, Melnyk left the draft table. Snider had a great deal of respect for Melnyk, who had played on the Flyers' inaugural team but had to retire after suffering a heart attack. Melnyk wanted to move home to Edmonton, so Snider hired him as a Western Canadian scout.

Snider sent Allen to follow Melnyk.

"Keith comes back and says Melnyk said he was shocked because there's this kid, Bob Clarke, plays for Flin Flon, that Jerry says could step on the ice and be our best player right now," Snider remembered.

Clarke had posted back-to-back seasons with 50 goals, 150 points, and 120 penalty minutes. He had the mix of skill, toughness, and physicality that Snider was looking for.

"I said to Bud Poile, what about this kid Clarke?" said Snider. "He said, 'I took Currier. A guy I know tells me he's great, a can't-miss guy.' I said our scouts, particularly Jerry Melnyk, think Bob Clarke is the kid. What if he's there in the second round? He said we already have a center, I don't need another center."

Snider was incensed. He told Allen that if Clarke was available in the second round, that he demand Poile select him. Clarke's diabetes had scared off the rest of the league, and in the second round, with the 17th overall choice, the Flyers tabbed Bobby Clarke.

Also in that 1969 draft, the team used its fifth-round pick (number 52 overall) on a winger from Waldheim, Saskatchewan,

**Bobby Clarke quickly became one of the Flyers' best players and leaders when they picked him in the second round of the 1969 draft.**

named Dave Schultz. One round later, the team picked 6'2" defenseman Don Saleski, a native of Moose Jaw, Saskatchewan.

The following year, the club drafted Bill Clement in the second round and "the Hound," Bob Kelly, in the third.

Allen, who had replaced Bud Poile as general manager following the 1970 season, knew of a defenseman playing for Hershey, the Boston Bruins' American Hockey League affiliate, that the Boston front office didn't think too much of. The Bruins saw Barry

Ashbee as nothing more than a broken-down career minor-leaguer, slow to recover from back surgery that had forced him to miss the entire 1966–1967 season. Allen saw a player who could provide toughness and veteran leadership, so on May 22, 1970, in his second trade as GM, Allen sent Darryl Edestrand and Larry McKillop to Boston for Ashbee.

Another Allen deal, a three-way trade involving the Bruins and Maple Leafs, allowed the Flyers to get winger Rick MacLeish. The cost, though, was high, as goalie Bernie Parent was sent to Toronto.

The Flyers, especially Snider, knew what they had in Parent, but it was a move that had to be made for the good of the organization.

"I cried when he left," Snider says of the January 31, 1971, deal. "I put my arms around him because the guy did everything right. He was a great guy, great player, but we didn't have any assets to build with....We would never win the Cup in Parent's lifetime if we didn't make some moves."

Snider wasn't the only one crying.

"It was a bad time," Parent says of the trade.

In January 1972 "Cowboy" Bill Flett and Ross Lonsberry came aboard in a seven-player deal with the Los Angeles Kings. That summer, the seventh overall pick in the draft was spent on a high-scoring winger from Callander, Ontario, named Bill Barber. Defensemen Tom Bladon and Jimmy Watson were picked in the second and third rounds, respectively. In December 1972 Andre "Moose" Dupont came from the St. Louis Blues in a trade.

Allen had hired Fred Shero in 1971 to lead the team. Shero had been coaching the New York Rangers' Central Hockey League affiliate in Omaha.

"I didn't know Freddie well, but I had followed his career, and he had won everywhere," Allen said in *Full Spectrum*. "The only thing that made me wonder was why [Rangers GM] Emile Francis had given other guys a chance [to coach the Rangers] and never given one to Freddie. But his record was so good, and I'd never heard anyone say a bad word about him."

Shero had schooled himself in the emerging Russian style of play, where teams attacked in five-man groups. But his Flyers took it to another level. They didn't just attack the other team's net. They attacked the other team.

"It was an eye for an eye, a tooth for a tooth," said Joe Watson on the *History of the Philadelphia Flyers* 40th anniversary DVD.

With Schultz, Kelly, Dupont, and Saleski, the Flyers didn't just beat teams, they beat them up.

They left a trail of bloody, broken players and teams in their wake, none more impressive than what Schultz did to Chicago's Keith Magnuson, who was among the elite tough guys in the early 1970s.

"Chicago came into the Spectrum, and Schultz kicked the shit out of Magnuson," says Snider, still smiling 30 years later at the image of Schultz's best punch bloodying the mouth of the Blackhawks' defenseman.

It was the beginning of things to come.

The Flyers marauded through the NHL, earning the scorn of many but pride and reverence from their growing legion of fans. The media also helped. Writers from other towns called the Flyers animals and barbarians. Shero called it smart, tough hockey. The Philadelphia press had another name for it, coined by *Philadelphia Bulletin* writer Jack Chevalier and editor Pete Cafone, who together created the name Broad Street Bullies in the paper on January 3, 1973. The club didn't really care about the nickname, but they relished the reputation.

"Intimidation was not my goal," says Snider. "We became intimidators because we were so strong and tough. My goal was...to [not] be intimidated. It was never to be the intimidator."

Teams grew fearful of the Flyers, afraid of their growing legion of loud, bloodthirsty fans, and afraid of coming into the lions' den known as the Spectrum.

Larry Hillman, a defenseman on that team, told writers, "You can see teams coming in here a little worried. They're hearing that we're a bunch of animals. Some guys don't want any part of that."

"Number one, you had the noise factor," remembers Gary Dornhoefer. "You couldn't even hear yourself talk on the ice, that's how loud it was. And because we played a very physical game, the combination of both made it a very intimidating place to play."

The Philly Flu became a common ailment among visiting hockey players.

"In that era, you come into the Spectrum, we think nothing about winning and we think nothing about taking advantage of you," says Kelly. "No one was going to come into our house and intimidate us or beat us."

"Everybody loved to hate us," said Orest Kindrachuk on the *History of the Philadelphia Flyers* DVD. "We loved to be hated. It inspired us even more. Going into someone else's building and taking two points from them was all we cared about. We didn't care how. We didn't care where. We just wanted to win the games."

With all the pounding the Flyers' bullies were doing, it was opening space for the team's highly skilled forwards.

In the 1972–1973 season Clarke had 37 goals, 67 assists, and a team-best 104 points, and after the season won the Hart Trophy as league MVP and the Lester B. Pearson Trophy as the league's best player, as voted by the players.

MacLeish became the eighth player in league history to that point to score 50 goals. Flett scored 43 times, and Dornhoefer and Barber netted 30 each.

## BULLIES NICKNAME

The Flyers marauded through the NHL in the early 1970s, and there to chronicle it was *Philadelphia Bulletin* writer Jack Chevalier.

After watching the Flyers ransack Atlanta like General Sherman, on January 3, 1973, he filed: "The image of the fightin' Flyers is spreading gradually around the NHL and people are dreaming up wild nicknames. They're the Mean Machine, the Blue Line Banditos, and Freddy's Philistines."

On the flight home, Chevalier called the newsroom and asked "Blue Line Banditos" be changed to "Bullies of Broad Street." Pete Cafone wrote the headline that accompanied the story that ran in the paper on January 4, 1973: Broad Street Bullies Muscle Atlanta.

They rode into the 1973 playoffs and a crucial first-round meeting with the Minnesota North Stars. Despite this being the franchise's fourth playoff appearance in six seasons, the Flyers had yet to win a series.

That was all about to change.

The best-of-seven series was tied 2–2, with Game 5 at the Spectrum on April 10, 1973. MacLeish netted his second power-play goal of the game early in the second period, giving the Flyers a 2–1 advantage.

The lead held until Bill Goldsworthy beat Doug Favell at the 13-minute mark of the third period, forcing overtime.

And that's when Dornhoefer scored one of the most memorable goals in team history.

He rushed down the left slot, eluded Barry Gibbs' poke-check attempt, pulled the puck from his forehand to his backhand as he cut in front of the net, and deposited a shot behind North Stars goalie Cesare Maniago, just before Tom Reid upended him. The goal gave the Flyers the win and the series lead, and two days later they closed out the North Stars for the first playoff series win in team history.

Dornhoefer's goal is immortalized in a large bronze statue outside the Spectrum—Dornhoefer parallel to the ground, arms and stick extended, as the puck sits in the back of the net.

"I don't even know how I scored," Dornhoefer told reporters that night. "I just remember getting the puck at center ice, and fortunately it stayed right with me. You could try that play again a hundred times and it wouldn't work."

The momentum from the Minnesota series lasted just one game and two days. The Flyers drew the powerful Montreal Canadiens in the conference finals. They won Game 1 on a MacLeish overtime score, but the Flyers dropped the next four games.

Despite the heartbreaking loss, there was a breakthrough.

"We went over the hump with Minnesota," says Barber. "We flew out of Minnesota and went right to Montreal. We beat them the first game, in their own building in overtime, then they beat us four straight. But there were games that we knew then that,

**Rick MacLeish was acquired in a trade to help beef up the Flyers' lines in January 1971.**

with maturity, there was something there. We woke them up. We woke the league up."

The next year would see them wake up even more people.

Favell had been the starting goaltender in what had been the Flyers' most successful season to that point in the club's history.

But team management thought that to reach the next level, an upgrade was needed in goal.

"It wasn't any particular goal or goals in the Montreal series," Keith Allen said in *Full Spectrum*. "It was just the realization that Dougie was the kind of goalie who could win you a series in four straight or lose you one in four straight."

While Favell was winning games in Philadelphia, Parent was remaking his game. What began as an unwanted move from Philadelphia became cushioned by a season and a half sojourn into the reservoir of hockey knowledge known as Jacques Plante, Parent's idol growing up and his teammate with the Leafs.

"I'm always one of those guys that looks at the glass as half full rather than half empty," Parent says today. "My approach there was, it was sad when I first heard [of the trade], but after a while, I concentrated on the team that made the trade for me rather than the team that traded me. Because you get traded, then you have sad feelings. But if you look at the other side of the coin, you're going to a team that made the move for you.

"At the same time, little did I know I was going to spend two years in Toronto with Jacques Plante. Spending two years with him took me from a raw goalie talent and he helped me become a better goalie."

In 1972 Parent returned to Philadelphia—as a member of the Philadelphia Blazers of the World Hockey Association. That stint lasted just one season, as once paychecks stopped coming, Parent stopped playing. He watched as his old teammates made their first significant playoff run.

"It's always difficult to be a spectator," Parent says. "All your life when you're playing, you're a performer. Just being a spectator was being difficult. Little did I know that the universe was guiding me with the right people, the right places, at the right time. Everything had to happen to put me in the right place at the right time with the Flyers."

The following season, Parent needed a job. And the Flyers needed an upgrade in net.

Since the Maple Leafs still owned Parent's NHL rights, Allen and Leafs GM Jim Gregory worked out a deal—Favell and a 1973 first-round draft pick for Parent and a 1973 second-round pick.

On May 15, 1973, the final piece of the puzzle was put in place as Parent returned to the Flyers.

"It was a great feeling," says Parent. "I knew the team, the team had gotten a lot better, and I knew the team had a chance to do something. I was going back to a team that was ready to explode."

"That was the great move," Snider says of bringing back Parent. "That was the greatest moment. To get him back was such a coup."

The Bullies were built. With the 1973–1974 season dawning, it was time to turn them loose.

# CUP I

The players reported to training camp in 1973 refreshed and feeling positive after the previous spring's playoff experience, plus the return of goaltender Bernie Parent added consistency in net.

"I went to Canada that summer and told everybody that I thought we were going win the Stanley Cup the next year," Don Saleski said in *Full Spectrum*. "Our whole club thought we had a chance."

"We had a good mixture, that was the key," says Bill Barber, who was starting his first full NHL season. "We had [veterans] Barry Ashbee, we had Eddie Van Impe and Joey Watson and Ross Lonsberry. Then we had the in-between group with Clarkie and Schultzy, guys a little older. Then there were guys like Tommy Bladon and myself, we were a younger group there. We had a mix of three different age groups. All of them complimented each other."

The 1973–1974 Flyers started with a bang as Kate Smith appeared live to sing "God Bless America." Opening night was Smith's first live performance for Flyers fans, but her rendition of the patriotic song already had become a regular event at the Spectrum. On December 11, 1969, Flyers vice president Lou Scheinfeld shocked the 10,059 in attendance by ditching "The Star-Spangled Banner" for Smith's song.

"I thought I'd do something to shake things up," Scheinfeld said in *Full Spectrum*. "I listened to tapes and records of various patriotic songs, tested them over the PA system in an empty Spectrum, and decided on Kate."

Ed Snider was furious, but the Flyers won that night. Scheinfeld returned to "The Star-Spangled Banner" two nights later, but the Flyers lost. When he played "God Bless America" before the next home game, the Flyers beat Pittsburgh 4–0, and newspapers noted the Flyers were 2–0 when Smith sang.

Over the following years, Snider and others within the organization had tried to get Smith to sing live, but to no avail.

Unbeknownst to the club was the fact that one of Smith's uncles, Fred Ditmars, lived in West Philadelphia and had been

When the Flyers realized they usually won the games in which Kate Smith opened by singing "God Bless America," a Philadelphia tradition was born.
*Photo courtesy AP Images.*

sending the singer newspaper clippings chronicling the "God Bless America" phenomenon. It was enough for Smith to tell her agent to make a deal with the Flyers.

"The cheers went right through me," Smith said after her opening-night performance. "I've played before larger crowds, but I've never had a bigger ovation. It was fantastic, and I'm sorry that is such a mediocre word."

The Flyers' beat the Leafs 2–0, running Smith's record, live or on tape, to 29–3–1.

The 1973–1974 Flyers cruised to their first 50-win season and won the West Division with 112 points.

Bobby Clarke led the team with 35 goals, 52 assists, and 87 points, the fifth-highest total in the league. Barber added 34 goals, and Rick MacLeish and Ross Lonsberry scored 32 apiece. Dave Schultz added 20 goals and a league-high 348 penalty minutes.

In net, Parent had arguably the finest season ever for a player at his position. He played a remarkable 73 of 78 games, setting a league record that stood for 17 seasons. He set another NHL standard with 47 wins in a day when there was no overtime or shootouts (the mark stood until the 2006–2007 season, when the rules had been changed so ties were eliminated). He also posted a league-low 1.89 goals-against average and an NHL-leading 12 shutouts.

Parent became the first Flyer to win the Vezina Trophy, sharing the award with Chicago's Tony Esposito, and he finished second to Phil Esposito in balloting for the Hart Trophy, awarded to the league MVP.

And for leading the Flyers to their best season ever, coach Fred Shero won the initial Jack Adams Award as league coach of the year.

The Flyers swept Atlanta in the first round of the playoffs, then took a 2–0 lead over the Rangers in the conference finals, but dropped the next two games. They also lost Bob Kelly to a season-ending knee injury in Game 3 and Barry Ashbee in overtime of Game 4 with what became a career-ending eye injury.

The Flyers, also now missing an injured Bill Clement, took Game 5 at the Spectrum, 4–1, but fell in Game 6 at Madison Square Garden by an identical score.

That set up Game 7 at the Spectrum. The Flyers drew first blood when Schultz pounded Dale Rolfe in the first period.

"That took something out of New York," said Shero to reporters. "They didn't do as much hitting after that."

The extra space allowed Orest Kindrachuk and Gary Dornhoefer to drive to the net for rebound goals to push the Flyers ahead 3–1. But at 8:49 of the third, Dornhoefer allowed Steve Vickers to get away from him and score to make it 3–2. Rather than berate Dornhoefer for his gaffe, Shero went a different way.

"Shero left our line [Dornhoefer, Lonsberry, and MacLeish] on the ice, and 30 seconds later I was able to get that goal back with a goal," says Dornhoefer. "He had confidence in the line by letting us stay out there after the goal was scored."

It actually took just 12 seconds, but Dornhoefer got in front of Rangers goalie Ed Giacomin and scored to restore a two-goal lead.

Pete Stemkowski scored for the Rangers to make it 4–3 with 5:26 left, but the Flyers kept the Rangers to the outside and milked the seconds off the clock. When it was over, the Flyers had become the first expansion team to beat an Original 6 club in a playoff series.

To win the ultimate prize, they'd have to do it again.

The Boston Bruins entered the Stanley Cup Finals a heavy favorite. They were well-rested, having a week to sit and watch the Flyers battle the Rangers after they had dispatched the Chicago Blackhawks in six games.

The Bruins' Phil Esposito was coming off a league-record 68-goal season, and his 145 points earned him the Art Ross Trophy as the league's leading scorer, as well as the Hart Trophy as NHL MVP. Bruins players took the top four spots in the league scoring race, as defenseman Bobby Orr had finished second with 122 points, followed by Esposito's linemates—Ken Hodge with 105 points and Wayne Cashman with 89.

Orr, though, was the key to the Bruins' success. Considered almost unanimously as the best player in the game at the time, he was in the midst of a stretch of six straight seasons finishing in the top three in league scoring, including a pair of Art Ross Trophies, and he had won the seventh of his eight straight Norris trophies as the league's best defenseman.

But rather than fear Orr, Shero devised a different plan: give Orr the puck at all times. Shero wanted Orr to carry the puck, which would allow the physical Flyers forwards to use him for target practice on the forecheck. Over a long series, the hope was Orr would wear down.

Game 1 started with Boston taking a 2–0 lead, but goals by Kindrachuk and Clarke tied the game 5:32 into the third period.

Cowboy Flett had a chance to put the Flyers ahead on a three-on-two break, but his shot hit the post. At the other end, Orr put the Bruins on top when his blast through traffic went between Parent's pads with 22 seconds left.

Despite the loss, the Flyers were confident.

"We'd outplayed them, and they knew it," said Clarke in *Full Spectrum.* "We were in better shape than the Bruins."

Game 2 saw the Bruins again take a 2–0 lead, but again the Flyers battled back. Clarke redirected a Flett shot past Bruins goalie Gilles Gilbert, and then an unlikely Moose Dupont score evened the game with just 52 seconds left to force overtime.

Midway through the extra session, the unlikely trio of Clarke, Flett, and Schultz got the puck in front of the Boston net, with Clarke lifting the winner over a sprawling Gilbert at 12:01. It was the Flyers' first win at Boston Garden since their first trip there in their inaugural season.

Despite losing Dornhoefer to a separated shoulder, the Flyers outworked the Bruins at the Spectrum, taking Game 3, 4–1.

MacLeish and Schultz gave the Flyers a 2–0 lead early in Game 4, but the Bruins tied the game before the first period was over on scores by Esposito and Andre Savard.

**Dave Schultz cross-checks Wayne Cashman in the 1974 Stanley Cup Finals.**

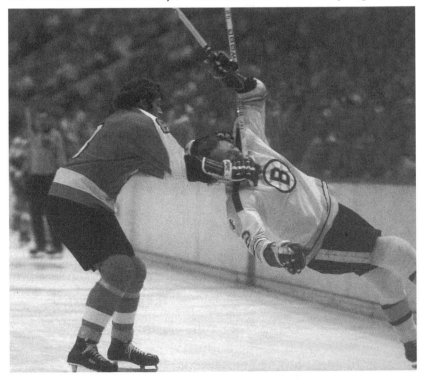

The game remained tied into the latter stages of the third period. Barber, a left wing playing on the right side for Dornhoefer, dumped the puck into the Bruins' end. Lonsberry held Orr up enough so the defenseman couldn't clear the puck, and Barber grabbed it off the boards and fired a shot over Gilbert's glove with six minutes left, snapping a nine-game goal drought and giving the Flyers a 3–2 lead.

Clarke then fed Dupont, who walked past Esposito and scored with 3:20 left, icing the 4–2 win and giving the Flyers a three-games-to-one stranglehold on the series.

Back in Boston for Game 5, Orr scored twice in the second period to snap a 1–1 tie and propel the Bruins to a 5–1 win.

Game 6 of the series was Sunday, May 19. The Flyers had a second chance to close the best-of-seven series, and no one in black and orange wanted to see Boston Garden until next fall.

"I don't think anybody would have been very comfortable going back," recalled Clarke.

When the players arrived in the locker room Sunday morning, there was a nine-word message scrawled on the blackboard: "Win together today, and we will walk together forever."

The Flyers were ready to throw everything they had at the Bruins in Game 6. They even brought in their secret weapon: Kate Smith, booked for an appearance on *The Mike Douglas Show* in Philadelphia the next day, was a no-brainer choice to sing "God Bless America."

"What could be better than being linked with something so wholesome as good, clean sport?" Smith rhetorically asked *Philadelphia Bulletin* writer Joe Adcock.

The Flyers gave the Bruins the game's first two power plays, but got a four-on-three advantage when Terry O'Reilly was sent off for tripping Barber at 13:58 followed by Orr and Clarke getting whistled for matching roughing minors at 14:22 after a goalmouth scrum.

Midway through the advantage, MacLeish beat Gregg Sheppard on a faceoff in the right circle, then got in front of the net and tipped a Dupont point shot past Gilbert at 14:48 of the first.

MacLeish, traded by the Bruins to the Flyers, described that night as "the best feeling I've had in my life."

"Only Rick could have done what he did," recalls Snider. "He had such great hand-eye coordination."

"It was a simple play, really," MacLeish said in *Walking Together Forever*. "Moose took a regular wrist shot, and I tried to tip it down, just change it up a bit, and wouldn't you know, it went in. It's something we practiced hundreds of times. In truth, it was a lucky goal."

Parent made the lead stand up. In one of the greatest big-game performances of all time, he stopped all 30 Bruins shots. His biggest save came with just under three minutes left, when Hodge ripped a low slap shot from the just above the left faceoff circle that looked destined for the inside of the far post, but Parent kicked out his right pad and kicked the shot aside.

"We threw everything we had at them in the sixth game and still needed a special effort from Bernie," says Clarke. "Parent in that particular game played the best game any player's ever played for the franchise."

As time ticked down, orange streamers started raining down from the Spectrum roof. Snider may have disagreed with the city's exaggerated ruling of the roof blowing off in 1968, but he was ecstatic that it might happen again.

Gloves, sticks, and players all flew into the air in celebration, and Gene Hart jubilantly screamed for all to hear, "The Flyers win the Stanley Cup! The Flyers win the Stanley Cup! The Flyers have won the Stanley Cup!"

Fans leapt the boards, some already with bottles of champagne, while the players engaged in the traditional postseries handshake. Many of the 17,000-plus were crowding onto the ice as Clarke and Parent, trailed by teammates, attempted a victory lap with the Cup.

They didn't get far, but that didn't mean they partied any less.

"I thought it was a wonderful thing when people stepped on the ice," says Parent. "I always said 75 percent of our success was our family at the Spectrum. I always felt it was 18,000 people and us playing against you. I was very happy when they jumped on the ice. It was as much their Stanley Cup as it was ours."

## POSTGAME ENTERTAINMENT

A city watched, listened, and cheered on May 19, 1974, when the Flyers won the Stanley Cup.

But no one beside the players, their families, and members of the organization know how beautiful the postgame celebration was. Rather than go inside the victorious locker room for interviews, NBC, which was televising the game, immediately cut to the movie *The Raiders*.

For his remarkable play, Parent was awarded the Conn Smythe Trophy as most valuable player for the playoffs. He went 12–5 with a pair of shutouts and a 2.02 goals-against average.

Parent also became the first goalie to win the Vezina and Conn Smythe trophies in the same season.

It was the first shutout in a Cup-clinching game in 20 years, and the 1–0 win was just the fourth time in league history the greatest title in sports had been won by the slimmest of margins. And it hasn't happened since.

The next day was the victory parade. Players, coaches, and other team officials piled into convertibles in the Spectrum parking lot for a ride up Broad Street and along Chestnut Street that ended at Independence Hall.

Police expected a crowd of a few hundred thousand for the first championship celebration since the 1967 Philadelphia 76ers won the NBA title; instead, a throng estimated at 2 million people overwhelmed the officers—and nearly overturned the cars carrying the players.

The car carrying Clarke and Ed Van Impe never made it to Independence Hall. Parent's car had to be stopped for fear of celebrating fans flipping it. Tom Bladon abandoned his car and walked, while MacLeish ended up with a bruised arm and Don Saleski had the sleeve of his jacket torn off by fans crazed at being so close to these champions.

Al Piazza was one of those 2 million. "I have a picture of Bernie Parent. It was something," the lifelong South Philadelphia resident and 40-year Flyers fan said. "I can remember that day, walking to Broad Street, it was bedlam. It was like that on the streets to Broad. It was just crazy. The day they won, South Philly was crazy, people hanging out of cars on Oregon Avenue.

"It was like the astronauts [returning from space]. In Center City, the tickertape was unbelievable. And it was played over and over on the news."

The parade was a special day for everyone associated with the Flyers. But it meant a little bit more to one three-year-old boy.

"My dad told me the first parade was for my birthday," said Brian Hart, Gene Hart's son.

Lauren Hart, Gene's daughter and currently the Flyers' sensational anthem singer, was only five years old at that first parade, but the memory of the event remains as clear today as it was on that day more than 30 years ago.

"When we got there, my father and Don Earl [Gene's broadcast partner] were supposed to ride in an open convertible right behind the Cup. The wives and children were all going to go on a bus behind. I remember my father grabbing us all and pulling all three kids and Don Earl's wife and my mom, and we all got into that two-seat convertible," she says. "Had he not done that, we would not have had that experience. And I remember people hanging from lampposts and street signs, and people wanted to shake my dad's hand."

When the parade—or at least most of it—reached Independence Hall, each player was introduced. Snider told the crowd, "They deserved the title. They've worked hard. We've got the number-one team in the world in the number-one city in the world."

Then it was Shero's turn, and the coach set the stage for the next season. "This is the greatest team in the league," he told the crowd, "and we're going to win it again next year."

# CUP II

Coach Fred Shero made the declaration that the Flyers would win the Stanley Cup again in the 1974–1975 season. It was up to GM Keith Allen to put the players in place to make it happen.

Allen wasn't interested in changing too much of a good thing. He did, though, believe the team needed more scoring, so five days after winning the Cup, he got a player he had been lusting after for a number of years: Reggie Leach.

Leach had been a teammate of Bobby Clarke's for two seasons with the Flin Flon Bombers, including one remarkable campaign when Leach had an amazing 87 goals and 131 points.

With Cowboy Bill Flett's scoring going down, and his alcohol consumption going up, Allen—living up to his nickname of Keith the Thief—sent Al MacAdam, Larry Wright, and a 1974 first-round pick to the California Golden Seals for Leach, and three days later moved Flett to the Toronto Maple Leafs.

Leach immediately was installed on Clarke's line, with Bill Barber completing the trio.

It was a gutsy move, both in the timing of the deal and for the player the Flyers acquired. Leach had unmistakable talent—the Boston Bruins thought so when they made him the third overall selection in the 1970 draft—but in five seasons his best output was 23 goals.

"[Leach] has never played with a good team or a good center-man as a pro," Allen said in making the deal. "He has a chance to be a star."

By Christmas the Flyers had reeled off 10- and 12-game unbeaten streaks. Backstopping their effort seemingly on an every-night basis was Bernie Parent. As great as the goalie had been the season before, he was even better in 1974–1975. In his first 37 starts, Parent had seven shutouts.

And not only was he making an impact on the ice, he was bringing newfound attention to the sport. On February 24, 1975, a masked Parent became the face of hockey when he appeared on the cover of *Time* magazine.

When the magazine hit newsstands, Parent had played in 53 of the Flyers' first 60 games, posting a 33–12–8 record with nine shutouts and a miniscule 2.11 goals-against average. The Flyers were 35–16–9 overall. Bumper stickers that read "Only the Lord Saves More Than Bernie Parent" began popping up on cars at all points in the Delaware Valley.

Bobby Clarke wasn't joking when he said in the *Time* story, "Bernie makes you feel like you can walk on water."

The Flyers ran roughshod over the league, with a 16–1–2 finishing kick, propelling them to league-highs of 51 wins and 113 points, one more in each category than the season before.

Parent, playing 68 of the 80 games, totaled 44 wins, a 2.03 goals-against average, and 12 shutouts.

Offensively, the Leach-Clarke-Barber triumvirate dominated the league. Leach, nicknamed the Rifle, finished with 45 goals. Clarke had 89 assists and 116 points, and won his second Hart Trophy. Barber finished with 34 goals, 37 assists, and 71 points.

Together, the LCB Line totaled 106 goals and 265 points, and had a plus-minus rating of plus-178. Leach, who had been a minus-61 in 1973–1974 with California, finished plus-53. Clarke was a stunning plus-79, while Barber was a plus-46.

"I think it was three different kinds of players," says Barber as to why the line worked so well. "Reggie had the cannon of a shot. I complemented in the sense of playing more detailed in all three zones and making sure I was accountable defensively. Clarkie was tenacious in his forecheck and anticipation of the puck. We all complemented one another. We knew where each other was, we always backed one another. We always took the sure route on things. We were three different players, but we could all score a little bit. We were tough to contain. Reggie could really gun the puck, so [defenses] tried to focus in on him. I was open a little bit. Reggie and I fed off ourselves quite a bit for rebound goals. It was one of those unique things."

The first-place Flyers opened the playoffs against the Toronto Maple Leafs. Parent was outstanding, keeping the Leafs off the scoreboard for a total of 143:16, covering the final 29 seconds of the second period of a 6–3 win in Game 1 and lasting through the first 2:47 of Game 4.

The Leafs made one last stand at home in Game 4. Barber scored in the second period to put the Flyers up 3–2, but Ron Ellis scored with 6:37 left in the third to force overtime.

Early in extra time, it was an unlikely pair combining to eliminate the Maple Leafs. Dave Schultz and Moose Dupont had combined for just 20 goals during the regular season, but it was Schultz who intercepted a Toronto pass and dropped the puck for Dupont, whose wrister from about 20 feet out beat goalie Gord McRae and closed the series.

On the flight home from Canada, the players danced to a new song that was set to debut on Philadelphia Top 40 AM radio—Schultz's single, "Penalty Box." Some of the lyrics: "Love is like an ice hockey game, sometimes it can be rough/You got me checking and holding and hooking and then you blow the whistle on me." Despite the lyrics and overall lack of singing ability, the fact that Schultz's name was attached sent the song soaring up the charts, and records flew off the shelves.

The Toronto challenge answered, it was on to the conference finals against the New York Islanders, who had just become the second team ever to overcome a 3–0 deficit in a best-of-seven series when they got past the Pittsburgh Penguins in the quarterfinals.

The Flyers felt confident—until a Gary Dornhoefer shot hit Parent on an unprotected part of the netminder's knee. Parent couldn't get back on his feet, and backup Wayne Stephenson, who had played just 12 games all season—and not at all in the previous six weeks—was pressed into action.

Stephenson was up to the challenge, shutting out a young Islanders squad—which featured much of the core of the dynastic team that would win four straight Cups in the early 1980s—and Clarke scored the overtime winner in Game 2.

With Parent back for Game 3, the only goal came from Leach, who looped a backhander over Chico Resch's glove 30 seconds into the third period.

Once again, the Isles were down 3–0 in a series. Once again, they mounted a comeback.

The Islanders won Game 4, 4–3, on an overtime goal by Jude Drouin, and they won Game 5 in a 5–1 rout, handing the Flyers their first home playoff loss in two years.

At Nassau Coliseum for Game 6, the teams were tied 1–1 early in the third when Flyers rookie defenseman Larry Goodenough gave the puck away to the Islanders' Gerry Hart, who rifled a shot over Parent's glove to give the Isles a series-tying 2–1 win.

Their season on the line, the Flyers brought in a little extra ammunition for Game 7. Kate Smith was secreted into Philadelphia, and once again her rendition of "God Bless America" drove the 17,077 Spectrum denizens into bedlam.

The Flyers' performance on the ice kept the good feelings rolling. Jimmy Watson forced Eddie Westfall to turn the puck over, and Dornhoefer fired a shot from 40 feet out that beat Resch to the short side, giving the Flyers a 1–0 lead just 19 seconds into the game. Rick MacLeish added a pair of goals, redirecting a Barber shot for a power-play goal at 2:27 to make it 2–0, and then again on a wrister to make it 3–1, 7:11 into the game. MacLeish capped his night with an empty-net goal, finishing the Islanders and sending the Flyers back to the Stanley Cup Finals.

The Flyers' foe in the final series was the Buffalo Sabres. The Sabres had eliminated the powerful Montreal Canadiens in their conference final, led by their French Connection Line of Gilbert Perreault, Rick Martin, and Rene Robert. As good as the LCB Line was, the Connection was better, combining for 131 goals and 291 points.

In Game 1 Barber snapped a scoreless tie in the third period and added an empty-net goal late, and Clarke had a goal and two assists in a 4–1 win.

In Game 2 Clarke set up Leach for the game's first goal midway through the second period. After Jerry Korab tied the game early in the third, Clarke took a pass from Barber and scored from the left side of the net at 6:43 of the third. Parent slammed the door the rest of the way, and the Flyers shuffled to Buffalo with a 2–0 series lead.

The fog got the better of the Fog and the Flyers in Game 3.

May 20, 1975, was an unusually warm spring day in Buffalo, and temperatures reached 90 degrees. As the temperature inside Memorial Auditorium—which did not have air-conditioning—matched the outside air, a mist began to rise as the ice started melting under the players' skates. The game was stopped 12 different times so players and arena workers, some holding bedsheets, could skate around the ice to try to dissipate the mist.

Adding to the surreal feeling was a bat that began buzzing the ice. Prior to a faceoff, Sabres forward Jim Lorentz slashed the bat with his stick. It dropped dead onto the ice as players and officials stared at it. Finally, MacLeish scooped up the carcass and dropped it in the penalty box.

Whatever the bizarre night held, the Flyers looked unstoppable early. Dornhoefer scored off a Barber takeaway just 39 seconds into the game, and then Don Saleski gave the Flyers a 2–0 lead at the 3:09 mark. Danny Gare and Martin scored 17 seconds apart to tie the game, but MacLeish put the Flyers back ahead when he scored with 5:47 left in the first. Don Luce tied the game 29 seconds into the second, but Leach put the Flyers ahead until Bill Hajt scored off a Martin rebound midway through the third, which forced overtime.

The longer play went, the thicker the fog got, making the puck harder to see. Play was stopped seven times just in the 18 minutes of overtime. Finally, Robert played a Perreault dump-in along the goal line in the Flyers' end, and from the sharpest of angles, he slid a shot past Parent's skates and into the net.

"I didn't see Perreault's pass," Parent told reporters after the game. "I saw Robert's shot too late for me to come out and stop it."

The Flyers remained confident heading into Game 4, and held a 1–0 lead after 20 minutes thanks to a Dupont goal. That would be as good as the night got for the Flyers, though, as Buffalo scored three times in the second period en route to a 4–2 series-tying victory.

In Philadelphia for Game 5, the Flyers bombarded Buffalo goalie Gerry Desjardins with shots, rather than look for nice set-ups to lead to goals. Dave Schultz started and finished what would become a 5–1 rout. He surprised Desjardins from a sharp angle just 3:12 into the game, and then closed the night with a break-away goal. With the win, the Flyers were one game away from their second straight Stanley Cup.

Game 6, on May 27, 1975, was scoreless through the first two periods thanks to Parent, who held off five Buffalo power plays.

Shero, worried that some of his players might be tiring from penalty-killing duties—the coach used his best players in all situations, including Barber and Clarke as his top short-handed forwards—took the advice of assistant coach Mike Nykoluk and subbed Kelly for Barber on the top line to open the third period.

Clarke won a faceoff back to his defense, with the puck ending up on Leach's stick along the right wall. He dumped the puck behind the Buffalo net, where Kelly beat Korab to the puck, but Korab momentarily pinned Kelly to the glass. Clarke joined the party behind the goal and bumped Korab hard enough to let Kelly spin away. Kelly bolted in front to the right of goalie Roger Crozier and slid a backhander to the far side of the net 11 seconds into the frame, and the Flyers held a 1–0 lead.

Kelly celebrated with teammates, but when he returned to the bench, he had a few words for Shero.

"I told Freddy he owed me five dollars," Kelly says.

The reference came from a drill frequently used by Shero in which players had to bull their way from behind the net and score a goal. They ran the drill during the final 15 minutes of every practice during the 1974–1975 season. And when the moment struck, all the practice time paid off.

The Flyers doggedly protected their goal, and Parent, as usual, was outstanding. His best save came late, when Barber failed to clear the puck and Craig Ramsay blindly whacked it with his backhand to an open Luce, who tipped it on net, but Parent made a juggling chest save with under five minutes left.

The Flyers got an insurance goal when Orest Kindrachuk blocked a Brian Spencer shot and raced the length of the ice to

## BILL CLEMENT TRADE

When Bill Clement scored the insurance goal in the Cup-clinching win over the Buffalo Sabres in 1975, technically speaking, Clement wasn't even a Flyer.

Earlier in the game, Flyers general manager Keith Allen had agreed on a deal that would send the young center to the Capitals, along with defenseman Don MacLean and a first-round draft pick, for the Caps' number-one overall selection in the upcoming draft.

corral the loose puck. Spencer and Korab chased Kindrachuk, and as Spencer caught him, he drilled the winger with a forearm to the head. But Kindrachuk was able to backhand the puck to a trailing Bill Clement, who shot the puck between Crozier's pads with 2:47 left to play.

The Flyers' bench emptied onto the ice to celebrate Clement's first—and last—playoff goal as a Flyer. When the final horn sounded, the Flyers again leapt off their bench and mobbed Parent. For the second straight season, he had backstopped a Cup-clinching effort with a shutout, the only netminder in NHL history to accomplish the feat.

Parent finished the playoffs 10–5 with four shutouts and a miniscule 1.89 goals-against average, numbers even better than the previous year. He again won the Conn Smythe Trophy as playoff MVP—the only goalie in league history to win it in consecutive years.

When Clarence Campbell handed the silver chalice to Clarke for a second consecutive season, the captain and the goalie finally got to skate their celebratory lap around the ice—something they didn't get to do the previous year at the Spectrum due to the overzealousness of the fans.

"It was really congested [the previous year]," recalls Barber. "There were so many people on the ice you never really had the true opportunity. The second time we did it, it was in Buffalo...it was pretty awesome. It's a memory that sticks with you. There's moments and memories. Memories are special things. Moments are everyday stuff you deal with. They're great memories that are with you the rest of your life."

They say you never forget your first time, but some players considered the second Cup just a bit sweeter.

"I can honestly say it's a better feeling to win two years in a row," Parent told reporters after the game. "When we won last year we were in the clouds. This year it was different because we knew what we were doing and where we were going. We proved to everyone that last year was no fluke."

More than 30 years later, Parent still feels the same way.

"The second one was better," he says. "We could appreciate more what happened. We had the Stanley Cup, and we flew back

**Bernie Parent (left) and Bill Clement (right) clasp hands as NHL President Clarence Campbell (second from left) presents them with the Stanley Cup after their victory over the Buffalo Sabres on May 27, 1975. Bobby Clarke (second from right) gives a big, gap-toothed grin.**

from Buffalo and had an hour and 15 minutes by ourselves to just reflect on this thing. It was beautiful."

For Kelly, he was just happy to be on the ice when the Cup was won. A knee injury had shelved him for the 1974 title series against the Bruins, and he didn't know until game time that he would be playing in Game 6, as Shero had considered kenneling the Hound.

"You have to be there in the end to feel like you made a contribution," Kelly told reporters that night.

Kelly then turned and told a man in a suit seated at his stall to get the heck out of there. The man, Pennsylvania Governor Milton Shapp, apologized and walked away.

After the near-riots of the previous year, Philadelphia police had the players ride on flatbed trucks for the parade down Broad Street to a rally at JFK Stadium.

There were 100,000 people packed into the stadium, plus an estimated 2.2 million lining Broad Street for the parade, meaning about 2.3 million—or 300,000 more people—saw the second parade.

There was none of the same pandemonium of the previous year, except for when Parent jumped off a truck and knocked on a door along South Broad Street and asked the homeowner if he could use the bathroom.

There also were none of the same pronouncements from Shero or anyone else. None were needed. Philadelphia was the center of the hockey universe. Anyone who didn't recognize it the previous year certainly knew it now.

# DEFEATING THE RED MENACE

The Broad Street Bullies were the ultimate bad guys, a hoard of rampaging monsters, beating and beating up people.

They didn't play classy, dignified hockey, but two straight Stanley Cups meant nobody in the City of Brotherly Love really gave a damn.

Ed Snider—credited or blamed, depending on your point of view—thinks the violence has overshadowed the legacy of the championship teams.

"The sad part is," Snider says, "that phase of it has detracted from our Stanley Cup championships. The truth of it is we had phenomenal talent on those teams, great coaching."

But the Flyers were the Broad Street Bullies, and no one likes a bully. But there was this one time...

In 1976 the Russian government sent a pair of all-star hockey teams to tour North America in their quest to show Communist supremacy over all things in the Western world. The final stop on the Russian Central Red Army team's barnstorming tour was a visit to the Spectrum to play the two-time defending Stanley Cup champions, on January 11, 1976.

The Red Army team had beaten the New York Rangers and Boston Bruins, and even the mighty Montreal Canadiens only could manage a tie.

"It was their all-star team against our regular franchises, and they were winning," says Snider. "They came in here, and we were the defending Stanley Cup champions. We were the team that everybody was hoping would finally beat these sons of bitches. The game had everything; it was mind-boggling."

Philadelphia, the cradle of liberty, the birthplace of the nation, put orange and black right next to the red, white, and blue.

Even other NHL teams were pulling for the Flyers.

"We were hated," recalls Snider, "And suddenly all of Canada wanted us to win."

"In those days it was defeating the Communist lifestyle," says Bob Clarke. "The Cold War was on. It was more than just a hockey game."

Clarke had initiated his own cold war with the Russians. During the famed 1972 Summit Series, he had slashed Soviet star Valeri Kharlamov hard enough to break the Russian legend's ankle.

"It wasn't premeditated," Clarke told reporters in the build-up to the 1976 game. "He had speared me, and it wasn't a clean series from the start."

After the Russians arrived in Philadelphia, the NHL hosted both teams and the press at a luncheon at the Blue Line Club at the Spectrum.

"The Russian players were on one side, and our players were on the other," recalls Snider. "Because of the cold war, the Russians were like slaves, they weren't allowed to do anything, very gruff, angry."

Gene Hart, who spoke some Russian, had taught Snider a few phrases to use to welcome the visitors to town.

"Gene taught me how to say in Russian, 'We welcome you to our fair city and we hope you're enjoying yourselves,' something like that. So I practiced and practiced, got up and I said [in English], 'We're looking forward to the game tonight, may the best team win,' and I sat down. Gene said, 'Did you forget?' I said I looked at those sons of bitches and I couldn't welcome them."

Fred Shero had been a disciple of the Soviet hockey style. Days after the Flyers' first Cup victory, Shero flew to Moscow to attend a coaching clinic led by Anatoly Tarasov, the father of Russian hockey. Shero spoke no Russian, and Tarasov spoke no English, but the pair somehow found a way to communicate.

Fred Shero coached the Flyers to two Stanley Cups and a memorable win over the Russians in 1976, but felt his ability to motivate the Flyers was waning by the late 1970s.

Shero believed the style of play used by the Flyers, where the third forward would stay high in the offensive zone, would cut off the Russians' favored long passes through the middle of the ice.

That, and the Flyers could bludgeon the Russians senseless.

"I'm not sure the Soviets wanted it with that type of attitude, but that was our type of attitude," says Clarke. "It was going to be ugly. We were going to beat you, and if you were going to beat us, you were going to pay a big price. And they weren't willing to pay the price."

There was more to it than just a hockey game. Clarke remembers people in Philadelphia imploring him and his teammates to do awful things to the Russians, including winning the game.

"We heard that all the time," he said.

While fans took it personally, so did forward Orest Kindrachuk. Kindrachuk's grandparents were of Ukrainian descent, and had told him about how the Soviets had mistreated their people.

"They told us stories about how tough it was for them over there," he said to reporters. "I was so happy to beat them. When I was out there, I didn't want to look at them, hear them."

Snider also had more than just the interest of an owner or a fan. Snider, a Jewish man, hated the Soviets for their treatment of Russian Jews, and long swore that he never would have a Russian player on his team.

Jewish activist groups marched outside the Spectrum on the day of the game, protesting the harassment and imprisonment of Russian Jews. Banners were hung inside the Spectrum, in Russian and English, demanding freedom for Russian Jews. But all the banners were taken down before the game, as the Russians said they wouldn't play if the signs were allowed to stay.

Off the opening faceoff, the Russians dropped back into their zone and made eight passes before coming forward. Meanwhile, the Flyers waited, like hungry lions watching gazelles at a watering hole.

"Shero had been over there and had a little understanding of them," remembered Clarke. "We had seen them play since 1972, and that's the style they played. Once you had the patience and discipline to just wait, they had to bring the puck to you eventually. They could keep going backwards all they wanted, but they have to come forward at some point if they want to score. And once they started coming forward, we took them physically, and then they weren't so eager to come forward."

The Flyers started on the attack early, outshooting the Russians 10–2, but world-renowned goalie Vladimir Tretiak was up to the challenge. The Flyers even got the game's first power play, when Boris Aleksandrov was sent off for elbowing Gary Dornhoefer in the head 2:24 into the game.

But with Ed Van Impe off for tripping Vladimir Lutchenko at 9:10 of the first, the serious hitting began. Moose Dupont threw a shoulder into Army captain Boris Mikhailov at the Flyers' blue line. Then Bill Barber, on the forecheck, rammed Valeri Vasilyev hard into the boards in the Russian end, and then cross-checked Kharlamov in the face.

As Van Impe jumped out of the box, he ran directly at Kharlamov, elbowing him in the head and leaving the Russian face-down on the ice in the Flyers' end.

"He basically ran into my elbow with his head," Van Impe joked in *Walking Together Forever*. "I've always said I just couldn't understand how a world-class player would have wanted to do such a thing."

Snider describes the incident a little differently: "Ed Van Impe put one of his famous checks on one of the Russians." He adds with a chuckle, "Ed Van Impe wasn't one of the cleanest hockey players."

The Russian players and their coach, Konstantin Loktev, screamed for a penalty, but the only one coming was a two-minute bench minor to the Russians for delay of game. Loktev then waved his team off the ice and into the locker room. There was still 8:39 left to play in the first period.

Snider immediately ran down to the locker room, where he met with NHL president Clarence Campbell and NHLPA president Alan Eagleson, who was coordinating the Russian tour.

"We went down, and they said we're not playing," remembers Snider. "They won't play, they're going to leave. I said, 'What's the status of the payment for this tournament?' They said we haven't given them anything yet. They get the check tonight for all the games. I said to tell them you're not going to pay them. I think we were the eighth game, and it was only, like, $25,000 a game in those days. They were supposed to get a couple hundred grand, but they hadn't been paid anything yet. It was supposed to be settled that night, so I said just tell them they're not going to get paid for the tournament. They told them, they started huddling, then they came back and said, 'We play.'"

After a 17-minute delay, the Russians returned.

"They cried it was too physical, but it wasn't any more physical than what we played against NHL teams," says Clarke. "It was just another form of quitting when they walked off. I don't think the players would have done that. It was their coaches and the people in charge who did that to the players. But the game was over....I think 10, 12 minutes into the game we knew."

The game resumed with the Flyers on the power play, and 17 seconds later, Reggie Leach tipped a Barber shot past Tretiak for the game's first goal.

The Flyers got another when Rick MacLeish's wrister went over Tretiak's glove with 2:23 left in the first.

Even when the Russians had a power play, they seemed to shy away from anything resembling physical play, allowing the Flyers to continue to dominate.

Early in the second, with Dupont in the penalty box for tripping Kharlamov on a breakaway, Don Saleski took a pass from Kindrachuk and cut wide on the Russian defense. He fired a shot from the right side that handcuffed Tretiak and dropped to the ice. Joe Watson knocked it in, giving the Flyers a 3–0 lead.

Watson, who was far from a prolific goal-scorer—NHL career totals: 835 games, 38 goals—recalled Shero coming into the locker room and saying, "That set the Russian hockey program back 20 years by scoring that goal."

The Russians got their only goal at 10:48 of the second, when Viktor Kutyorgin scored on just their sixth shot of the game. That was all the Russians could manage, as the Flyers' forechecking and tight defense continued to stifle them.

The Flyers made it 4–1 after Clarke drew a hooking penalty on Alexei Volchenkov, and on the ensuing power play fed a cutting Larry Goodenough, who sneaked in from the point and beat Tretiak with a wrist shot at 4:01 of the third.

Shero told reporters after the game that he felt as good after beating the Russians as he did after beating the Bruins in 1974 to win the Stanley Cup.

The final shot tally was 49–13 for the Flyers, and despite the claims of the Red Army coach, who said the Flyers played "like animals," the animals had just two more penalty minutes than the Russians, 14–12.

"We made every place they went on the ice miserable for them, and they quit," recalls Clarke. "They didn't compete."

In the days following the game, something strange happened. The phone calls and letters that used to decry the players and the organization as thugs and bullies had a different tenor.

The players were heroes, avenging the honor of their league brethren.

"Probably the only time the league was cheering for us," Clarke says with a smile. "To this day."

## THE KIDS AND THE CUP I

The first seeds for the Flyers team that grew to make the 1984–1985 Stanley Cup Finals were planted in the summer of 1979.

With their first pick, at number 14 overall, the Flyers chose high-scoring winger Brian Propp. In the third round, they made what some considered a reach and others viewed as shocking: they took a relatively unknown Swedish goalie named Pelle Lindbergh.

Jerry Melnyk, the scout who in 1969 fought so hard to convince the Flyers to take a diabetic center from Flin Flon, Manitoba, named Bobby Clarke, raved about Lindbergh. The Flyers knew they wouldn't be getting Lindbergh for at least a year so he could play in the 1980 Olympics, but that was fine by Melnyk. Overshadowed by the U.S. team's Lake Placid miracle was the fact that Lindbergh was the only goalie to face the Americans and not lose.

Lindbergh played eight games for the Flyers in 1981–1982 and 40 relatively unimpressive games the following season. Then a rocky start in 1983–1984 saw him serve a four-game sentence with the AHL's Springfield Indians. But with the dawning of the 1984–1985 season, rookie coach Mike Keenan declared the 25-year-old Lindbergh his number-one goalie.

When Keenan convened his first training camp in 1984, he was looking at the youngest team in the league. The oldest player on the roster was 33-year-old defenseman Miroslav Dvorak, but it was only his third NHL season.

Mark Howe was a veritable graybeard at 29. Ilkka Sinisalo and Brad Marsh were 26; Propp, team captain Dave Poulin, and Brad McCrimmon were 25; Tim Kerr was 24; Ron Sutter and Rick Tocchet were 20; and Peter Zezel was only 19.

And not only were the players young, it was Bob Clarke's first year as general manager, and for Keenan, just 34, the 1984–1985 Flyers were his first NHL team.

He already had a reputation for having a tongue as sharp as a skate blade. But he had taken Peterborough to the Memorial Cup championship, and won an AHL title with Rochester, Buffalo's minor-league affiliate—beating Maine, the Flyers' minor-league club, in the finals—and led the University of Toronto to the Canadian university title.

"Everybody I talked to said that his style would cause some problems with players, but that he had always won," Clarke said in *Full Spectrum.*

The Flyers entered the 1984–1985 season with a first-time NHL coach, a first-time general manager, and a roster of kids. They hadn't won a playoff round in three years, all of which added up to low expectations—but not for Keenan.

"Some form of excellence," was Keenan's answer to reporters who asked what his goal was for the coming season. Meeting that level excellence would not be an easy task.

"He was willing to do whatever it took to get the best out of someone," Poulin says of Keenan. "It's a difficult proposition because there are times you don't want to do what's necessary as a coach. I think the best coaches in many respects have to be unreasonable about what a player goes through. The demands on a player have to be so extreme, and it's very hard to get to that point. That's not a reasonable demand, and Mike was able to make unreasonable demands."

They gave Keenan what he wanted early, roaring out of the box with a 6–2–3 start through the season's first month.

"Everybody is so enthusiastic," Kerr told reporters. "The expectations, at least from the outside, aren't as great they've been the last few years, and so far we're having fun."

Kerr was having more fun than most. He posted the club's first four-goal game in four seasons October 25 against St. Louis, and a pair November 15—Bob Clarke Appreciation Night—gave him 17 in 15 games.

By December 8, the young Flyers had blazed to a 17–4–5 mark, but over the next two months, they sputtered along at 14–12–2. They recovered to enter early March second to Washington in the Patrick Division, but facing a three-game set that featured a trip to Long Island and a home-and-home series with the Caps.

The Flyers topped the Islanders in overtime when Propp intercepted a pass and fed Poulin for the game-winner. Two nights later at the Spectrum, the Flyers fell behind the Capitals 4–2 midway through the second, but hat tricks by Poulin and Kerr—the latter notching goals 49, 50, and 51 on the season—keyed a 9–6 win.

The next night in Washington, Sinisalo and Derrick Smith scored early, Murray Craven added a goal in the second, and Howe notched an empty-net goal with five seconds left as the Flyers finished with a 4–2 win.

The Flyers shotgunned their way through the rest of the schedule, blowing away 13 of their final 14 foes. Trailing Washington by 11 points February 9, they won the Patrick by 12. They finished with a team-record 53 wins, and their 113 points was four better than Edmonton for tops in the league.

Despite missing four games down the stretch with a knee injury, Kerr led the team with 54 goals—matching his total from the previous season—and 98 points. Propp added 43 goals and 97 points. Sinisalo had 36 goals, and Poulin had 30 with 44 assists.

Howe finished a remarkable plus-51 and added 39 assists and 57 points. His defense partner, McCrimmon, posted a plus-52.

In goal, Lindbergh was nothing short of sensational. Playing 65 games, he went 40–17–7 with a 3.02 goals-against average, .899 save percentage, and two shutouts. He was rewarded with the first-ever Bobby Clarke Trophy as Flyers team MVP, and later added the Vezina Trophy as top goalie in the league.

The Flyers opened the playoffs against the New York Rangers. They had swept the seven-game season series, averaging more than four goals per game, while the Rangers had sneaked into the playoffs with a 26–44–10 record, the second-worst record ever for a playoff team. The Rangers had amassed just 62 points—51 fewer than the Flyers.

Despite their dominance over their neighbors to the north, Keenan said he sensed fear in his young team.

Some of that could have been the fact that only three players—Kerr, Propp, and defenseman Thomas Eriksson—had

# THE GUFFAW

Brian Propp was known as much for scoring goals as he was for his celebration, the Guffaw.

Propp got the idea while attending a Howie Mandel show in Atlantic City during the summer of 1986. Mandel suggested the Guffaw—a short left-to-right wave followed by extending the arm straight up to the ceiling—instead of laughing to confuse the next comic on stage. Propp had other ideas.

"I was thinking about the Guffaw and finally scored my first of the year," Propp writes on his website. "I had the usual crowd of players congratulating me after the goal; then, as I broke away from the pack and headed to center ice, I put my right glove under my left arm and did the 'Guffaw' as I skated toward center ice."

Propp continued the Guffaw for the rest of his career, and does it today for fans at golf outings.

won a playoff series as a Flyer, and only four others—blueliners Doug Crossman, Brad Marsh, Ed Hospodor, and McCrimmon—had won a playoff series at all.

"I could feel the nervousness," Keenan recalled in *Full Spectrum*. "After all we had accomplished, as strongly as we had finished, they weren't sure they could win."

It didn't take them long to figure out they could.

Ron Sutter scored on an odd-man rush just 4:04 into the game, and then Todd Bergen's long shot deflected off Rangers defenseman Grant Ledyard and past goalie Glen Hanlon. McCrimmon finished a three-on-two break to give the Flyers a 3–0 lead after 20 minutes of hockey.

The Rangers rallied, and when Don Maloney deked Lindbergh and scored 1:17 into the third period, the game was tied.

Kerr put the Flyers back ahead, scoring off a Hanlon giveaway, but Anders Hedberg tallied with 26 seconds left to force overtime.

Any apprehension from regulation was washed away during the intermission, as the Flyers came out flying, outshooting the

Rangers 8–1 to start overtime. As the midpoint of the extra session neared, Sutter beat Reijo Ruotsalainen to a McCrimmon dump-in and passed from behind the net to Howe, who had crept to the top of the right faceoff circle. With Lindsey Carson providing a screen, Howe fired a shot that went between Hanlon's pads, giving the Flyers a 5–4 win.

The Rangers drew first blood in Game 2 when George McPhee tipped a Ron Greschner shot past Lindbergh 61 seconds into the second period. Bergen redirected a point shot by Crossman past Hanlon to tie the game, and then knocked in Marsh's rebound 5:23 into the third. Sinisalo converted a Sutter pass with 2:20 left to ice the 3–1 victory.

Home for Game 3, the Rangers took a 2–0 lead on goals by Ruotsalainen and Maloney. Zezel got a goal back late after Hedberg was sent off for tripping, and then Crossman scored on a delayed penalty early in the second to tie it. With Kerr off for tripping, Willie Huber scored off a rebound to put the Rangers back up 3–2.

But Kerr would make up for his gaffe in a historic way.

Over the next 8 minutes, 16 seconds, Kerr put four pucks into the Rangers' net, three on the power play, and a one-goal deficit became a 6–3 advantage. The offensive explosion set an NHL playoff record for fastest four goals in a game.

Maloney and Hedberg scored in the first four minutes of the third period, but the Flyers played flawless defense for the final 16, and skated into the second round of the playoffs for the first time since 1981.

The Flyers' foe in the Patrick Division Finals was the New York Islanders.

Poulin, who had partially torn knee ligaments in Game 2 against the Rangers, was out, so into the scoring breach stepped Propp. The winger had just three goals and eight points in the three previous spring flameouts, but he set up second-period goals by Tocchet and Kerr, and Lindbergh stopped all 22 shots he faced as the Flyers took a 3–0 win in Game 1.

The Islanders opened Game 2 hot, throwing 14 shots on Lindbergh and earning three power plays in the first 20 minutes.

The Flyers hung tough, as Propp had a hat trick and Kerr had a goal and three assists. The Flyers took a 5–2 win and a 2–0 series lead.

The Isles took a 1–0 lead in Game 3 when Lindbergh accidentally knocked Anders Kallur's pass into his goal. But with Paul Boutilier and Ken Morrow in the penalty box, Crossman scored on a five-on-three power play to tie the game. Tocchet scored with 1:12 left to give the Flyers a 2–1 lead after one period.

Sutter and Propp scored to make it 4–1 eight minutes into the second, but Brent Sutter and John Tonelli answered with two of their 27 second-period shots, making it a one-goal game with 20 minutes of hockey left.

Rather than wilt, the Flyers strengthened, limiting the Islanders to just four shots in the third, and Sinisalo iced it with an empty-net goal. The 5–3 win put the Flyers one game away from the Wales Conference Finals.

These Islanders had rallied from 3–0 deficits before, and they made a nice first step in that regard in Game 4. Tonelli set up first-period goals by Pat LaFontaine and Bryan Trottier, and when Mike Bossy scored at 8:53 of the second to make it 4–0, Keenan pulled Lindbergh for Bob Froese in what became a 6–2 loss.

After a scoreless first period in Game 5, the Flyers turned on the jets in the second and outshot the Isles 17–8. Just under seven minutes into the period, Zezel entered the zone, dropped a pass for Crossman, and drove to the net, where he got tangled with goalie Kelly Hrudey. Hrudey stopped Crossman's shot, but Sinisalo dumped the rebound into an open net.

From there it was all Lindbergh, as he closed the series the same way he opened it, stopping 25 shots to earn his second shutout of the series.

The Quebec Nordiques stood between the Flyers and a berth in the Stanley Cup Finals. In an odd quirk of the schedule, the series started in Quebec due to Adams Division teams winning more regular-season games in head-to-head battles with Patrick Division clubs.

Poulin returned for Game 1, but it didn't help as Peter Stastny snapped a 1–1 deadlock at 6:20 of overtime when he rang a long shot past Lindbergh and under the crossbar.

Not only did the Flyers trail in a series for the first time, they also lost Kerr to a sprained right knee ligament in the first period.

While Game 1 had little anger to it, the teams wasted little time finding their hate in Game 2. Tocchet and Pat Price dropped the gloves 30 seconds in, and there were four fights in all.

Between all the fisticuffs, Poulin suffered cracked ribs when Mario Marois sticked him, but the grinding captain took a feed from Craven and scored shorthanded at 11:16.

Craven and Sinisalo notched goals in the second, and after J.F. Sauve scored for the Nords, Joe Paterson, playing in place of the injured Kerr, added an insurance goal and the Flyers evened the series with a 4–2 victory.

As the series shifted to the Spectrum, Paterson's solid play continued. He set up Craven for a first-period goal, and after Quebec took a 2–1 lead after one period, he scored 1:41 into the second to tie it, and then drew the second assist on Sinisalo's game-winner. Propp notched an insurance marker, and the Flyers, despite playing without Kerr, Poulin, and McCrimmon, who was lost after a first-period blast into the boards by Wilf Paiement left him with a grotesquely separated shoulder (Dr. John Gregg said the defenseman's shoulder blade was next to his ear), took home a 4–2 victory and a 2–1 series lead.

The Flyers' good fortune ran out three nights later. Quebec jumped to a 2–0 lead, and after Howe's goal early in the third tied it at 3–3, the Nordiques scored twice more to take a 5–3 win back to Quebec City.

"You can't be great every night," Lindbergh told reporters.

But he was just that in Game 5. The Flyers had just 12 shots over the first 40 minutes, but trailed just 1–0 thanks to stellar play by Lindbergh, who allowed only Sauve's goal at 7:02 of the second.

Keenan ranted and raved between periods, imploring his young team to push further than they thought they could— another of what Poulin called Keenan's "unreasonable demands."

Whatever he said worked, as Paterson knocked in a Howe pass 60 seconds into the period to tie the game. With five minutes left,

Propp sent Craven in alone on goalie Mario Gosselin, and the winger shot high off Gosselin's shoulder for the deciding goal and a 3–2 series lead.

The Flyers returned home with a chance to clinch the series but knew they had to play better.

They did just that, limiting the Nords to five shots in the first period, and taking a lead when Tocchet tipped a Howe drive into the net. After penalties 37 seconds apart to Paterson and Propp put the Flyers two men down early in the second, Poulin, wearing a flak jacket to protect his cracked ribs, intercepted a lazy pass by Marois, raced the length of the ice, and buried one of the biggest goals in club history behind Gosselin.

Crossman added a goal as the Flyers and Lindbergh, facing just 15 shots, needed little effort in closing his second straight playoff series with a shutout.

The Flyers, the youngest team in the league, were going to play for the oldest prize in hockey.

With Kerr back in the lineup for Game 1, plus the home-ice advantage, the Flyers seemed like a team of destiny. But standing in their way were the defending Stanley Cup champion Edmonton Oilers in all their future Hall of Fame glory—Wayne Gretzky, Mark Messier, Jari Kurri, Esa Tikkanen, Paul Coffey, Kevin Lowe, Grant Fuhr, Glenn Anderson.

"I don't know if there was an awe factor, maybe more of a scared factor," says Propp. "They were all in their prime, and all Hall of Famers. I don't think there was awe, it was, we all have to play our best games if we're going to beat that team."

They didn't look intimidated in Game 1. With a two-man advantage late in the first period, Bergen threw a puck into the crease that Sinisalo knocked in.

In the third, with the score still 1–0, Ron Sutter stole a Coffey pass and scored, and then Poulin stole the puck from Anderson and fed Kerr, who scored to make it 3–0. Poulin added an empty-net goal as the Flyers took a 4–1 victory and the series lead.

The victory extended the Flyers' win streak over the Oilers to nine straight, a streak that dated back three seasons. But one Flyer knew things wouldn't be easy.

"Historically, in the regular season we beat the Oilers the majority of the time," recalls Howe. "But the team you saw in the finals was a completely different team. The Oilers were a highly skilled team that played loose and open hockey in the regular season, but in the playoffs, when you talk about all the small details of the game, their attention to detail was as good as any team I've ever seen."

Gretzky found a keen eye for the newspaper, especially something written in *The Philadelphia Inquirer* by Al Morganti.

Morganti wrote, "Unless they are total frauds, the Oilers should be able to play a lot better." It wasn't meant to be insulting, just Morganti's way of saying that the Oilers were the better team and still should win the series.

"That's just how Wayne was, finding motivation from nothing," Morganti says now.

The Great One notched the first goal of Game 2, recovering his centering pass from between Howe's skates and scoring.

Kerr, his knee suffering, tied the game after Poulin poked the puck away from Messier, but Willy Lindstrom put the Oilers ahead when he scored from in close, and Dave Hunter added an insurance goal in the Oilers' 3–1 win.

The series moved to Alberta for Game 3, which Gretzky took over in the first period, scoring three times. The Flyers managed a Derrick Smith tally after Gretzky's first two goals. Philadelphia trailed 4–1 entering the third, but they limited the Oilers to just two shots, and Howe and Propp each scored to make it a one-goal game.

That was as close as the Flyers got, though, as their last, best chance ended a bounce short. With 15 seconds left, Craven nearly sprung Tocchet on a breakaway, but the pass was just behind the winger, and he stumbled trying to reach back for the puck. The Oilers escaped with a 4–3 win and the series lead.

The Flyers may have trailed just 2–1 in the series, but they were at the end of their collective rope by the start of Game 4. Kerr's knee was bad enough to end his season, and Poulin's ribs had made the captain a shell of himself. Despite that, Craven's short-handed goal midway through the first gave the Flyers a 3–1 lead.

But their injuries and inexperience, combined with the Oilers' superior skill, allowed the home team to tie the game early in the second, and two goals by Gretzky gave the Oilers a 5–3 win and put the Flyers on the brink of elimination.

Game 5 was an Edmonton whitewash. Lindbergh, who had taken a shot off the back of his knee in the Quebec series, took another when a Mike Krushelnyski drive caught him in the same spot in Game 4. Doctors diagnosed a partially torn quadriceps tendon, meaning Froese, who was less than 100 percent after December knee surgery, had to step into the breach.

The Oilers, smelling blood, poured eight goals past the helpless Froese. Rich Sutter scored twice, and Propp added a goal, but it was the Oilers who celebrated their second straight Stanley Cup at home.

"We knew how great they were as individuals, but we were really beat up," says Howe. "McCrimmon was out, Timmy Kerr was out, Dave Poulin was out with broken ribs. I think the only two big scorers we had on our team were Brian Propp and Sinisalo. When you're playing a juggernaut, it's kind of a tough task."

## THE KIDS AND THE CUP II

When the Flyers reported for camp in 1986, it was much the same group that had gone to the Stanley Cup Finals two seasons prior.

The kids who had ridden their youthful exuberance to that 1985 final were two years older in age, but they were a far more mature and hardened group after dealing with the tragic death of teammate Pelle Lindbergh a year earlier in a car accident.

"The core of the group was the same, but it was two different teams," says Dave Poulin. "That team went through so much with the death of Pelle that it was a more mature team in 1986–1987."

Helping the group awake from that nightmare was a rookie goalie who couldn't have been more different from Lindbergh: Ron Hextall. Where Lindbergh was relaxed, Hextall brought a level of intensity that bordered on the fanatical.

"His competitive edge in practice—he wouldn't let you score in practice 10 seconds after the whistle blew and he was skating toward center ice," recalls Poulin.

**Fiery coach Mike Keenan guided the Flyers to a pair of Stanley Cup Finals.**

"He was such a good competitor," adds Howe. "Not only in the games, but every day at practice. The only way you're going to get better as a scorer or a defenseman is to have someone working with you. If I'm trying to keep the puck out of the net, I'm going to want a goalie that's working with me in practice. If I can keep the puck out of my net in practice, I can do it during a game."

"Every time he stepped on the ice, he was full out," recalls Kjell Samuelsson. "Even in practice, if you shot high on him he'd get irritated. He tried to stop every puck coming at him."

Besides Hextall, there were other changes. Rich Sutter, Dave Richter, and a draft pick went to the Vancouver Canucks for defenseman J.J. Daigneault. Rambunctious forward Scott Mellanby, a second-round pick in 1984, was signed away from the University of Wisconsin. And undrafted Western Hockey League graduate Craig Berube was signed to a minor-league deal.

It all added up to increased expectations, as Clarke said during training camp, "I think it's time for this team to do something."

Hextall gave a glimpse of what was to come opening night against Edmonton at the Spectrum. Jari Kurri gave the Oilers an early lead, but Hextall stoned Wayne Gretzky on a breakaway, and held the fort as Ron Sutter and Peter Zezel gave the Flyers a 2–1 win.

They won their first six, and were 13–4–2 when Tim Kerr scored four in a row against Chicago on November 20, his fourth hat-trick-plus-one.

Slowly, though, injuries began whittling away at their lineup. Brian Propp had 41 points in 27 games when he fractured his left knee. Ilkka Sinisalo went down with a knee injury, and back issues sidelined Howe and Sutter.

Despite the injuries, the Flyers went 17–10–2 from the beginning of December through the end of January. Propp and Sinisalo returned in mid-February, Howe was back by the end of the month, and the Flyers finished with 100 points and the Patrick Division title.

Kerr totaled 58 goals—his fourth straight 50-plus season—Zezel had a career campaign with 33 goals and 72 points, while Propp had 31 goals in just 53 games.

The revelation, though, was Hextall, who finished with a 37–21–6 record, a 3.00 goals-against average and a .902 save percentage, good enough to earn him the Vezina Trophy (but oddly, not the Calder Trophy, which went to Los Angeles's Luc Robitaille).

Hextall also finished with six assists and 104 penalty minutes—the sixth-highest amount on the team—foreshadowing a historical future in both categories.

The Flyers were due to open the playoffs against the New York Rangers, a team they finished 24 points ahead of in the regular season, but there was a bit of trepidation from how the regular season ended—a 9–5 embarrassment against the Islanders. All season there had been tremors of a rebellion against the ultra-intense, volatile Keenan.

"Mike ran such a tight ship," says Al Morganti, who covered the team for *The Philadelphia Inquirer*. "It was very tense with Mike all the time. There wasn't much fun and games with Mike. It was pretty serious all the time.

"Mike took every loss personally, like, 'They f*cked me.' I said, 'Mike, sometimes you lose,' but he looked at me like I had three heads. He wouldn't back off."

The Rangers had allowed 323 goals in the regular season, the second-most in the NHL, but the Flyers couldn't get any past goalie John Vanbiesbrouck in a Game 1 loss.

The Flyers got on the scoreboard in the first period of Game 2, went ahead with four seconds left in the second on a Rick Tocchet goal, and dominated in the third en route to an 8–3 series-evening victory.

Hextall was the star in Game 3, holding off a 12-shot Rangers first-period attack. He stopped all 34 shots he faced for the game, and Zezel and Howe scored 13 seconds apart early in the second as the Flyers earned a 3–0 win.

The goalie was his own worst enemy in Game 4, allowing an early Tomas Sandstrom goal, and then getting into a shouting and taunting match with Rangers coach Phil Esposito in a series-knotting 6–3 defeat.

Game 5 at the Spectrum could have turned ugly again after Hextall was whistled for clearing the puck over the glass moments after Samuelsson had been sent off for holding, but the netminder kept the game scoreless until Tocchet jammed in the rebound of a Derrick Smith shot 2:02 into the second period.

Another Hextall gaffe, when he lost a race into the corner to play the puck, allowed the Rangers to score into an empty net to tie it. Kerr put the Flyers back ahead with about six minutes left in the second, and Tocchet scored into an empty net in the third to ice the 3–1 victory.

Game 6 started with the Flyers losing Poulin four minutes in when he needed X-rays on his ribs after being driven into the boards by Ron Duguay. Even without their captain, the Flyers got first-period goals from Smith and Doug Crossman. Brad Marsh and Kerr tallied in the second, and Lindsay Carson scored early in the third. Hextall stopped all 34 Rangers shots to register the series-clinching 5–0 shutout.

The Islanders arrived at the Spectrum an aging, tired club that had survived a four-overtime Game 7 win just two days earlier.

The visitors were missing Mike Bossy and Denis Potvin, but out for the Flyers were Poulin with broken ribs and Murray Craven, who broke his foot during Game 6 against the Rangers.

Kerr was healthy, though, and his hat trick pushed the Flyers to a 4–2 win in Game 1.

Game 2 featured a goaltending duel between Hextall and Kelly Hrudey, which the Isles won when Mikko Makela scored a power-play goal with three seconds left in regulation to hand the Flyers a 2–1 loss.

Al Hill tipped Howe's long shot past Hrudey to open the scoring midway through Game 3, and then Propp, who had just one goal in his previous 13 playoff games, scored off the rebound of a Tim Tookey shot as the Flyers cruised to a 4–1 victory.

Propp scored again in Game 4 after Alan Kerr had given the Islanders an early lead. Hill scored with 1:25 left in the first to tie the game, but Trottier beat Hextall 2:50 into the second to put the Isles back on top.

Tim Kerr tied the game with a power-play goal, and then Tookey, the leading scorer in the American Hockey League making his first foray in the NHL playoffs, scored off a Propp set-up to put the Flyers ahead for good. Kerr and Tocchet added goals as the 6–4 victory gave the Flyers a 3–1 series lead.

The Flyers looked to be on their way to clinching a spot in the next round in Game 5 when Carson blocked a Ken Morrow shot, raced in alone, and beat Hrudey 5:56 into the second period for the game's first goal. Instead, the Islanders tied the game late in the second and won it in the third.

Game 6 saw the Flyers lose the game, 4–2, and Kerr, whose season-long shoulder issues finally forced him out of the lineup.

"It got to a point in that Isles series," he says, "my arm sitting by my side, [my shoulder] would separate. I couldn't even hold a stick."

Without Kerr, Poulin put aside the pain from his broken ribs and set up goals by Dave Brown and Propp, and the Flyers advanced to the Wales Conference final with a 5–1 win. Their foes would be the Montreal Canadiens, the defending Stanley Cup champs.

Montreal coach Jean Perron went with goalie Brian Hayward in Game 1, rather than Patrick Roy, giving the Flyers a huge edge in net.

Despite not having Poulin—his Game 7 heroics against the Islanders proved a personal setback—a red-hot Propp one-timed a Crossman pass into the back of the net with 2:09 left in the first. Montreal scored the next two, but Sinisalo tied the game, and after the Canadiens' Bobby Smith and Derrick Smith traded goals in the third, overtime was needed to decide the contest.

Midway through extra time, Samuelsson sent the puck up the boards to Zezel. As Zezel cut to the net, Guy Carbonneau tackled him. The puck momentarily was lost under the pile of bodies and sticks, but it emerged behind Hayward, with Sinisalo getting credit for the game-winning score.

Montreal scored early and often on Hextall in a 5–2 win in Game 2, and they came out fast again in Game 3, firing 21 shots on net and getting rebound goals from Chris Nilan and Chris Chelios. Pelle Eklund scored twice to spark a three-goal rally that gave the Flyers a 3–2 lead midway through the third, but a Mats Naslund power-play tally tied the game. Tocchet, who committed the penalty that led to Naslund's goal, fed Propp at the hash marks for a score with 3:09 left for a 4–3 Flyers win.

Perron turned to Roy for Game 4, but it made little difference as Eklund snapped a 2–2 tie with a goal with less than five minutes left in the second, and Mellanby scored 14 seconds into the third. Perron yanked Roy for Hayward, but Eklund scored twice more for his first playoff hat trick as the Flyers took a 3–1 series lead home to Philadelphia.

Larry Robinson's power-play goal through a Claude Lemieux screen sparked a 5–2 Canadiens win in Game 5, sending the series back to Montreal.

Fireworks started in Game 6 before the puck dropped, as a pregame brawl sparked by Shayne Corson and Lemieux scoring into the Flyers' net at the end of warm-ups saw players spill out of both dressing rooms to brawl on the ice. Flyers defenseman Ed Hospodor was ruled the instigator in the attack and was the only player ejected; he subsequently was suspended for the remainder of the playoffs.

## WATER BOTTLE

Pelle Lindbergh had suffered from dehydration in the past, so coach Mike Keenan gave him a water bottle, which the goalie kept on top of the goal during games. No netminder ever had done this before, and the league never objected.

Edmonton coach Glen Sather unleashed one of the more comically famous quotes in Stanley Cup history the day before Game 2 of the 1985 Stanley Cup Finals.

"Maybe we want a bucket of chicken on our net," he said. "Maybe hamburgers. I mean, if you have a water bottle out there, let's have lunch."

Once the game started, it looked like the Canadiens could safely pack for one more trip to Philadelphia. Mike McPhee scored for Montreal less than a minute in, but Poulin, whose busted ribs forced him out of Game 5, scored shorthanded to tie the game.

The game was tied 3–3 seven minutes into the third period when Tocchet finished a two-on-one with Propp, and the Flyers held on over the final 12-plus minutes to celebrate a 4–3 win and a second chance in the Stanley Cup Finals in three seasons.

Just like 1985, their final opponent would be the dynastic Edmonton Oilers.

The Flyers felt many of the lessons learned in losing to Edmonton two seasons prior would be put into practice in the upcoming series.

"We were mentally stronger, mentally tougher, and with the emergence of the Cravens, the emergence of the Tocchets, and the other younger players, we were all better as a group," says Howe. "We were tougher mentally as a team, which I think makes you better as a team overall."

All the experience, though, couldn't compensate for the injuries that had decimated their roster. Already without Kerr and with Poulin nursing broken ribs, Howe was hobbled by a charley horse suffered on his first shift of Game 1.

The Oilers' Wayne Gretzky opened the scoring, but Propp answered late in the second, when his long shot handcuffed Grant Fuhr and dropped into the net. But the Oilers responded with three goals in an 8:23 span of the third to earn a 4–2 win.

Gretzky scored early in the second in Game 2 on a five-on-three advantage, but the Flyers rallied. Ron Sutter dug a puck out of the crease and Derrick Smith pushed it over the line. Then Propp redirected a Tocchet shot into the back of the goal, and after two periods, the Flyers led 2–1. But in the third, Anderson walked past Crossman to score and force overtime.

The Oilers continued to swarm like white-sweatered hornets, as a Gretzky drop pass to an open Paul Coffey caught the Flyers with four skaters down low. Coffey got deep and fed a diagonal pass to Kurri, who beat Hextall for a 3–2 win and a sweep of the first two games at Northlands Coliseum.

For Game 3, the Flyers trotted out a video performance of the late Kate Smith singing "God Bless America" to pump up the fans and hopefully court Lady Luck.

It looked like the Lady had run out on the Flyers early when the Oilers took a 3–0 lead. Craven, back in Game 3 from the broken foot that had sidelined him for the previous two series, got the shaft of his stick on a Tocchet shot for the Flyers' first goal, and then a puck bounced off Edmonton's Craig Muni and into the net to make it 3–2.

Mellanby scored through Fuhr's pads 4:37 into the third to tie the game, and 17 seconds later, with the celebration of Mellanby's goal still echoing through the Spectrum, Brad McCrimmon took the puck from Esa Tikkanen, received a return pass from Mellanby, and lifted the puck high above a sprawling Fuhr to give the Flyers a 4–3 lead.

Propp scored into an empty net, and just like that, the Flyers had a heartbeat again.

The loss only served to anger the Oilers, who took a 2–0 lead in the first period of Game 4. McCrimmon answered with a long one-timer off an Eklund feed to make it 2–1, but Randy Gregg and Mike Krushelnyski scored to give the Oilers a 4–1 victory.

Hextall, angry at his own play, snapped when Anderson poked him as he was juggling a shot. He took out his frustration on Kent Nilsson with a two-handed stick chop across the back of the winger's legs as he skated near the goal. Hextall was assessed a five-minute major, but stayed in the game.

"That was basically a frustration moment for me," Hextall says in retrospect. "We were getting beat, and I had taken a lot of abuse over the course of the playoffs, and my frustrations came boiling out at that point. Glenn Anderson slashed me right before that, and I said that was enough. [I swung at the] first blue jersey I saw."

Knowing his team was running on fumes—Game 4 had been the Flyers' 23rd playoff game, at the time a league record—Keenan dug deep into his bag of motivational tricks for a special locker room guest for the morning skate prior to Game 5.

The Stanley Cup.

The message was simple: there it is, boys. Go get it if you want it.

Early goals put the Flyers down by two for the third straight game, but Hextall kept things close, and Tocchet scored to halve the deficit. Marty McSorely answered to make it 3–1, but a Crossman rocket over Fuhr's glove got the Flyers back within a goal, and Eklund scored on his own rebound to tie it in the second.

Edmonton came out firing in the third, but it was the Flyers who got the go-ahead goal. Propp took the puck from Muni in the Edmonton zone, walked in front, and backhanded a pass to Tocchet, who poked the puck past Fuhr to make it 4–3.

There still was 14:34 on the clock and the best team on the planet facing them, but Hextall was up to the challenge, and the Flyers survived for a return trip to Philadelphia.

Game 6 at the Spectrum followed the same script as the previous three games. The Oilers took a 2–0 lead, but with Hextall as the last line of defense, the ever-resilient Flyers fired back.

Brown pushed the puck between Kevin Lowe's skates to Carson, who deposited the disk behind Fuhr at 7:12 of the second, and then Propp tied the game with a power-play goal at 13:04 of the third.

Moments later, on a Flyers rush into the Edmonton end, Kurri picked off a Zezel pass and tried to throw it out of the zone. The puck hit the wall short of the blue line and dribbled toward the edge of the zone.

Daigneault had been trailing the play and was headed for the bench for a line change, but Keenan waved him back on the ice. That allowed him to pounce on the dying quail and one-time a low shot through a Mellanby screen. The Spectrum shook as the Flyers once again had survived to reach a remarkable, previously unthought-of Game 7 back in Edmonton.

"I guess we had a little more to give than everybody thought," Brown said after the game.

There was a two-day break before Game 7 due to scheduling issues at Northlands Coliseum, but the Flyers didn't seem to mind. Back-to-back penalties on Mark Messier and Coffey gave the visitors a two-man advantage, and they capitalized when Craven banked in a shot off Fuhr's skate as the Flyers scored first for the first time in the series.

Messier answered to tie the game, and at 5:01 of the second, Kurri put a shot between Zezel's skates and inside the right post to put the Flyers into one final hole.

With the lead, the Oilers put the pedal to the floor while the weight of 80 regular-season games and 26 exhausting playoff contests in 54 nights dropped like an anvil on the Flyers' backs. After putting 12 shots on Fuhr in the first period, they managed just 14 the rest of the game.

As Jay Greenberg wrote in *Full Spectrum*, "Hextall and heaven were the only things that could help the Flyers now."

The rookie netminder was brilliant with one exception, when Anderson fired a wicked, sinking slap shot from about 35 feet that went between Hextall's pads with 2:24 left to play.

When the final horn sounded, it was the Oilers parading around the rink with their third Stanley Cup in four seasons. Hextall, for all his brilliance, became just the second player from a losing side to take home the Conn Smythe Trophy as playoff MVP.

"That was the best goaltending I've ever seen," says Howe. "He was incredible his first year. For the most part, especially in the Finals, as good as we played and as close as we came, it wouldn't have been that close without Ron Hextall, there's no doubt about it."

# SUPRIMEAU

Coming down the stretch of the 2003–2004 season, the list of injured Flyers was growing like a pile of broken sticks.

And when the playoffs started, the Flyers drew about the worst opponent possible for them, from both an on-ice standpoint as well as a psychological one—the New Jersey Devils.

An aging, injured team with an inexperienced goalie needed a hero, someone who could throw a team on his back for a two-month death march through the playoff minefield.

Far down the list of hero candidates would have been Keith Primeau. The team captain, he had played just 54 games due to a series of injuries, including a concussion that sidelined him for seven weeks. He had just seven goals during the regular season, and since his epic fifth-overtime goal against Pittsburgh in the 2000 playoffs, Primeau had scored exactly one postseason goal.

"It's hard to score in the National Hockey League even in the best of times. It's even harder to score in the playoffs," says Primeau. "A lot of factors go into why numbers are the way they are. I didn't play any different [in 2004]."

But scoring wasn't Primeau's role on this Flyers team. With Ken Hitchcock's arrival as coach, Primeau was given a new role, that of checking center.

"I think I started to buy into the idea that I was a different player as he was coming in," Primeau says. "But he gave me the opportunity to really shine in that [defensive] role."

Primeau also had a much larger job, one possibly harder than anything he would encounter on the ice: providing the buffer between the abrasive Hitchcock and the delicate egos of some of his teammates.

"My message to the guys was, don't listen so much to the delivery as the message," he says. "If you hear the message, 99.9 percent of the time the message is right."

It also helped that he accepted his changing place on the team without complaint. When Primeau came to the Flyers in 2000, he was a top-line center expected to perform offensively. Four seasons later, he was a checker, a mucker, and a grinder.

"He became an excellent captain and leader because he first made himself accountable and then made everyone else accountable," says Hitchcock. "He had no problem doing that, and that's why our team played to its potential on a nightly basis, because he made the team play."

"When they see me accept a lesser role, a different role from what I was accustomed to, what was their excuse? That's where we transformed," says Primeau.

That transformation changed Primeau from an ordinary hockey player into a new man—Suprimeau.

As all journeys do, Primeau's started with a first step—or in his case, a long stride. Many of them, in fact, as midway through the first period of Game 1 against the Devils, he raced into the corner to support Simon Gagne, who had beaten an icing call, and worked the puck back along the wall to Sami Kapanen. Goalie Martin Brodeur stopped Kapanen's shot, but Gagne scored on the rebound, and just like that, the checker had helped set up the game's first score.

Early in the third, he rushed the puck into the offensive zone. He barreled down the right side and around Devils defenseman Brian Rafalski, turning him into a red-clad traffic cone. He cut hard on the goal line, and in one deft motion slid the puck under Brodeur, giving the Flyers a 3–0 lead.

The Flyers held on for a 3–2 win, and as would become the norm, Primeau's play was the difference.

Primeau didn't score in Game 2, but was dominant in the faceoff circle, winning 14 of 22 draws, as the Flyers won again. He was just as good in Game 3, but it took a stellar lunging save by Brodeur to keep Primeau off the score sheet and preserve a 4–2 victory.

In the loss, Primeau's supremacy still could be seen. *Philadelphia Daily News* columnist Rich Hoffman called him a "runaway destroyer," while Devils coach Pat Burns said the best way to stop him was with "a couple of bricks and some cement."

Burns' players tried to take their coach literally in Game 4, showering Primeau with all manners of hacks and whacks, from elbows to gloves to sticks. Primeau took it all with a smile.

"That's good. I like that," he told reporters. "If they're focused on me, it frees up J.R. [Jeremy Roenick], it frees up Rex [Mark Recchi], it frees up Alex [Zhamnov]—those guys—to create a little more."

They did just that as Zhamnov scored the second goal of a 3–0 win, a game capped by Primeau tipping a Kapanen pass off Brodeur, then knocking the puck from between the goalie's skates and into the net.

But it was more than goals and points for Primeau.

"He has presence, he has accountability," Hitchcock told reporters. "When he sits in the locker room, nobody dares not play. He knows that he's carrying a message from the coaching staff through to the players. That's what captains do....He has accountability on both sides, in the locker room and in the coach's office. Players know that."

Primeau looked at it as his duty to not just play well, but to excel, because he owed that much to his teammates.

"They had really pulled up their socks when I was out with my concussion, and I felt they really carried the load that I had left," he says. "I was in an important role, and now I wasn't there. They found a way to persevere. I felt I owed it to them more than anything. That's why I really dug in, because I really felt they carried my weight while I was out."

A 3–1 series lead brought back all the talk of the 2000 collapse, but Primeau quickly and efficiently chased away the ghosts of failures past, playing physically over 200 feet of ice, dominating in the faceoff circle (winning 16 of 23 draws), and being on the ice in the crucial final minutes of a 3–1 series-clinching victory.

Next was the Toronto Maple Leafs, the team that had extended the Flyers to seven games in the first round the previous year. And with seven overtime periods, it was more like nine games.

"I thought I played better the year before [2003] in the Toronto series," says Primeau of his one-goal, one-assist performance.

He was on the ice for Gagne's late goal in a 3–1 win in Game 1, and again did yeoman's work killing off penalties. In Game 2 he added his fourth playoff point, drawing an assist on Donald Brashear's power-play goal in a 2–1 victory.

The Flyers were pushed around in Games 3 and 4, both losses in Toronto, but when the series shifted to Philadelphia for Game 5, Primeau had a little something extra attached to his black sweater.

A cape.

The day before Game 5, Primeau called a team meeting.

"He stepped up in the meeting and laid some things on the line," said goalie Sean Burke. "He told us he would be great today and told us to jump on for the ride."

It turned into the ride of their captain's life.

With just three playoff goals in 40 games as a Flyer entering the night of May 2, 2004, Primeau equaled that amount in just 60 minutes. It started, appropriately, when the Flyers needed him the most: leading 2–0 but shorthanded in the final two minutes of the first period.

Leafs defenseman Bryan McCabe fumbled the puck at the blue line, and Primeau pounced. He poked the disk loose and streaked in alone on goalie Ed Belfour. He held off defenseman Brian Leetch, deked Belfour out of the goal, and slid a backhander into the gaping net with 1:06 left in the frame.

Goal number two came 44 seconds into the second, when he stepped around the Leafs' Aki Berg and redirected a Gagne pass past Belfour.

He completed his night by shrugging off a Joe Nieuwendyk slam into the boards to finish a give-and-go with Gagne for the hat trick at 3:50 of the third.

Caps rained down on the ice, carried by the throaty, loving screams for their team's newest hero. Besides his three goals were an assist, 10 wins on 15 faceoffs, and a number of bone-rattling body checks.

"He's been our leader on and off the ice," Roenick told writers. "That's what you need from your captain. He had something to prove after Games 3 and 4. He was a real treat to watch."

Primeau didn't score in Game 6, but he didn't need to record a point to earn the second star of the game. He won faceoffs, killed penalties, and turned the Leafs' leader, center Mats Sundin, into the Invisible Swede. He refused to budge on puck possession, at one point taking about 20 cross-checks between the numbers from the Leafs' Gary Roberts during a second-period scrum in the corner.

And it was Primeau, more than any netminder, who made the save of the night—and maybe of the season. With their defense corps decimated by injuries, Kapanen, Primeau's closest friend on the team, had been shifted back to defense. In overtime, Kapanen stretched to hold the puck in the offensive zone, leaving himself vulnerable. Toronto's Darcy Tucker arrived with a hit more felt than seen. The force of the blow lifted Kapanen off his feet and turned him parallel to the ice. For a split second he remained airborne, pinned between the Leafs' forward and the wall. When Tucker skated away, Kapanen fell like Wile E. Coyote, landing with an audible splat. Kapanen's body may have landed in Toronto, but his head was in a faraway place. He attempted to skate back to the bench, but instead stumbled toward center ice. Primeau opened the bench door, and with one skate barely scraping the rink, he used his stick to hook Kapanen back toward the bench.

"I could see he had no clue as to where he was," Primeau told reporters. "He wasn't sure which way he was facing."

The save allowed Roenick to jump on the ice and score the series-clinching goal.

Thanks to Primeau, the Flyers were back in the Eastern Conference Finals for the first time since 2000, where they faced the Tampa Bay Lightning.

Primeau didn't score in the first two games of the series in Tampa, but his presence on the penalty kill enabled the Flyers to return to Philadelphia with a split. They lost Game 1, but killed four of five Tampa power plays in Game 2 and got a short-handed goal from Kapanen—he used Primeau as a decoy before scoring—in a 6–2 rout.

With the Flyers down 2–0 in Game 3, Primeau knocked a pinballing puck past goalie Nikolai Khabibulin to halve the lead, but it was as close as the Flyers would get in a 4–1 loss.

# SHUT YER YAP

Ken Hitchcock not only knows how to irritate his players, but opposing coaches, as well.

In the 2004 Eastern Conference Finals against Tampa Bay, Lightning coach John Tortorella took the bait.

The day after Game 2, Tortorella accused Hitchcock of yelling at one of his players, and famously told the coach to, "Shut his yap."

While Tortorella steamed, Hitchcock laughed, replying that the Tampa coach should, "Mind his own business." And when asked if he would take Tortorella's advice and shut his yap, he chuckled and said, "You know me better than that."

In writing about how Primeau had carried the team on his huge shoulders to that point, *Philadelphia Inquirer* columnist Phil Sheridan asked, "How many more of those does Primeau have in him?"

They didn't have to wait long for the answer.

Midway through the first period of Game 4, he helped kill off a double-minor on Simon Gagne followed by a slashing call on Robert Esche, all of which left the Flyers down a man for nearly four straight minutes. Tampa scored just once, and Kapanen, who served the penalty on Esche, jumped out of the box and dragged the puck up the ice. He was stopped near the red line, but Primeau, following the play, jumped on the loose puck. He cut to the middle in the Tampa zone and sent a pass across to John LeClair, who rocketed a shot past Khabibulin to tie the game.

After Recchi's goal late in the first put the Flyers ahead, Suprimeau stepped out of the phone booth one more time.

On a Tampa power play, Lightning captain Dave Andreychuk couldn't control a bouncing puck at the Flyers' blue line. Primeau saw the fumble and jumped toward the play, and when Andreychuk batted the puck in the air, the Flyers' Captain Clutch was at full speed when he gloved it down and dropped it on his stick. Gagne broke out with Primeau, who rushed the puck up the right side of the ice and into the Tampa end. He looked to pass across to Gagne, but when Dan Boyle slid down to take away the lane, Primeau rock-eted a shot high and just inside the right post for a 3–1 lead.

The goal was his seventh of the playoffs, matching in 15 games his 54-game regular-season total.

Vincent Lecavalier got a goal back with 33 seconds left in regulation, and as the Flyers teetered, Primeau again steadied things. After losing the ensuing faceoff, he charged into the Tampa end, tipped away passes, and pushed the puck into the corner. Taking whacks and hacks, Primeau held possession along the wall, milking the final precious seconds off the clock.

"There are certain stages in your season and certain stages in critical playoff series where captains have to step up, and he stepped up again," Hitchcock told reporters.

"Preems has been that guy we've been looking to and following," added LeClair. "Today he did the same thing. He was the difference out there each time he was on the ice."

And he was out there a lot. He played 31 shifts totaling 22:28 of ice time. It was five shifts and four minutes more than any other Flyers forward.

"Every time I came off the ice, I looked around to Hitch and wanted to go back out again," Primeau said. "I felt I could have played 60 minutes."

In Tampa for Game 5, he only played 20, but it was a night he'd like to forget as he indirectly assisted on a pair of Brad Richards power-play goals—sitting in the penalty box for one, the other bouncing off his shin pad on a faceoff—as the Flyers fell behind 3–0. He set up Patrick Sharp's second-period goal that got the Flyers back to 3–2, but that was as close as they got.

The Flyers flew home to Philadelphia, knowing their season was one game from ending.

The day of Game 6, uncertainty filled the Philadelphia air. It wasn't just about one game for the rest of their season. It was so much more than that. The dark cloud of impending labor Armageddon had hung over the entire season. The 2003–2004 campaign was the last of the collective bargaining agreement between the players and the clubs. There was more talk of war chests and lockouts and lost seasons than there was of goals, assists, and points.

The funeral for the 2004–2005 season was being held before it even was born.

And with a veteran group, many of whom were playing in the final years of their contracts—and their careers—some knew this was their last, best chance to get their names on the Stanley Cup.

LeClair, Recchi, and Vladimir Malakhov already had their names on the Cup, but for many others—Roenick, Burke, Zhamnov, Primeau, Danny Markov, Tony Amonte—they could see more road behind them than ahead. They had no way of knowing it then, but of those nine distinguished veterans, only Primeau still would be wearing a Flyers sweater when the 2005–2006 season began.

"We're not sure where this group will be not only a year from now but three months from now," Primeau said the day before Game 6. "Odds are that there will be changes. And on top of that, there's the collective-bargaining agreement. We don't know what to expect. So it's important to take advantage of the opportunity right now."

It wouldn't just take a supreme effort. It would take a Suprimeau one. And the Flyers' Captain Fantastic had one more memorable night in a two-month run of them.

With his team trailing 1–0, Primeau took a bouncing pass from Roenick into the Tampa end. Unable to control it with his stick, and with a pair of Tampa players hanging on him like a clothes-line, he kicked the puck to Gagne, who scored to tie the game. And with 2:59 left in the first, Roenick forced Darryl Sydor to throw a clearing attempt through the slot to Malakhov, who fed Primeau on the doorstep for goal number eight in his remarkable run.

But the Flyers trailed 4–3 when the game's final 20 minutes began.

As the clock ticked down under two minutes remaining, the Flyers got the puck deep in the Tampa end, but Martin St. Louis emerged from the scrum and tried to push the puck to Andreychuk. It skittered past him and onto Mattias Timander's stick at the left point. Timander fired a shot that went off Sydor and Khabibulin's blocker, where it dropped to the ice and onto Primeau's right skate. In a play that was one part Pele, one part

Gretzky, Primeau kicked the puck across the goal line behind Khabibulin, circled behind the net, and tapped it in for a remarkable game-tying goal with just 1:49 left in regulation.

Primeau described his magical goal: "I kind of directed it with my skate and then I thought, 'Oh, don't go in.' I wanted it to go in, but I didn't want it to go in, because I was thinking, 'They are going to review it, and it's going to be disallowed.' And all of a sudden, it kept coming across the crease, and I was coming out the other side, and I got an easy whack at it."

The Wachovia Center shook with the excitement of 19,910 rabid fans proudly clad in their Orange Crush T-shirts.

Those fans might not have known it, but their heroes on ice would coax one more deafening roar out of them.

With 1:42 left in overtime, Primeau, Roenick, and Gagne controlled the puck deep in the Lightning end. Gagne sent a pass behind the net to Primeau, who skated out and slid the puck to Roenick. Roenick threw it across the crease to Gagne, who buried the shot and gave life to Game 7 back in Tampa. Primeau drew an assist, his second of the game. The four-point night was his biggest scoring output of a remarkable postseason. And he saved it for when his team needed him the most.

## GAGNE GAME 6

Five games into the 2004 Eastern Conference Finals, Simon Gagne had one assist. In a newspaper story the day before Game 6, GM Bob Clarke went right after his young forward.

"He has to make the decision whether he wants to become a great player in the NHL or whether he will be satisfied being a good player," Clarke said.

Gagne answered with a pair of goals in Game 6, including the overtime winner.

"Usually I don't read the papers, but I got calls from back home and read it," Gagne said. "It was a message he was trying to tell me. I had to find a way to put the puck in."

"You knew if he was on the ice, he'd find a way to win that game," recalls Chuck Gormley, the longtime Flyers writer for the *Courier Post*. "And he was on the ice a lot that game. They kept sending him over the boards, and he said let's go. He was obsessed with winning that game, and he did. He did it on his own."

Looking back now, Primeau says that game not only was his best experience with the Flyers, but possibly in his hockey career.

"I know how many people remember the fifth-overtime game, but for most memorable game, for me, was Game 6 against Tampa Bay. I was so much more involved offensively on the score sheet from start to finish, as opposed to just scoring an overtime goal. That game I remember very vividly, especially being at home. It was such a great atmosphere. That's a point in time I'll never forget."

Neither have the fans. In a 2006 online poll, Game 6 of the 2004 Eastern Conference Finals was voted as one of the 10 greatest in the 40-year history of the Flyers.

But beyond the fans, Primeau's peers stood in awe of what he accomplished.

"What pleases me about that [Game 6], people tell me what kind of performance it was, how dominant and all those things. But the two greatest compliments I got were from Steve Yzerman and Phil Esposito. Both those guys have told me face to face that it was the most dominating performance they had ever seen in the playoffs. To receive those kinds of accolades from those people and players is pretty special."

That the dream died in Game 7 doesn't diminish what Primeau accomplished in the 2004 playoffs.

"Probably the best individual performance that I had seen by a Flyer," says Gormley, who has covered the team since 1990. "He literally carried that team on his shoulders. And he was not a Joe Sakic/Wayne Gretzky/Mario Lemieux kind of player. He was a mucker and a grinder and he did things that were uncharacteristic for him."

Adds Hitchcock, "Players have a sense that they might not ever get an opportunity to win a championship again. He knew this was the best chance he'd have in his life and he was going to do everything in his power to pull the rest of the players along.

All the players in the world, he was a cut above everybody in the whole playoff run."

Primeau finished with nine goals and seven assists, 16 points in 18 games. Of the 234 players who had played at least 100 playoff games to that point, Primeau was the first player in league history to match his career playoff goal total in just one postseason.

He also was a plus-11 while averaging nearly 19 minutes per game. He killed penalties, played on the power play, and skated over 20 minutes in five games, including three of the final four games of the Tampa series. Oh, and he did it all while suffering possibly two concussions during the run.

"It was by far the best period or stretch of my career," he says. "For many reasons: one, it's playoff time; two, the way I was able to produce offensively, especially after the regular season and the role I had taken on under Hitch's system; and because I was getting older, and I didn't think I wouldn't ever play again, but I didn't know how many more opportunities I would have. It was an exciting run and a very memorable point in my career."

But when asked to explain how an otherwise ordinary career playoff performer can turn into Superman—or Suprimeau—for two months, he's at a loss.

"Other than coming off a concussion that year, I was healthier than I'd been in a long time because I had just missed six weeks before the playoffs started," he said. "And pucks just started to go in and kept going in. I really don't feel I played any different, but statistically it was a lot different."

LeClair, who had one of the best seats in the house during the historic run, summed it up simply and succinctly: "With the team we had, we needed someone like that. Without someone stepping up like that, we would have been out of the playoffs a lot earlier."

.

# THE COMEBACK

When the Flyers reported for training camp in September 2007, no one knew what to expect as new faces dotted the roster.

There was Danny Briere, the team's new $52 million center, imported to add front-line scoring. And Kimmo Timonen, the

All-Star defenseman added to bolster a blueline corps that had been embarrassed and outskated the previous season.

Other additions included scoring wingers Joffrey Lupul and Scott Hartnell, and Jason Smith was brought in for his toughness and leadership along the blue line. He was appointed the 16th captain in club history prior to the start of the season.

The chemistry experiment would be how the newcomers would blend with those left over from the previous season's league- and team-worst 22-win, 56-point campaign.

"It's a little bit of the unknown," goaltender Martin Biron told the team's website on the first day of training camp. "In the [scrimmages], in the workouts and all of that, you never really know what is going to happen, so you kind of come in pretty much ready for anything."

What coach John Stevens wanted them to be ready to do was work.

"Our motto coming into the season is we have to be willing to earn it," he said. "We have to be willing to earn the respect of the league again."

Their quest for respect got off to a bumpy start. In a preseason game against the Ottawa Senators on September 25, rookie forward Steve Downie, looking to earn himself a spot on the team, instead earned himself a 20-game sentence in NHL jail when he launched himself like a cruise missile at the head of Ottawa's Dean McAmmond.

The Flyers got a little extra bonding time when they traveled to Western Canada prior to starting the season in Calgary. If anyone was wondering how the new players would jell, that question was answered in the affirmative when Briere scored two goals, including the game-winner with less than two minutes left in a 3–2 win against the Flames.

"It's a great feeling right now,"' Briere told reporters after the game. "I can't even explain it. To start like this on a new team is an unbelievable feeling."

The good feelings were tempered six nights later when another belligerent play overshadowed an 8–2 win over the Vancouver Canucks. Mike Richards scored twice and added two

## CHANGING THE ROOM

One of the Flyers' worst losses of the season came March 16 in Pittsburgh, a 7–1 beating reminiscent of the 2006–2007 disasters.

Coach John Stevens, looking for some way to shake the team up, called equipment manager Derek Settlemyre and told him to rearrange the dressing stalls in the locker room.

"The next day at practice, we walked in the room and everything was rearranged," said Daniel Briere. "We kind of laughed about it. John didn't say anything, [but] it changed the mindset. Instead of thinking about the last game, we were talking about who's my new stall neighbor. I thought that was pretty clever."

The coach looked even smarter when the team went 7–1–1 the rest of the season.

assists, but the night was marred when Jesse Boulerice cross-checked the Canucks' Ryan Kesler in the face in the third period, breaking his stick on the center's jaw and earning himself a 25-game suspension.

While the Flyers were pilloried for their overly physical play, they also were winning games. Biron earned back-to-back shutouts of the Atlanta Thrashers and New Jersey Devils, and when Simon Gagne scored 48 seconds into overtime for a 3–2 win against the Carolina Hurricanes, the Flyers had swept their season-opening four-game homestand.

The good feelings wouldn't last long, though. A season-long 15-day road trip started badly and only got worse. During their first stop, Gagne was leveled by a hard hit from Florida Panthers defenseman Jay Bouwmeester that left the forward with the first of what would begin a season-long fight with concussion problems.

Three nights later in Boston, the Flyers had their third major suspendable offense, when Randy Jones drove Bruins forward Patrice Bergeron face-first into the boards behind the Flyers' net. Bergeron suffered a broken nose and what became a season-ending concussion; Jones was given a two-game suspension.

When the teams met in Philadelphia a month later, there was another incident. Bruins defenseman Andrew Alberts dropped to his knees to stop a puck from leaving the zone when Hartnell barreled into him. Alberts was knocked out of the game with a concussion, and Hartnell earned a two-game suspension.

The suspensions didn't put a damper on the Flyers' physical play, but their winning certainly subsided, as they won consecutive games just once between November 1 and December 22.

They rebounded, though, with an 11–2–1 streak leading into the All-Star break that pushed them to the top of the Atlantic Division and second overall in the Eastern Conference.

The success wouldn't last, however, as the club flopped out of the break, losing 10 straight games to plummet from second to 10th in the conference.

Along the way, they lost Gagne for the season due to recurring concussion issues. After sitting out most of November and all of December, he wasn't the same player when he returned in early January, playing a perimeter game and scoring just three power-play goals in 15 games; his season ended February 10 against Pittsburgh, when Jordan Staal hit him from behind on the first shift of the game.

Gagne's prolonged absences not only took a 40-goal scorer out of the lineup but sent Briere into a tailspin that nearly ruined his first season in Philadelphia.

Briere had spent his offseason studying Gagne—where the forward wanted the puck, where his scoring zones were. When they were together, it was beautiful to watch—in the first eight games of the season, Gagne had four goals and eight points, while Briere had four goals and 12 points. Without Gagne, though, Briere struggled to jell with other linemates. Stevens tried Briere with just about every other forward on the roster, and even shifted him to wing for a short time.

"It was frustrating," said Briere, "because for the past four years I had been in Buffalo, I had three different wingers the whole time I was there."

The low point came February 23 at the Wachovia Center. Briere scored his third goal in 18 games to give the Flyers a 1–0 lead, but by the end of the night, the Flyers had lost the game—Bouwmeester tied the game with 3.7 seconds left and Olli Jokinen scored in overtime—and Richards, the team's leading scorer, to a torn hamstring, and Briere was a mind-boggling minus-23.

"We're just going to have to deal with it right now," Flyers general manager Paul Holmgren told the media. "We're in a tough spot. There's no sense waving the white flag. Everyone else is just going to have to pick it up."

"You're just hoping for a break somewhere," said Briere. "When things start to go wrong or go bad, everything is magnified. All I was hoping for was just a break somewhere, somehow."

That break came in the most unexpected spot.

On February 25, the Flyers toted a 10-game losing streak into Buffalo. It looked like the skid would hit 11 when they fell behind 3–0 14 minutes into the game, but Jeff Carter and Scottie Upshall scored 1:48 apart late in the first, and then R.J. Umberger scored a power-play goal in the third to tie it.

After a scoreless overtime, the game went to a shootout, with the outcome resting on the stick of Briere, the former favorite son who now was booed every time he touched the puck.

"All I was thinking was, this is perfect," Briere said that night. "I can't be in a better position."

Briere skated in on goaltender Ryan Miller, baited him out of position with a forehand deke, and deposited the puck inside the right post.

On one shot, Briere lost about 700 pounds off his narrow shoulders.

"Going in, it was a big game personally," said Briere. "We had been struggling, 10 in a row we lost....That game was probably the turnover of the season for us.

"If it wasn't the biggest game of the year, it was close to it. And personally, that was the break I needed to turn things around."

It continued to get better for Briere and the Flyers hours later, when the team dealt promising defense prospect Alexandre Picard and a draft pick to the Tampa Bay Lightning for forward Vaclav Prospal. Installed on a line with Briere, magic happened almost instantaneously.

"The way we were doing drills, he was just throwing the puck without looking into areas I like to hang out," said Briere of their first practice. "And for him, he had played with Marty St. Louis and Vinny Lecavalier in Tampa, and that's the way they played. For me, I was just trying to find that chemistry with different guys. I remember that first practice getting really excited. It just felt like we were thinking the same way.

"I think what happened was you start feeling lighter, quicker, more comfortable. That's when things started happening positively for you. Instead of forcing plays and forcing passes, you let things happen. And that helped me play better, play more relaxed, and enjoy myself out there."

There was little to enjoy, though, on March 16, when the Flyers were embarrassed 7–1 in Pittsburgh. With their playoff hopes slipping away, GM Paul Holmgren didn't hide his frustration.

"That was painful to watch," he said. "You've got to question a lot of things. It was a big game; we're in a fight for a playoff spot. To have that type of performance is alarming."

What bothered him most?

"Preparation," he said. "We weren't ready to play in a game. The players certainly need to look in the mirror right now, and I'm sure the coaches are looking very closely at their preparation."

Stevens didn't disagree with his boss.

"It starts with me," he said. "I'm the head of this snake, if you want to call it that, and we have a staff here that works diligently to get this team ready to play. At the end of the day I have the responsibility to make sure these guys are ready."

They were ready after that game. With a new look to the locker room—Stevens ordered the layout of the room changed—they won four straight and finished the season on a 7–1–1 streak.

They shut out the New Jersey Devils in the second-to-last game of the season to get back into the playoffs, and two days later, after a season-closing 2–0 shutout of the Penguins, the Flyers had the number-six seed in the playoffs and an opening-round date with Southeast Division champion Washington Capitals.

The Flyers took a two-goal lead into the third period of Game 1 in Washington, but defenseman Mike Green scored twice to tie it.

And then forward Alexander Ovechkin, displaying the sublime skills that had earned him the league's scoring title and MVP award, won it with less than five minutes to play. Ovechkin poked the puck away from Jaroslav Modry, and then lifted Lasse Kukkonen's stick to steal the puck and score for a disheartening 5–4 loss.

"To start that series, not a lot of people believed we had a chance or that we could win," said Briere. "But that wasn't the mindset in our room. It was totally different in our room....Even though we lost and people saw we blew that two-goal lead, for us, it was a step in the right direction. We knew if we could play like we did in the first two periods, we could win."

They made the right next step in Game 2. Biron stopped everything thrown his way, and Carter and Umberger scored as the Flyers evened the series with a 2–0 victory.

A raucous Wachovia Center crowd was delighted by a three-point night from Briere and a penalty-shot goal by Richards in a 6–3 win in Game 3. Two nights later, Briere tied the game with a power-play goal midway through the third, and Mike Knuble scored off his own rebound 6:40 into the second overtime for a 4–3 victory and a commanding 3–1 series lead.

Washington took Game 5, forcing Game 6 back in Philadelphia. Ovechkin, held mostly in check since Game 1 by outstanding defensive work by Timonen and Braydon Coburn, scored twice, including the winning goal 3:46 into the third period to force Game 7 back in Washington the next day.

More questions were asked of Biron. The goalie was 0–5 with a 5.95 goals-against average in back-to-back games during the regular season, and his confidence had to be wavering after the team surrendered what had looked to be a commanding series lead, right?

"One of Marty's strengths to me is he's able to brush it off when things go bad," said Briere, who played with Biron in Buffalo and has been a close friend for years. "It always seems like he's happy. When we lost Game 6 and everyone got on his back and said he can't do this, he can't do that, I knew this is where his personality is going to come into play and help us win this game. He's going to forget about what happened yesterday and he's going to come in and have fun in Game 7."

Biron had more than just fun in Game 7—he had the game of his life.

The Flyers took a 2–1 lead when Patrick Thoresen shoved Shaone Morrison into goalie Cristobal Huet, giving Sami Kapanen an open net to score into. Ovechkin tied the game, but that was all Biron would allow. He stopped the next 21 shots, including a 16-shot third-period bombardment.

The game went into overtime, and turned when Caps defenseman Tom Poti was sent off for tripping at 4:15. On the ensuing power play, Timonen fired a shot from the left point that Huet stopped, but Lupul, who hadn't scored a goal to that point in the playoffs, poked in the rebound at the 6:06 mark, and the party was on.

Lupul was the hero, but Biron was the real star.

"I guess he answered those questions about back to back," Stevens told reporters. "He was terrific, and he had to be."

Next for the Flyers was the top-seeded Montreal Canadiens, who had beaten the Flyers in all four regular-season meetings. They made it five straight in Game 1, but in irregular fashion.

The Flyers jumped to a 2–0 lead on goals by Umberger and Jim Dowd, but started a series-long trend of handing those leads back by the third period. Andrei Kostitsyn scored midway through the second, and Alex Kovalev used a controversially magical piece of

## THAT'S THE TICKET

After the worst season in franchise history, the Flyers wanted to do something different for their fans. So they took their tickets and made them something more than a piece of paper with a seat location on it.

"One thing we realized is, the fans are what make the organization," said Shawn Tilger, the club's senior vice president, business operations, "so why not do a tribute to the fans, especially the season-ticket holders?"

Through an email campaign, the club received more than 200 photo submissions from it's season-ticket holders, and put the best 44 (preseason and regular season) on the tickets.

eye-hand coordination to tie the game near the period's close. Tomas Plekanec fired a shot off a short-handed rush, and the rebound popped in the air. Kovalev appeared to play the puck with a high stick, but replays showed that while the blade of his stick came down on top of the crossbar, the puck hit the middle of the shaft—which was below the crossbar—and was ruled a goal.

Lupul scored 19 seconds into the third to put the Flyers ahead, but Montreal got another break when Richards was whistled for kneeing Kovalev with 1:09 left. Replays, though, showed Richards hit the Canadiens forward with a clean shoulder check when Kovalev tried to jump around him.

Carter lost the ensuing faceoff when his stick broke, allowing Kovalev to score again to tie the game with 29 seconds left. The Canadiens' Tom Kostopoulos won it with a goal 48 seconds into overtime.

Just like he did in Game 2 of the first round, Biron rose to the occasion in Game 2 against Montreal. He stopped 15 of 16 shots in the first period and made 34 saves for the game, while Umberger scored twice as the Flyers took a 4–2 decision and a tied series home to Philadelphia.

Game 3 easily was the wildest of the series. The Flyers took a 3–0 lead in the second period as Scottie Upshall capped an end-to-end rush by Lupul, Richards scored off a short-handed two-on-one break, and Umberger scored off a Carter rebound. But the lead nearly came unraveled 5:17 into the third period as Derian Hatcher was given a five-minute major and a game misconduct for drilling the Canadiens' Francois Bouillon face-first into the boards.

Montreal cashed in twice in 1:12, but that was all they would get. Biron was outstanding as the Flyers were outshot 17–2 in the third period, but skated away with the 3–2 victory and the series lead.

Hatcher breathed a sigh of relief when the final horn sounded.

"It was a horrible feeling," the veteran defenseman said. "Watching those 15 minutes that I wasn't playing, that was a lot more exhausting than playing the game. Mentally it was a lot more stressing."

There was more stress in Game 4, as the usual script unfolded—the Flyers scored the first two goals, the Canadiens tied the game in a short burst, Biron played like a superhero, and the Flyers eked out a victory.

This time it was Umberger scoring twice more—giving him six in the series—and Briere netting the game-winner in a 4–2 victory.

Biron, though, was the story.

"Marty has set a standard of play for himself that he's able to consistently achieve," said Stevens. "Until you have success this time of year, you really don't know what your standard is. Marty has never been in this situation, he never had a reference point, and now he has a reference point that he can play at a very high level and be the difference in a hockey game, and he was tonight."

The series moved back to Montreal for Game 5. Up 3–1 again, the Flyers were determined not to make the same mistakes they made against Washington.

"The last Game 5, we played like we were an unsure team," said Lupul. "They [Washington] came out hard, and we should have been prepared for that. We'll be prepared for that [against Montreal]."

They didn't look prepared early, as the Canadiens scored the game's first goal for the first time in the series. It actually was the first time they had played with a lead the entire series to that point. Umberger scored his seventh of the series to tie it, but midway through the second, the Canadiens led 3–1.

That's when the Flyers turned the offense loose, scoring three times in a 2:58 span to take a 4–3 lead. Umberger continued his dream series, as his wild shot from the point hit Richards's glove and dropped into the goal. Moments later, Umberger took the puck from Montreal defenseman Roman Hamrlik in front of the Montreal net and scored to tie the game. Hartnell completed the comeback when he lasered a shot past Montreal rookie goalie Carey Price to put the Flyers ahead.

Kostitsyn scored early in the third to tie the game, but Upshall tipped a Carter shot behind Price, and Knuble outraced Christopher Higgins to a loose puck for an empty-net goal for a final 6–4 margin.

The Flyers became just the second team in NHL history to win two rounds in the playoffs the season after finishing with the league's worst record.

"For the guys who were doubted last year, it's been a lot of fun, and it's a vindication," said Knuble. "We're thrilled where we are and now we can really start thinking, 'Why not us?'"

The Eastern Conference Finals would be dubbed the Keystone Clash, an All-Pennsylvania series between the Flyers and Penguins.

As high as the Flyers were riding, a huge dip came the day before the team was scheduled to leave for Pittsburgh, when they learned they would be without Timonen due to a blood clot in his ankle, suffered when he blocked a shot late in Game 5 against the Canadiens.

Facing the Penguins' offensive juggernaut, it was a crushing blow.

"We feel like we've battled through adversity all year long," Briere told reporters just before the series started. "Yes, Kimmo is a big part of our team, but at the same time we've been faced with those situations before. We've found ways to pull through, to come together. We believe we can do the same thing."

For a while in Game 1 it looked like they would, thanks to a pair of Richards goals that put them up 2–1 midway through the first period. But the Penguins scored twice before the period ended and added another goal when a cherry-picking Evgeni Malkin scored a short-handed goal for a 4–2 final score.

Less than two minutes into Game 2, Coburn would join Timonen on the sideline after a tipped puck slammed into the left side of his head, leaving him with a face that looked like it came from a Halloween nightmare. A gash in the middle of his face that needed more than 50 stitches to close left him with a scar that resembled a question mark, and his left eye looked like he had gone 12 rounds with both Rocky Balboa and Apollo Creed. He also suffered a concussion and didn't play the rest of the series.

Playing the rest of Game 2 with just five defensemen—three of whom were 34 or older—the Flyers held as best they could. The game turned midway through the third when Downie didn't fight hard enough to clear a puck from the Flyers' end, and then compounded the mistake by chasing Gary Roberts behind the net. No one covered Maxime Talbot in front, and he netted the winner off Roberts's pass in what became another 4–2 defeat.

Despite the mistake, Stevens wrote Downie's name into the lineup for Game 3. "There'll be lots more good days for Steve Downie," the coach said.

Game 3 wasn't one of those days.

Pittsburgh jumped out early, scoring twice in a 2:37 span early in the first, but Umberger scored his 10th of the postseason when he knocked in a Prospal rebound midway through the period.

The game turned in the third when Downie went one-on-four in the Pittsburgh end. Trapped, he threw a lazy pass into the middle of the ice that Malkin intercepted and started back the other way, leading to a Ryan Malone goal that started the Pens to a 4–1 victory and left the Flyers in a 3–0 series hole.

"You've just got to keep going," said Carter. "We had a 10-game losing streak this year. We learned from it. We just have to keep battling. You can't let up, you have to keep going, work harder. We've got one game here to turn things around."

Their season on the line, the Flyers came out angry and effective. Lupul scored when his shot ticked off the stick of Penguins defenseman Hal Gill, and Briere made it 2–0 when he found a sliver of space between Gill and goalie Marc-Andre Fleury to knock in a rebound. Carter made it 3–0 when he whacked his own rebound out of mid-air.

The Pens got a pair of Jordan Staal scores in the third period to make it a one-goal game, but Biron backstopped a furious final 5:49, and the Flyers remained alive with a 4–2 victory, and even felt a little confident.

"This is the weirdest group I've ever been around," said Lupul. "We seem our most confident when it looks like we're down and out. We're kind of a weird team that way. We play our best when our backs are up against the wall."

Timonen was cleared to play in Game 5, but there was no extra lift from the return of their best defenseman, as the Penguins' over-abundance of offensive firepower ended the Flyers' fairy-tale season with a 6–0 shellacking.

## GUTTING IT OUT

Players will do whatever it takes to get their name on the Stanley Cup.

For veteran defenseman and team captain Jason Smith, it was playing through two separated shoulders while leading the team in the playoffs with 56 hits and 45 blocked shots, while for fellow blueliner Derian Hatcher, it was blocking out the pain from a broken leg and needing fluid drained from his knee every other day and still playing more than 21 minutes per game.

"I get shivers thinking about it," said GM Paul Holmgren. "It was almost like we'd have to shoot him [Smith] for him not to play. That was his attitude. I've been around hockey a long time, and I don't know that I've ever seen anything like that. I don't know how he did it.

"They both are ultimate pros. What they bring to a team, you can't define it."

While there were tears in the aftermath of their season ending, the 2007–2008 campaign was a wild ride that shows the Flyers' future is a bright one.

"To win the Cup, you have to be a good team, but you need some breaks to go your way," said Briere. "I believe at some point things will fall in line with us. That's the way you have to see it. We made some great strides. We gained a lot of experience this year. It's tough to see right away, you're fighting so hard to get to the Stanley Cup Finals, it's a tough blow when it happens, when you lose that game that sends you home. But when you sit back and look at all the strides we made this year, the organization is definitely headed in the right direction."

# THE BAD

## 1976

The Flyers' quest for a third straight Stanley Cup in 1975–1976 got off to a dreadful start.

Bernie Parent, the hero of the previous two title runs, reported to training camp in 1975 complaining of neck and elbow pain. He was given massages and muscle relaxants, but even a few days in traction at a hospital did little to ease the netminder's aching body. Further tests revealed a herniated cervical disc. Surgery was performed, sidelining Parent until late February.

Little-used Wayne Stevenson was pressed into service, but he didn't exactly get a ringing endorsement from his coach.

"Unless we get somebody better, we'll go with him," said Fred Shero.

Despite Parent's absence, the Flyers flew out of the box, winning their first four and not losing consecutive games until the end of December, and only twice did they go more than three games without a victory. When the calendar turned from 1975 to 1976, the Flyers were 22–6–8.

By then Reggie Leach had 23 goals, Bobby Clarke had 17 goals and 36 assists, and Bill Barber had 18 goals and 23 assists.

"It's so easy," Leach told reporters. "All I have to do is get in the slot and wait for Clarkie to get me the puck."

After beating the Russian Central Red Army team on January 11, 1976, the Flyers finished the regular season going 24–7–8 over their final 39 games. Included was an NHL record-tying 23-game unbeaten streak, during which they went 17–0–6. Leach became the 13th player in league history to net 50 goals, and Barber went over 100 points.

They clinched the Patrick Division title March 21, one game after the streak ended, when Barber and Terry Crisp each scored twice in a 4–2 victory over Toronto.

The Flyers finished 51–13–16, their third straight 50-win season, and their club-record 118 points was second overall to the Montreal Canadiens.

They led the league with 348 goals, and the high-flying LCB Line—Leach, Clarke, Barber—set records with 141 goals and 322 points. Leach established a team record with a league-leading 61 goals. Barber added 50 goals, 62 assists, and 112 points. Clarke led the league with 89 assists, finished second to Montreal's Guy Lafleur with 119 points, and won his second straight Hart Trophy as league MVP.

Despite having Parent for just 11 games, only two teams—Montreal and the New York Islanders—allowed fewer goals.

Stephenson starred in Parent's absence, winning 40 games with a 2.58 goals-against average.

The playoffs started for the second straight season with a first-round matchup with the Toronto Maple Leafs. And just like the previous season, the Flyers took the first two games at the Spectrum. Parent, getting the playoff nod over Stephenson, made 23 saves to backstop a 4–1 win in Game 1, and in Game 2, goals 70 seconds apart by Ross Lonsberry and Don Saleski early in the second period pushed the Flyers to a 3–1 win.

The Leafs turned up the hitting in Game 3 and lured the Flyers into giving away 16 man-advantages, which allowed Toronto to score all its goals in a 5–4 win. And despite a pair of Mel Bridgman goals, Parent played poorly in a 4–3 loss in Game 4, returning the series to Philadelphia tied 2–2.

Beside the losses, the Flyers were angry about what they viewed as mistreatment by the Toronto fans and police. During Game 3, Saleski was sitting in the penalty box when he was hit by a piece of ice thrown by a fan. Saleski turned to look into the crowd, and an overzealous police officer grabbed his stick. Joe Watson, coming to the defense of his teammate, swung his stick over the glass and smacked the cop on the shoulder. Both players were charged with crimes in the mêlée, as was Bridgman, who had decked Leafs defenseman Borje Salming.

Game 5 saw the Flyers score three times in 1:33 in the second period to blow open the game, and Saleski capped the 7–1 win with a hat trick.

The Flyers returned to Toronto with a chance to clinch, but Darryl Stitler scored a league record–tying five goals in an 8–5 rout, which featured more Flyers arrests.

Dave Schultz, who took a record-tying 42 penalty minutes, was elbowed by a fan while leaving the ice. While Schultz was held back from attacking the 65-year-old knucklehead, Bob Kelly threw his glove into the stands, but accidentally hit an usherette in the face. Kelly and the fan who smacked Schultz were charged with assault in the fracas.

Clarke ripped his teammates after the game, saying, "We didn't play like Stanley Cup champions. We were undisciplined, unorganized."

After falling behind 2–1 after one period of Game 7 back at the Spectrum, something clicked for the Flyers. They scored four times in the first eight minutes of the second, including a pair by Bridgman, and the Flyers cruised to a series-clinching, sigh-of-relief-inducing 7–3 win.

Next were the Boston Bruins. Despite not having Bobby Orr, who was recovering from knee surgery, the Bruins took a 4–2 Game 1 win powered by third-period goals by Dallas Smith and Gregg Sheppard against a deteriorating Parent.

Prior to Game 2, Parent took himself out of the lineup, telling reporters, "I'm tired. I'm not in playoff shape. I don't want to cost the team a game. Let's make the move before it happens."

When the game started, Saleski gave the Flyers an early 1–0 lead, and Stephenson, who hadn't played in nearly a month, held the fort until 13:17 of the third period, when Johnny Bucyk scored through a screen. In overtime, Leach knocked in the rebound of Jimmy Watson's shot off the end boards at 13:38.

With Game 3 tied 2–2 after two periods, Bridgman scored off a Larry Goodenough rebound to give the Flyers the lead, and Leach and Tom Bladon added late goals for a 5–2 victory. Leach scored 23 seconds into the second period in Game 4, and Orest Kindrachuk and Joe Watson tallied in the third for a 4–2 victory.

The Game 4 score was Leach's 10th goal of the playoffs and gave him a goal in eight straight games. He wasted little time extending both numbers.

The Flyers returned home for Game 5 one win from their third straight trip to the Stanley Cup Finals, but Leach started his celebration a little early. After no-showing the morning skate, teammates found him passed out in the basement of his South Jersey home. When coffee and a shower didn't completely revive the winger, a few more beers did the trick.

"We stayed at a hotel down in Valley Forge the night before that game," Leach recalled in Jim Jackson's book *Walking Together Forever*. "I got in a big argument that night with one of the coaches, so I got drunk and went home. I don't even remember going home. The next morning Clarkie found me passed out in the basement of my house and got me up. I had a couple of beers to revive me and told him to take me to the rink so I could play."

Clarke had to talk Shero into letting Leach play in Game 5.

"When we got to the Spectrum, Freddy saw what shape I was in, and he wasn't going to play me," said Leach. "Clarkie told him, 'Let him play. He will probably score a bunch of goals.'"

Leach was suffering from what he called an alcohol-induced "concussion," but he magically cleared the cobwebs when he stepped on the ice. At 5:45 of the first period, he scored off a Barber feed to open the scoring.

Sheppard beat Stephenson 59 seconds into the second, but then Leach scored three times during the frame to give him a hat-trick-plus-one.

After Don Marcotte scored 6:09 into the third to cut the Flyers' lead to 4–2, Leach made it a five-goal night when he finished a Clarke feed at 8:07.

Two weeks after Stitler became the first player in more than 30 years to score five in a playoff game, Leach turned the trick. Of his handful of goals, three came on backhanders: one to the short side, one to the wide side, and one under the crossbar. He stuck forehanders to the stick side and between the pads of flustered Bruins goalie Gilles Gilbert. Three of the goals came after he crossed over from right wing to left.

And with nine goals in five games, Leach set a post-expansion record for goals in a series.

More importantly, the 6–3 victory sent the Flyers back to the Stanley Cup Finals, against the Montreal Canadiens, where their playoff experience made them a favorite in many eyes.

Leach's record output against the Bruins gave him 15 goals in the playoffs, but the Flyers that faced Montreal were a beat-up bunch. The team's top three centers were hurt or out—Clarke was slowed by strained ligaments in his knee, Rick MacLeish hadn't played since February after surgery to repair torn ligaments in his left knee, and Kindrachuk was playing through a major back injury. Add to that Parent's shattered confidence, and the Flyers were far from a full team when the series started at the Montreal Forum on May 9, 1976.

Leach scored just 21 seconds into Game 1, and Lonsberry added a first-period goal, but Montreal's speed allowed them to tie the game with a pair of goals in the second period. Stephenson kept the game tied until Goodenough's power-play goal put the Flyers back on top, but Jacques Lemaire knocked a loose puck in the slot under Stephenson at 10:02 of the third, and Guy Lapointe notched the game-winner with just 1:22 left for a 4–3 Canadiens win.

In Game 2 Montreal's checking line of Doug Jarvis, Bob Gainey, and Jimmy Roberts held the LCB Line to one shot by each player, and all the Flyers could manage was a Dave Schultz bad-angle goal with 2:25 left in the third of what ended as a 2–1 defeat.

Home cooking helped early in Game 3. After Steve Shutt scored from 70 feet away to give Montreal the lead, Clarke fed Leach to tie the game, and Leach turned a Bill Nyrop turnover into his NHL-record 18th of the playoffs. Newsy Lalonde of the Montreal Canadiens had scored 17 playoff goals in 1919.

# AL HILL'S MEMORABLE DEBUT

In one day, Al Hill went from minor-league nobody to NHL record-holder.

Playing for the AHL Springfield Indians, Hill arrived home at 4:30 AM from a game in Rochester, New York. At 11:00 AM, he was told to report to Philadelphia to suit up for the Flyers. He got to the Spectrum at 5:30 PM, and was on the ice by 7:35 PM. By the time he punched out for the night, he had two goals, three assists, and a league record for a debuting NHL player.

By the time the league learned of his mark, three scoreless games passed, and Hill had been returned to the minors.

Shutt scored again, knocking in his own rebound at 1:09 of the second period, but Stephenson kept the game tied, turning aside 12 of 13 Montreal shots in the second, including breakaways by Murray Wilson and Yvan Cournoyer. But at 9:16 of the third, Pierre Bouchard took a pass out of the corner from Wilson and scored through a Rick Chartraw screen. The tight-checking Canadiens limited the Flyers to just 13 shots over the final two periods, and anything that did get through, goalie Ken Dryden turned aside.

"We played our best," said a pained Barber after the game, "but there wasn't much we could do."

Down three games to none, the goal had changed to just winning one to avoid the embarrassing sweep. Kate Smith was on hand to sing "God Bless America" for the fourth time live, and she seemed to serve as Lady Luck as Leach beat Dryden from 45 feet out just 41 seconds into the game.

Shutt and Bouchard answered for Montreal, but Barber deflected a Bladon shot past Dryden with 1:40 left in the first to tie the game at 2–2.

With Guy Lapointe off for tripping, Moose Dupont put the Flyers ahead at 13:59 of the second, and with Lemaire off for hooking at 17:20, the Flyers had a chance for an insurance goal, but Gary Dornhoefer was penalized for hooking Jarvis just 33 seconds later, negating the Flyers' last, best chance. Four seconds before Dornhoefer was set to step back on the ice, Cournoyer tied the game with 11 seconds left in the second.

With time running down in the third and the game tied, Dornhoefer hit the crossbar behind Dryden, and on the next shift Lafleur tapped in a puck in the crease with 5:42 remaining to put Montreal ahead 4–3. Pete Mahovlich added an insurance goal 58 seconds later, and the celebration was on for the visiting team.

The Canadiens won the Cup, but Leach took home the Conn Smythe Trophy as playoff MVP. His record of 19 goals in 16 games has been matched one time since, by Edmonton's Jari Kurri in 1985, but it took the Finn 18 games to do it.

The record and individual bauble was little consolation to the Flyers. They had seen their team at less than 100 percent stopped by a total of five frustrating goals.

"I thought the '76 team was loaded," says Joe Watson. "The reason we didn't win in '76 was we didn't have Bernie and we didn't have MacLeish. We go against Montreal in the finals and we lost to them before the playoffs started. Wayne Stephenson did an admirable job, but he wasn't Parent. There was nobody like Parent."

"I think the 1975–1976 team was better than the two that won the Cup," says team chairman Ed Snider. "But when Bernie went out, and we had Wayne Stephenson in goal, Bernie would have won that. I think that team was better than the teams that won the Cup."

## THE FOG ROLLS OUT OF PHILADELPHIA

After the Flyers were eliminated from the 1978 playoffs by the Boston Bruins, the Broad Street Bullies' days were coming to a close.

Already gone were Ed Van Impe and goalie Bobby Taylor, who had been traded to Pittsburgh in 1976, and Dave Schultz, dealt to Los Angeles in 1977. Barry Ashbee had passed away, and Gary Dornhoefer and Terry Crisp had retired.

And before the 1978–1979 season started, Tom Bladon, Ross Lonsberry, and Orest Kindrachuk were shipped to Pittsburgh, and Joe Watson was sold to Colorado.

But the Bullies' days really ended on June 2, 1978. That was the day the Fog cleared in Philadelphia.

Sports experts claim that after five seasons with the same club, regardless of the sport, a coach begins to lose his effectiveness. The players have heard all the stories, all the motivational speeches; there's nothing new, and the relationship can get stale, boring, and repetitive.

The end of the 1977–1978 season marked Fred Shero's seventh season behind the Flyers' bench. And after a disheartening five-game semifinal-round loss to the Boston Bruins—the second straight time the Bruins had ended the Flyers' season—general manager Keith Allen was pondering whether a coaching change was needed.

"I'm sort of a believer that you have to change coaches every once in a while, and I did wonder if [the players] were still getting Freddie's message," Allen told Jay Greenberg in *Full Spectrum*.

Shero had a year left on his contract, and Allen was content to let it run its course, knowing Bob McCammon was gaining experience with the franchise's American Hockey League affiliate in Maine after being hired in 1977. But a week after the 1978 playoffs ended, Allen found an envelope waiting for him from Shero. Enclosed was the coach's letter of resignation.

Two days later, Shero and his agent met with Sonny Werblin, the new president of Madison Square Garden, at Pimlico Racetrack in Baltimore, the site of the Preakness Stakes. Owner Ed Snider learned of the meeting after it happened, and suspected Mark Stewart, Shero's agent, of trying to orchestrate Shero's move from Philadelphia to the New York Rangers; the Rangers had been rumored during the playoffs to have interest in hiring Shero.

Snider told scouting director John Brogan to write a reply to Shero, stating that his resignation would not be accepted, and that the coach would be expected to honor the final year of his contract.

Shero took his case to the press, saying, "I feel my effectiveness to motivate the players has been exhausted. The organization needs a change, whether they realize it or not. Most of the players have been with me too long and I've been with them too long."

He then added, "I really believe I don't want to coach anymore. Coaching anywhere else would be a demotion."

The next week, Snider took a phone call from Werblin, who said he had read about the Flyers' coaching situation and asked if he could talk to Shero about coaching the Rangers. Snider's reply was for Werblin and the Rangers to stay away because Shero was Flyers property.

Snider hung up from Werblin and called Rangers president Bill Jennings and asked him to help set up a deal that worked for both teams. Snider asked for $100,000 and the Rangers' first-round choice in the 1978 draft, the number-seven overall selection. He settled for $50,000 and the pick, which was used to select Ken Linseman.

Years later, Snider said dealing away the only coach to lead his team to a Stanley Cup was a good move.

"The time had come to make a change," Snider told Jim Jackson in *Walking Together Forever*. "Everything worked out beautifully for us. We basically suckered the Rangers. We ended up with a first-round pick for a coach we probably were going to fire anyway."

So the Flyers got what they wanted, and so did Shero. Shero had played parts of three seasons for the Rangers in the 1940s and was coaching one of their minor-league affiliates when he was hired by the Flyers.

"My heart has always been here," Shero told reporters the day he was hired by New York.

"He said he had enough of coaching and he obviously wasn't telling the truth," a disappointed Bobby Clarke told reporters. "It's fairly obvious he had an idea of where he was going all along. He probably knew during the playoffs. You wonder how much he could concentrate on what we were doing."

Both teams moved on after the coaching change. Shero's first trip back to the Spectrum was for a preseason game. The Flyers ripped Shero's Rangers 8–2, and the fans ripped their old coach, hanging signs reading, "Rangers: Beware, He Lies," and, "Win Today and Renegotiate Forever," from the Spectrum rafters.

Meanwhile McCammon, tabbed as Shero's replacement, was himself replaced after 50 games, by Maine coach Pat Quinn.

Quinn had been Shero's assistant during the coach's final Flyers season, and then sent to the AHL club when McCammon was promoted. Ironically, McCammon returned to Maine to fill Quinn's spot.

Quinn led the Flyers to an 18–8–4 finish and a three-game preliminary-round playoff win over the Vancouver Canucks.

But that was as far as the 1978–1979 Flyers would go, as Shero's Rangers knocked off the Flyers in five games, outscoring them 28–8, thanks in part to John Davidson's magnificence in the Rangers' net and the Flyers missing Bernie Parent from theirs.

Shero guided the Rangers past the New York Islanders and into the Stanley Cup Finals, where they lost to the Montreal Canadiens.

The following season, the Flyers eliminated the Rangers in five games in the 1980 quarterfinals. That would be the old coach's last hurrah—he was fired 20 games into the 1980–1981 season

Though there were hard feelings at the time, Shero's son Ray said his father held no bitterness toward his former team.

"There was no sense of revenge or anything like that," he said in *Walking Together Forever*. "My dad was just trying to do the best he could for the Rangers at the time. We all wish the parting with the Flyers could have been handled a little better, but it was in the past. Everybody had agreed it was time to move on."

Fred Shero was diagnosed with stomach cancer in 1983, but recovered enough to work as a radio color analyst for New Jersey Devils broadcasts, and felt well enough to coach a team in Holland in 1987.

On March 22, 1990, Shero was inducted into the Flyers' Hall of Fame.

"Once a Flyer, always a Flyer," he said that night. "I knew the day I left here [in 1978] that I had made a mistake." Shero's words struck a chord, and he was hired by the team as a senior adviser.

His health took a turn for the worst months later; the cancer had spread to other parts of his body, and on Saturday, November 24, 1990, the greatest coach in team history passed away.

Fred Shero is remembered for many things, but it was his words from that memorable 1974 playoff run—"Win together today and we will walk together forever"—that blinked back into focus at his funeral.

"Forever didn't stop Saturday," said Clarke. "Freddie left a piece of himself with every one of us."

# LEON STICKLE

Mention it to any Flyers fan, and the name Leon Stickle still brings dirty looks and dirtier words.

The 1979–1980 campaign was Stickle's 11th in the NHL, and he drew the assignment to work Game 6 of the Stanley Cup Finals between the Flyers and the New York Islanders at Nassau Veterans Memorial Coliseum on May 24, 1980.

Up to that point, the Flyers looked like they had an outstanding chance to win their third Cup.

Powered by their record-setting 35-game unbeaten streak, they had finished 48–12–20, their 116 points the most in the league. A reinvigorated Reggie Leach scored 50 goals, Bill Barber had 40, and Ken Linseman had a team-best 57 assists and 79 points.

The Flyers swept a young Wayne Gretzky and the Edmonton Oilers in the best-of-five preliminary round, and then took the first three games in the best-of-seven quarterfinals against the New York Rangers, including a 29-save Game 3 shutout by goalie Pete Peeters. The Rangers took Game 4, but the Flyers clinched the series two days later. Against Minnesota in the semifinals, the Flyers lost Game 1 but came back to rout the North Stars in four straight to set up a final match between the Flyers and Islanders.

In Game 1 the teams traded goals through the first two periods, and were tied 2–2 when Rick MacLeish scored off a Paul Holmgren pass at 13:10 of the third. The Flyers were just 3:42 from taking the game when the Islanders took advantage of a hooking penalty on Al Hill. Mike Bossy sent the puck into the slot where Stefan Persson beat Peeters for the tying goal.

Just 2:08 into overtime, Jimmy Watson was whistled for holding when he grabbed John Tonelli around the shoulders. In those days, overtime penalties were rare, and fans were unhappy

# TERRY GREGSON

A persecution complex has seemed to exist in the minds of members of the organization since the Broad Street Bullies days.

Many of the conspiracy buffs point to referee Terry Gregson and May 2, 1999.

With 2:54 left in a scoreless playoff game with the Toronto Maple Leafs, John LeClair got his left elbow up on the Leafs' Mike Johnson. Gregson's arm went up, and the Flyers' season went down—with Toronto up a man, they got the game's only goal with 59.2 seconds left.

An enraged Mount Snider erupted, calling Gregson "a coward."

"As far as I'm concerned, I'm sick of this crap," the chairman added. "When an official decides to decide the game, when the players are playing their hearts out, that's a disgrace to this team and to this league, and I won't put up with it anymore.

"They call this chicken you-know-what on John LeClair, one of the cleanest players in the league. It's a disgrace....Gregson, I hope he can sleep well tonight, because he knows damn well what he did."

despite the clear infraction. Just one second before Watson could get back on the ice, Tonelli fed a pass to Denis Potvin, who scored the NHL's first overtime power-play goal to give the Isles a 4–3 win.

The Flyers came back in Game 2. Trailing 1–0 early, the Flyers went ahead when Holmgren and Bob Kelly scored 1:15 apart, and Bobby Clarke added a goal before the period's end to make it 3–1 for the Flyers. Keyed by Holmgren's hat trick—the first American-born player to score three in a playoff game—the Flyers tied the series with an 8–3 knockout.

Coach Pat Quinn surprisingly tabbed Phil Myre for Game 3 ahead of Peeters, but the move didn't work as Myre was ripped for six goals, including five on the power play, as the Flyers fell 6–2.

Peeters was back in goal for Game 4, but it didn't change much. Watson suffered a broken collarbone, and Holmgren had torn knee cartilage during Game 3 and didn't play. John

Paddock and Linseman scored to keep the game close, but Bob Bourne blocked a Bob Dailey shot and fed Bobby Nystrom, who finished a two-on-one break, and Clark Gillies finished the 5–2 Islanders win.

Down three games to one, the Flyers returned home with their season on the line. All the good they had accomplished during the 35-game unbeaten streak was 60 minutes away from going out the window.

"We knew if they don't win the Cup, they either would be the streak team or the Cup winner," recalls longtime Philadelphia media member Al Morganti, who covered the team for *The Philadelphia Inquirer*.

Holmgren, wearing a bulky knee brace, returned for Game 5, as did Watson. But when Holmgren went to the penalty box for slashing, followed by Moose Dupont 1:37 later for holding, the Islanders had a five-on-three power play, and Persson scored off a Mike Bossy pass for the lone goal of the first period.

The Flyers had just six shots in the stanza and went 16 minutes without any, but a different team took the ice in the second period. Clarke one-timed a Behn Wilson pass 1:35 into the frame to tie the game, and MacLeish beat Isles goalie Billy Smith over his glove to put the Flyers ahead. Bryan Trottier tied the game, but just 48 seconds later Mike Busniak popped out from behind the Islanders net to give the Flyers back the lead, 3–2, heading into the third period.

## ARVEDSON HITS THE WALL

One of the more gruesome injuries in Flyers history occurred January 20, 2000, when Flyers forward Marc Bureau checked Ottawa Senators winger Magnus Arvedson into the frame of the bench door.

Arvedson was rushed to Pennsylvania Hospital, where he had three inches of his bowel removed to repair a hole in his small intestine. He spent a week in the hospital and lost 20 pounds, but was able to return two and a half months later for the playoffs.

MacLeish and Brian Propp scored to push the lead to 5–2, and after Persson scored again, a one-legged Holmgren answered with his 10th of the postseason to finish the 6–3 win and send the series back to Long Island.

The Flyers felt the momentum swing heading into Game 6. And their smiles got even bigger when Nystrom was given an extra roughing minor after fighting Kelly, and Potvin was whistled for cross-checking 34 seconds later. Leach scored on the five-on-three advantage, and the Flyers looked like they were on the way to forcing a Game 7 back in Philadelphia.

Their smiles would be wiped away four and a half minutes later. Peeters stopped a Bossy shot, but the rebound popped into the air, where Potvin smacked it into the net. The Flyers claimed Potvin's stick was above his shoulders when he made contact with the puck, which would have nullified the goal. The officials disagreed, and the goal stood.

It only would get worse for the Flyers.

Just 2:12 after the Potvin goal, Gillies skated the puck into the Flyers' end and dropped a pass that drifted about two feet beyond the blue line and into neutral ice, where Goring grabbed it and crossed into the Flyers' end. Gillies never left the zone, so when Goring crossed the blue line, the whistle should have blown for offside. Dupont pointed at the line, assuming play was about to be stopped. Propp, who was backchecking Duane Sutter, slowed down, assuming play was about to be stopped.

"I definitely know the offside one was way offside," recalls Propp. "It was so obvious that I slowed down for a second."

Linesman Leon Stickle, though, never blew his whistle. Play never stopped.

Goring sent a pass past Dupont and Propp to Sutter, who beat a stunned Peeters under the crossbar.

The Flyers, incredulous about the non-call, composed themselves, and Propp scored with 1:22 left in the first to tie the game.

Between periods, a fuming Ed Snider stormed into the officials' room and confronted Frank Udvari, the supervisor of officials, and spoke to him in what Snider gingerly calls, "A very strong manner."

"Udvari said the officials felt the puck, when he [Potvin] hit it, hit our player first before it went in. I said it's still a high stick, and the whistle should have blown. He said our player touched it, and we had control and then it went in. The film showed that didn't happen, and the officials changed their tune. They said it wasn't a high stick when he made contact, it was below the crossbar. That's bullshit. It was pure BS....Every time a guy raised his stick and hit the puck, it was a high stick. There was no technology, there was no replay. Anytime a player had his stick up and smacked the puck, nobody tried to gauge where he hit it, it was a high stick.

"We got screwed out of two goals in that game."

Bossy gave the Islanders the lead with a power-play goal 7:34 into the second, and with 14 seconds left, Tonelli got past Clarke and fed a pass to Nystrom, who got behind Leach and scored to give the Islanders a 4–2 lead with one period to play.

Summoning one last bit of strength, Dailey scored from the point 1:47 into the third, and then Dupont's slap shot hit off MacLeish and then Paddock before finding its way behind Smith at the 6:02 mark.

The teams played into overtime, with Linseman and Al Hill having chances to win it, but Smith denied both. Just over seven minutes into the extra session, Hill's soft clear out of the zone was picked up by Lorne Henning, who backtracked and then sent a pass to Tonelli that trapped the line of Hill, Mel Bridgman, and MacLeish too far up ice. Dailey skated after Tonelli, missing Nystrom, who cut down the backside. Dailey tried to recover and get back to Nystrom, but Tonelli sent a pass over Dupont's stick right to Nystrom, who had a stride on Dailey and tipped the puck with his backhand over a sliding Peeters.

The Islanders had won the first of their four straight Stanley Cups.

Snider went on the warpath after the game, telling the *Philadelphia Bulletin*'s Ray Didinger: "It was an absolute, total [expletive] disgrace. Anybody who's impartial knows we took a screwing today. I believe the [officials] who come out of Montreal and Toronto don't want [us] to win. I believe that right down to

## AN AWFUL ACCIDENT

The Flyers nearly were witness to an on-ice fatality January 23, 2000.

In a game at the Molson Centre in Montreal, Canadiens forward Trent McCleary dropped to block a Chris Therien slap shot. The puck hit the winger in the throat, fracturing his larynx and causing massive bleeding that led to a collapsed lung. A tracheotomy was performed to keep McCleary alive. He later needed his larynx and windpipe reconstructed.

"He was making a sound like a muffler on a car," Therien said the next day.

David Mulder, a Canadiens team doctor, said, "Until we performed the tracheotomy, he was in great danger. It was as close [to death] as I think you could come. It was a matter of seconds."

the pit of my stomach....The problem with this league is [referee-in-chief] Scotty Morrison. He should be shot."

General manager Keith Allen was just as bitter, but slightly calmer, than his boss: "You can say they [referees] are human and they make mistakes, but this was the Stanley Cup Finals, and [the offside goal] wasn't even close. I know people think we cry a lot about the officials, but just look at it. You can see it."

For his part, Stickle admitted the Flyers had a legitimate gripe. "I guess I blew it," he said that night. "Maybe I was too close to the play. Maybe there was tape on the stick and it confused me."

Today, Snider is a bit calmer when he looks back on the events of May 24, 1980.

"We had the Cup taken away from us that year," he says. "That team would have won the Cup."

Dating back to the prime days of the Broad Street Bullies, the Flyers always have felt a bit of a persecution complex. Most hockey people, including the media, always have ignored it as whining. But this time, though, they had a point.

"That wasn't a case of crying," says Morganti. "They got screwed, they really did get screwed. They legitimately got screwed."

## "A CHOKING SITUATION"

The 1997 Stanley Cup Finals was supposed to be the crowning achievement for the Legion of Doom–led Philadelphia Flyers.

The threesome of Eric Lindros, John LeClair, and Mikael Renberg had used their abundant size and skill to run roughshod over the rest of the NHL.

The Legion had meant doom for Eastern Conference competition, as the Flyers walked through their postseason battles with the Pittsburgh Penguins, Buffalo Sabres, and New York Rangers in five games each. In the first three rounds of the playoffs, Lindros had racked up 11 goals and 11 assists; LeClair had seven goals and 10 assists, and Renberg had four goals and five assists.

And with players like Rod Brind'Amour, Joel Otto, Dale Hawerchuk, and rookie Dainius Zubrus, the Flyers had ample size, strength, and scoring depth. Eric Desjardins, Chris Therien, and Paul Coffey, acquired in December to add mobility to the defense, anchored the back end.

The Flyers' only weak spot looked to be in goal, but coach Terry Murray had pushed all the right buttons in alternating Ron Hextall and Garth Snow.

"The Flyers had that big question in goal," recalls Chuck Gormley, who covered the series for the *Courier Post*. "It was like [spinning] the roulette wheel and every time you'd get the right number. Terry Murray, for the criticism he received, he played that [perfectly]. How he got that team to the finals with that kind of goaltending situation was amazing. He knew the call to make each time."

The Detroit Red Wings, the Flyers' foe in the championship series, were seen as just another speed bump on the road to the Cup.

It was thought the Red Wings didn't have the size or strength to handle the Flyers, especially down low in the offensive zone, and over time the Flyers would push the Wings off the ice.

With the left-wing lock trapping system, the Grind Line of Darren McCarty, Kris Draper and Joey Kocur, and high-skill defensemen Nicklas Lidstrom and Larry Murphy, the Red Wings needed only the first period of the first game to make that view seem as erroneous as someone who believed the sky was orange.

On a Flyers power play 6:38 into the game, Draper stripped Lindros of the puck and started a two-on-one break with Kirk Maltby, who scored over a flopping Hextall.

The Flyers answered 59 seconds later when Lindros slid a Janne Niinimaa rebound to Brind'Amour, who tied the game.

Another turnover by the Flyers, this time by Kjell Samuelsson, allowed Kocur to score with just over four minutes left in the first. Then Coffey fumbled the puck away to Murphy, and Sergei Federov finished a three-on-one to put the Wings ahead 3–1.

LeClair scored between goalie Mike Vernon's pads late in the second to cut the deficit to 3–2, but 56 seconds into the third period, Steve Yzerman beat Hextall from long distance to finish the Wings' 4–2 win.

Murray opted for Snow in Game 2, but it made no difference, as more poor Flyers decisions put the Wings up 2–0 before the game was 10 minutes old. First, Brendan Shanahan picked off a Samuelsson pass, and with Coffey backpedaling, fired a shot from about 50 feet out that ticked off the defenseman's skate and went behind Snow just 97 seconds into the game. With Coffey off for hooking, Yzerman smacked a puck from between Samuelsson's skates and past Snow to make it 2–0.

The Flyers woke up late in the first when consecutive Red Wings penalties allowed Brind'Amour to score a pair of power-play goals 1:09 apart.

Rather than build on the momentum, though, the Flyers allowed the Wings to come back. Snow blocked an Yzerman shot, but the long rebound went out to Maltby. With Coffey again giving too much ground, the winger's 50-footer got behind Snow, giving the Detroit a 3–2 lead just 2:39 into the period. Shanahan scored again in the third, and the visitors' stifling defense allowed them to go home up two games to none.

"I saw this team really struggling to break though the pressure of the event," recalls Murray. "It wasn't just the spotlight of the Stanley Cup Finals, it was a heat lamp. We started off here in Philadelphia, and for two or three days before the first game, this is where all the media was because Detroit was coming here. They [Detroit] came the day before the game, had their press conference, and played Game 1. We had three days of intense pressure."

Murray believed in the hope of a comeback of historic proportions—at that time, only two teams had ever lost the first two Cup finals games at home and won the series—and that getting away from home would help his team.

It seemed to work early in Game 3, as LeClair banged in the rebound of a Desjardins shot at 7:03 of the first. It was the Flyers' first lead of the series. It lasted exactly two minutes.

Another awful turnover, this time by Karl Dykhuis, led to an Yzerman power-play goal. And just 2:05 later, Dykhuis coughed the puck up to Federov, who sped past Dykhuis and Samuelsson and beat Hextall.

The Flyers had a chance to answer, as back-to-back Detroit penalties gave the Flyers a 90-second five-on-three advantage, but they could muster just one shot. Another penalty moments later, on Martin Lapointe, gave the Flyers another power play, but again they came up empty. To add insult to the injury of missed opportunity, Lapointe jumped out of the penalty box and scored with 60 seconds left in the period to give the Wings a 3–1 advantage.

Things only got worse, as Detroit sucked all the life out of the Flyers, holding them to just 14 shots over the final 40 minutes of hockey and skated away with a 6–1 win.

"We got beat very soundly," Murray says today. "We didn't really have any kind of a game going. It was very frustrating for the team, for the whole organization, because we had put every part of our game in place in the other three series. We weren't able to get a forecheck going, we weren't generating any offensive-zone time, we weren't generating chances. There were a lot of things building, and it didn't look like it was going to clear up."

Reaching into his bag of coaching tricks, Murray recalled watching Bowman during the 1995 final, when the Wings were whacked by the New Jersey Devils.

"I remember very clearly," he says, "when Detroit played the New Jersey Devils. And [the Devils] killed them, they shut them

## NIINIMAA-METALLICA

One of the urban legends surrounding the Flyers is how Metallica got a Flyers defenseman benched.

Prior to a game against the Ottawa Senators on October 11, 1997, defenseman Janne Niinimaa was seen rocking in the CoreStates Center parking lot as the heavy metal band played a free pregame concert.

That night, Niinimaa took a seat in the press box, and the assumption was coach Wayne Cashman benched the blueliner as punishment. Niinimaa said he only went to the show because Cashman previously had informed him that he wouldn't be playing that night.

down. As great a team as Detroit was, they [New Jersey] gave them no sniff whatsoever. And Scotty Bowman, in the media press conference following that series, went after his team and his players big-time. But it was a learning process, and they broke through. A lot of the players that were key players on that hockey team, over the next several years, [scored] a lot less points, [had] a lot less individual statistics, became more of a team, and look where they ended up. They became a great franchise."

Following Bowman's lead, Murray tore into his team in a meeting the day after Game 3. Then, in an interview session with the press, Murray was asked about his team's confidence. His attempt at psychoanalysis failed miserably.

"Many teams have been through this problem before, and it is basically a choking situation that I call it for our team right now," he said.

In public, a coach had just called his players chokers. Jaws could be heard dropping like anvils.

"All of us couldn't believe those words would come out of a coach's mouth," said Gormley, speaking for the majority of the slack-jawed press corps.

Murray's players equally were stunned, leading to a classic reaction by Desjardins—"Aye-yi-yi-yi-yi-yi-yi"—to which the written word truly can't give justice.

Forward Daniel Lacroix, told by a reporter that he was shocked by the statement, replied, "You think you're [expletive] shocked!"

Desjardins was left to answer the horde of questions following Murray's statement, since Lindros, the team's captain and supposed point man for media inquiries, had slipped out of the building through an exit under the Joe Louis Arena stands after the initial meeting broke up.

"Nobody likes to be called that," said a seething Desjardins of the choker label. "I don't want to start a big war in the paper, but of course it hurts. It hurts to hear that."

"I don't think anybody liked it," says Hextall, today the assistant GM of the Los Angeles Kings. "The media made a bigger deal and twisted it more than it was meant to be. I remember Murph [Murray] coming to me shortly after that, and he asked me if he needed to address the team, and I said, 'What's the big deal?' We're playing in the finals and to me, I didn't care. That didn't bother me, it didn't affect me. It was something Murph said that he didn't mean the way it came out. Not a big issue to me."

"I didn't care," added Brind'Amour. "I don't believe he meant we were chokers. He meant we weren't playing the way we're capable of, because we hadn't hit that adversity. I don't think he meant we were choking. But of course everything gets turned into a big deal. That's just an unfortunate choice of words. I didn't care. It didn't bother me."

"We're trying to get one win," Murray says today in explaining his choice of words. "We went out the next game in Game 4, and I said we're not trying to win the Stanley Cup right now, we're trying to win the first game. It was trying to find a way to win the first game, to try to kick-start our team again and start to play the way we had, [the way] I knew that we could play."

Regardless of what he meant, all the goodwill Murray had built with his team had been thrown away. And any kind of motivation he hoped would come from an angry bunch of players never materialized. Although the Flyers came out hard and fast in the first period of Game 4, all the energy got sucked out when Lidstrom's long shot eluded Hextall with 33 seconds left in the frame.

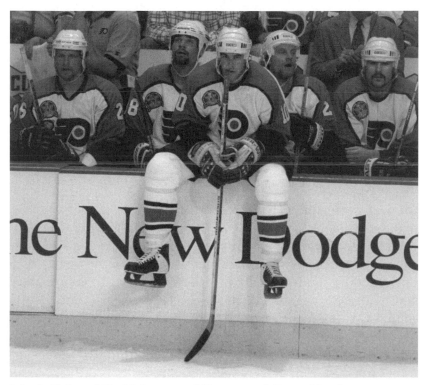

**John LeClair and the high-powered Flyers were left searching for answers after losing in a sweep against the Red Wings in the 1997 Stanley Cup Finals.**

The second period capped the series when McCarty scored one of those highlight-reel goals you see every year during playoff time. Taking a pass from Tomas Sandstrom, McCarty turned Niinimaa inside-out and then finished by pulling the puck away from a diving Hextall and scoring into an open net 13 minutes into the stanza.

The Flyers continued to attack, but all they could manage was Lindros' only goal of the series, with 15 seconds left in the game and with Hextall pulled for an extra attacker.

"That was a negative, no doubt about that," Murray says now of his "choking" comment. "Some of the players, they did bring it up. They felt it did have an impact on their performances. We were a little bit better in Game 4 than we were in Game 3, [but] it didn't have the effect because we didn't win the game and the series was over."

In reality, there were a number of reasons the Flyers lost to the Red Wings, with Murray's caustic remarks ranking far down the list.

"I don't think people knew how good that team was," says Hextall of the victorious Red Wings. "I look back, and there's a lot of us who didn't play up to expectations, but I think a big part of that was how good that team was." The core of that Red Wings group went on to win Cups in 1998 and 2002.

At five-on-five, the Flyers were outscored 11–1. The goaltending was awful, the defense committed far too many turnovers, and the power play went one-for-10 over the final two games. And the Legion of Doom, which scored at ease during the first three rounds of the playoffs, was rendered pointless in the finals—figuratively and almost literally, with Lindros, LeClair, and Renberg combining for a total of just three goals, seven points, and a minus-12 rating.

When the team met back in Voorhees for breakdown day, Murray made what became his final statement to his team.

"I stood in front of the team and I apologized to the team for saying it [choking]," he recalls. "I tried to explain what my position was in the moment that I said it. Players came up to me afterward and said, 'We appreciate you explaining it and we understand. Let's just move on.'"

But it was Murray who would do the moving. Six days after the series ended, general manager Bob Clarke told Murray his contract would not be renewed. Clarke never gave a reason, but it was easy for Murray to figure what led to his demise.

"It was assumed on my part," he says. "How can you get fired after going to the Stanley Cup Finals? You lose four straight? Detroit had just lost four straight to New Jersey two years before that, and they weren't making the change. In fact, Scotty got extended. Absolutely that entered into it, but I was never told that at the time."

Murray spent two and a half seasons as the head coach of the Florida Panthers, but his brother, Bryan, was the GM who hired him. Both were fired during the 2000–2001 season.

He returned to the Flyers and worked as a pro scout and assistant coach under Ken Hitchcock and John Stevens, but as numerous head coaching positions came open over the next decade, he rarely, if ever, was considered. The drought ended when the Los Angeles Kings hired him as their head coach in July 2008, but he believes his words from that 1997 press conference haunt him to this day.

"It always will [follow me]," he says. "It was the wrong thing to say. Maybe it was a deer-in-the-headlights kind of effect. Maybe that statement would have been more appropriate. But it was the reality of the situation."

## PRIMEAU BOWS OUT

The Flyers led the league in games lost to injury in 2005–2006, but no ache or pain hurt worse than the loss of captain Keith Primeau.

Primeau finally was feeling better after suffering as many as three concussions between February and June in 2004. He was knocked out for 21 games in February after a nasty collision with the New York Rangers' Bobby Holik, and suffered possibly two more head injuries, against Toronto and Tampa Bay, during his amazing playoff run.

The lockout gave him time to recover at his own pace, and by October 2005, Primeau felt like any remaining fogginess had cleared.

That all changed on Tuesday, October 25, 2005, in Montreal, when Primeau was leveled by a high, vicious elbow to the head by the Canadiens' Alexander Perezhogin.

"All I remember is we were killing a penalty, and a shot comes off the boards, and the rebound comes into the slot, and I turned," recalls Primeau. "The puck comes to my left side, so I turned to the right. I'm going to try and find the puck, so I'm not looking at who's coming, and I turn right into Perezhogin, and I go down."

Primeau was encouraged by how he felt in the immediate aftermath of the hit, saying, "I'm actually excited because I was leery of when the first hit I was going to take, when it was coming, and how I would react. I was excited because I thought I got through it. After the game I got on the bus, I called my wife, I called my parents, and said I feel good, I'm fine. I think it was a good thing. I got hit hard and I'm okay."

The good feeling wouldn't last.

"The next day wasn't too bad," he recalls. "The following day was a game day, Thursday. We were at home against Florida, and in the game I was in a daze. I was sluggish. I remember Hitch hollering at me to get into it, get involved, and I just couldn't. I thought it was because we had been off for a year."

That night the Flyers flew from Philadelphia to North Carolina for a game the next day against the Carolina Hurricanes, but Primeau says, "I wasn't good."

He played that Friday night in Carolina, but registered just one shot and was an uncharacteristic minus-3 in over 17 minutes of action in an 8–6 loss.

The team had a day off before a game in Ottawa on Sunday, October 30. When Primeau woke up that morning, he knew something was wrong.

"That morning I went to Hitch and said, 'I don't feel right,'" he says.

Primeau sat out that game, but thought it wouldn't be long before he was back in the lineup.

"I literally thought it would be a game or two," he says, "but after I removed myself and started paying attention to the symptoms, I knew I was in trouble."

That day in Ottawa started a nine-month odyssey of trips to doctors throughout North America in a quest to find some way, somehow, to continue his career.

"It was torture because I continued to expect to get better," he says. "That year was a very frustrating time because I continued to hold out hope I would heal and I would be back in the lineup."

Months of work culminated in an ordinary early April day when he shockingly took the ice with teammates. That one, hour-long appearance began fueling rumors of a playoff return for a team that by the spring of 2006 looked to be running out of gas.

Primeau advised people not to take it too seriously, but that didn't stop rampant rumors of an impending return, Suprimeau stepping out of the phone booth to rescue his troubled teammates from impending playoff doom.

It never happened. Days later, Primeau gathered the media in a closed locker room and unleashed his anger in a post-practice, closed-door rant at a press corps that he thought was being unfair to the fans and causing a distraction to his teammates. As he spoke passionately, he clenched and unclenched his long fingers around a Power-Ade bottle, nearly choking the fluid out of it.

"I said to everyone, I'm not better," he recalls, although that day he used much saltier language. "There's no ulterior motive here. I'm just trying to put myself in a position to be ready if I'm healed. Everybody kept saying, 'He's coming back, he's coming back,' and it became a distraction, and that's not what I wanted. Not at all."

Primeau went back into hiding during the Flyers' aborted playoff run. He would arrive early in the morning, before the press and most of his teammates, work out alone, and leave before anyone could talk to him.

This continued into the summer, when Primeau retreated to his cottage outside Toronto. His workouts continued, with a return targeted for the 2006–2007 season.

"I really thought I was turning the corner [over that summer], and I took a few days off to spend with my family [at home in Canada], and I figured when I get up north, I'll be up there, it'll be quiet, the environment will be good, I can put my work in and get myself ready."

Like most people who go the gym for the first time after a long layoff, though, Primeau did too much too fast.

"The first day I worked out," he says, "I pushed it too hard, like I was trying to get my conditioning back in one day, and it laid me up for a week."

Too much work, combined with a summer flu bug, led to a return of all the bad, old feelings: pressure in his head, dizziness, nausea, exhaustion.

It was so bad, a planned trip in August to Finland, where he was going to work out with a professional team part-owned by teammate and close friend Sami Kapanen, was scrapped. Instead, he returned to South Jersey to meet with team neurologist Gary Dorshimer. Dorshimer explained to Primeau that the concussions had left an open door into his body; since his brain was his most vulnerable part, it was the first place any virus would attack.

Dorshimer instructed Primeau to take a week off, but after seven days, "He [Dorshimer] checked with me, and I said I'm just not there."

Dorshimer took that message to GM Bob Clarke, who confronted Primeau about his health.

"Clarkie called me and said 'Keith, I hear you're not doing well.' I said I don't think I'm going to be able to do this. I said I'm going to keep working out, my intentions haven't changed, I'm still coming back in August. I'm not going to Finland, but I'm going to try and skate. So I did, I came back and skated again. I was out there practicing with the guys, trying different treatments again."

Watching was Jim McCrossin, and it was the trainer who had traveled with Primeau to doctor's appointments, who had helped him through the worst of the dizziness and the headaches, who helped him with all the experiments—from different-colored visors to massages—who finally told Primeau the cold, hard truth.

"I remember Jimmy calling me into his office and saying, 'Keith, it's been a valiant effort, but even if you got yourself in a position to play, I could never personally give you permission to go back out on the ice,'" Primeau recalls.

A gamer, a warrior in every sense of the word, Primeau could have thrown chairs and books and trashed the training room; instead, he listened. And understood.

McCrossin was right. It was over.

"I think it was relief," he says of his feelings that day. "I needed somebody to make the decision for me. I was going to keep going and going until they said stop. That's what I needed. As much as it hurt, it was the right decision. I guess for the first time it was the first cold, hard slap of reality. I needed someone to give me the finality of it. Because everyone's saying, 'Okay, Keith, you can do it. Way to go.' I was kind of embarrassed by it, because I thought, maybe I was being naïve, and everybody felt bad for me, and I didn't want that."

Instead, he got the truth, from McCrossin and then from Clarke. And days later, on the eve of training camp, Primeau said the words himself: he was done.

# 2007: A DISASTER OF HISTORIC PROPORTIONS

The 2006–2007 season marked the 40th anniversary of the birth of the Philadelphia Flyers. It was to be a campaign of great celebration, bracketed by the release of a pair of momentous DVDs, one highlighting the 10 greatest games in the franchise's history, another the definitive 40th anniversary DVD, showcasing the greatest moments in the club's illustrious history.

The 40th season of Flyers hockey would go down in history. But not in the way anyone would have hoped.

The seeds for the disastrous 2006–2007 campaign were planted in the days following the lockout that caused the cancellation of the 2004–2005 season. The settlement of the labor dispute saw the implementation of a salary cap for the first time. That meant GM Bob Clarke had to pare a payroll that hovered around $60 million to the cap ceiling of $39 million. To do so he bought out veterans John LeClair and Tony Amonte, chose not to re-sign productive players like Mark Recchi and Vladimir Malakhov, and dealt away Danny Markov and Jeremy Roenick.

As teams struggled to get under the cap, Clarke jumped headfirst into one of the deepest pools of unrestricted free agents ever. He emerged with three giant catches.

First came defensemen Derian Hatcher, with a four-year, $14 million contract, and fellow blueliner Mike Rathje, signed away from San Jose to a five-year, $17.5 million deal.

A day later came the biggest prize, all-world center Peter Forsberg, who left Colorado for a two-year, $11.5 million pact.

The moves were swift, stunning, and thought not to be possible in a salary-cap world. In a matter of days, Clarke had cut a third of his payroll while improving a team 14 months removed from the Eastern Conference Finals.

He also re-signed Keith Primeau, Robert Esche, Eric Desjardins, Kim Johnsson, and Simon Gagne, and was poised to add highly regarded rookies Jeff Carter and Mike Richards to the mix, as well as jumbo-size free-agent forwards Mike Knuble and Turner Stevenson, signed before the lockout.

Clarke, sticking to traditional Canadian values, tried to downplay his new and improved team, saying in the summer of 2005, "I think starting this year we're a pretty good team. I'd say we're one of the teams that can compete for it. But so much can happen along the road that I can't say we're closer to a Stanley Cup than anybody else right now."

He might not have said it, but others certainly did: the Flyers were the heavy favorite to win the 2006 Stanley Cup.

The financial landscape wasn't the only thing to change coming out of the lockout. The game on the ice underwent a massive transformation. Referees were empowered to crack down on obstruction-type penalties. No longer would defensemen be able to use their sticks to hook or impede an offensive player, so skaters now would be allowed to use their speed and skill.

The days of the large, immobile defensemen who could hack, whack, and maul opposing forwards into submission were gone. The winning formula—seemingly overnight—had become speed and skill over size and strength.

Teams like the Buffalo Sabres got the message; the Flyers did not. Hatcher and Rathje quickly were exposed as 6'5", 235-pound twin towers of immobility, and combined with the orange on their sweaters, they resembled the world's largest traffic cones.

On top of that was a seemingly non-stop injury soap opera that started before training camp, when Sami Kapanen injured his shoulder and needed surgery that sidelined him until Thanksgiving. Hatcher missed the early part of the preseason with a knee injury, and Forsberg missed time having a bursa sac removed from his ankle. Carter struggled early while recovering from a summer-long bout of mononucleosis and a position change from center to wing on the team's top line.

Real devastation hit October 25, 2005, in Montreal, when Primeau was leveled by a high, vicious elbow to the head by the Canadiens' Alexander Perezhogin. Primeau played twice more, but just nine games into the season, the captain stepped out of the lineup with another concussion, his second documented (and possibly his fourth) in 20 months.

That left three of the Flyers' four lines being centered by rookies Carter, Richards, and R.J. Umberger, who was recalled from the minors when Primeau went out. Off the ice, the players were left without their emotional leader, as well as the buffer between themselves and the ultra-abrasive Hitchcock.

The Flyers muddled on, and despite the rash of injuries, embarked on the franchise's longest-ever road trip, an 11-game odyssey that bridged the end of December and early January. Wins in their first four games sparked an 8–2–1 trip, which pushed the Flyers to the top of the Eastern Conference with a 28–10–6 record.

But just when the Flyers hit the top, the floor dropped out from under them.

With goalie Robert Esche missing the entire trip with a groin injury, it meant rookie Antero Niittymaki was forced to start 18 straight games, including all 11 on the road trip, leaving him out of gas once the team returned home.

And there were a slew of injuries that decimated the defense corps: a concussion suffered by Johnsson, sports hernia surgery for Joni Pitkanen, and shoulder surgery for Desjardins. In addition, Hatcher played through knee pain, and Rathje tried to skate through a nerve problem in his back.

Up front, Forsberg missed the final eight games before the Olympic break, Stevenson was out with a degenerative hip condition, Branko Radivojevic seriously injured his ankle, and Gagne had a sore hip.

It got no better after the Olympics as the club's ironman, Michal Handzus, missed the first two weeks after the break with a torn rotator cuff.

"That's when we went from being the top dog into complete survival mode," recalls Hitchcock. "That's the way we played the rest of the season and playoffs. We were wondering every day who could play and who couldn't."

The Flyers barely survived, going just 17–16–5 down the stretch. They earned the fifth seed in the playoffs, where they met the Buffalo Sabres in a worst-case scenario matchup.

# HI, MY NAME IS...

Injuries and poor play led the 2006–2007 Flyers to dress 49 different players, obliterating the previous team record.

Among that group were five different goalies—Robert Esche, Antero Niittymaki, Martin Houle, Michael Leighton, and Martin Biron—and 12 rookies.

The Sabres were the poster boys for the New NHL. Their game was based on skill and speed. Their forwards attacked in waves; their defense, while not physically imposing, made smart decisions; and they were backed by an emerging star in goaltender Ryan Miller.

The Flyers had beaten the Sabres just once in four regular-season games, but the one win was in Buffalo, providing a glimmer of hope. Game 1 of the playoffs had a chance to be number two. The Flyers fell behind 2–0 early, but Knuble got a goal back in the second period, and Gagne tied the game with 1:51 left to force overtime.

Esche was nothing short of brilliant, stopping 55 of the first 57 shots he faced, but he couldn't stop the last one, when Daniel Briere tapped in a Jochen Hecht pass 7:31 into the second overtime.

Game 2 was a disaster. The Sabers scored five times on 10 shots in the first period and completely outclassed the Flyers in an 8–2 rout. The Flyers didn't help themselves, handing the Sabres 12 power plays, more than half of which came on obstruction-type holding, or tripping calls—lazy penalties that left an apoplectic coach Ken Hitchcock to say, "Our team was embarrassed tonight. We were embarrassed for our fans, and we were embarrassed for the city of Philadelphia at the way we played. We've got to make amends when we go home."

Forsberg, a non-factor in the first two games, was the best player on the ice in Game 3, scoring a pair of goals and setting up Gagne's empty-netter. He also threw his body around with reckless abandon, including a head-high shot on Briere that set the tone in a 4–2 win.

They tied the series with a gut-wrenching Game 4 victory, 5–4. Umberger, knocked senseless by a massive Brian Campbell hit in the first overtime of Game 1, notched the game-winner, scoring off a two-on-one break with Carter. Forsberg scored twice more and had an assist, and the Flyers packed the series momentum with them for the return to Buffalo for Game 5.

All the good, though, went out the window in the initial 20 minutes, as the Sabres held them to just three first-period shots, and Miller recorded a 3–0 shutout that sucked all the life out of the Flyers.

"The way we showed up today, we might as well have just gone home after warm-ups," defenseman Denis Gauthier told reporters.

Game 6 in Philadelphia was the coup de grace, and a harbinger of the disasters to come. The Sabres scored three times in the final nine minutes of the first period, and the 7–1 humiliation matched the worst home playoff loss in club history.

It was so bad Esche received a mercy ovation when he was pulled from the game in the second period. Philadelphia fans understood the netminder had no chance on the five goals he allowed, and was receiving no support from his teammates.

Despite the way the series ended, Hitchcock today believes his team lost more because of injuries than the Sabres' superior skill.

"We made the decision, rather than operate [on injured players] and be done, we opted to rehab players and continue to play," he says. "Those players weren't able to perform near their capabilities during the playoffs. They gave us what they had the first four games, and Buffalo took advantage in Games 5 and 6. Buffalo was a better team, but health-wise they were better than us."

Confident there was enough front-end talent, GM Bob Clarke did little to upgrade the team in the summer of 2006. Even with Primeau's retirement, Clarke felt he had enough depth at center that he could trade the versatile, valuable Handzus to the Chicago Blackhawks for winger Kyle Calder. On defense, Desjardins retired, and Johnsson signed with Minnesota. To replace them, Clarke signed Lars Jonsson, a 2000 first-round pick of the Boston Bruins who had been playing in Sweden the last six years, and Nolan Baumgartner, who had played his first full NHL season in his 11th professional campaign. The previous summer's Neiman Marcus–like shopping spree became a visit to Wal-Mart that saw Clarke add low-cost fringe players like forwards Marty Murray, Randy Robitaille, Mark Cullen, and Geoff Sanderson.

Most of the nine new players Clarke added came on the cheap, and early in the 2006–2007 season, the club looked to have gotten what it paid for.

Four losses in five games to start the season was the prelude to a return to Buffalo on October 17. It turned out to be one of the blackest days in club history, as the Sabres eviscerated the Flyers 9–1.

"The character on this team is not showing right now," Richards told reporters. "We're getting behind in games and we seem to implode."

Changes were needed, so Clarke waived three players; Baumgartner, veteran center Petr Nedved, and fringe forward Niko Dimitrakos all were sent to the minors. It didn't help as two more losses on a swing through Florida followed. The Flyers staggered home with a 1–6–1 record.

Watching the Buffalo game from home, team chairman Ed Snider had seen enough, and wanted to make even more changes. Early on a Sunday morning, October 22, 2006, Snider accepted Clarke's resignation as GM, something he had first offered two weeks earlier. Paul Holmgren replaced Clarke, and his first move, with Snider's approval, was to fire Hitchcock.

"Homer called me into his office and said he was making a change," Hitchcock recalls. "When you're not winning, the pressure starts, and then the evaluation has to start—how good is the team and can it play better for another coach. The Flyers thought they could play better for another coach."

That other coach was John Stevens, eight games into his first NHL coaching stint as Hitchcock's assistant after spending the previous six years coaching the club's minor-league team, the Philadelphia Phantoms.

"We're very confident we can turn this thing around," Stevens said then. "I'm very good at getting players to relax and play."

More changes came; separate deals with the Islanders saw young defenseman Freddy Meyer go for veteran blueliner Alexei Zhitnik, and Robitaille was sent packing for forward Mike York. Zhitnik did little to help, and York was a complete bust, arriving overweight and undermotivated.

The team's stock tumbled faster than Enron's. Injuries, poor play, and the seemingly nonstop saga over Forsberg's right foot—mostly, his inability to find a skate to fit his surgically repaired appendage—sent the club to never-before-seen depths. The season turned into a slow-speed, 82-car accident.

As the losses piled up like cordwood, the feeling in the locker room was one of distinct lack of leadership or direction. Some of that is directly attributable to Forsberg. Named captain during the summer, the talented Swede wore the C like a scarlet A.

"It can be a burden," Primeau says of being a captain. "It's a big responsibility, and not everyone is cut out to carry that responsibility. We saw that with the last guy through here," he said, meaning Forsberg.

The foot issues limited him to cameo appearances in the lineup, and combined with his impending free agency—the two-year deal he signed coming out of the lockout was due to expire at season's end—Forsberg became more of a story off the ice.

History, seemingly ever-repeating in Philadelphia, once again meant teammates were left to answer questions about another injured captain. Kapanen went so far as to tape off his dressing stall at the team's Voorhees practice facility as a media "no-fly" zone.

Despite flying Forsberg all over North America in search of the perfect skate, and despite all the losing, the Flyers wanted him to sign a new contract. Frustrated with his foot and his play, Forsberg said he didn't know what he was going to do next season and wouldn't make any long-term commitments.

Snider took one last stab at signing him to a new contract in late January, but not even that went right. Hours after a Saturday night game, Forsberg confirmed he had a meeting scheduled with

Snider for the next morning, but the team chairman called reporters in the press box to claim no get-together was planned.

The pair did, indeed, meet the next day, a Sunday morning, at Snider's office at the Wachovia Center. Snider pressed Forsberg to sign a new contract. Forsberg stubbornly held his ground, repeating that he wouldn't make a decision on his future until the summer, at the earliest.

After that meeting, Holmgren asked Forsberg for a list of teams he would be interested in playing for; the Nashville Predators were at the top of the list.

At noon on Thursday, February 15, hours before the Flyers were to play the Toronto Maple Leafs and two weeks before the trade deadline, Snider made one last plea to Forsberg to sign a new deal. When the All-Star again refused to change his mind, Forsberg volunteered to waive his no-trade clause, and Snider told Holmgren to make the best trade possible.

When the players came off the ice after warm-ups a little before 7:00 PM, Holmgren walked into the locker room and informed Forsberg he had been dealt to Nashville in return for winger Scottie Upshall, defense prospect Ryan Parent, and first- and third-round draft picks.

"It was literally five, seven minutes before the game," Knuble, Forsberg's linemate, told reporters. "I've never seen that, a guy getting yanked out of the locker room as you're tightening up your skates."

Those weren't the only trades before the deadline, as Holmgren set his sights on shedding salary and making the club younger and faster. Zhitnik was sent to Atlanta for young defenseman Braydon Coburn. The disgracefully disappointing Calder was jettisoned to Detroit in a three-way deal that netted the club defenseman Lasse Kukkonen. And in a move to shore up the future, a second-round pick was traded to Buffalo for goalie Martin Biron.

The Flyers lost the night Forsberg left, as they did most nights during the 2006–2007 campaign. The team won back-to-back games only four times all season, and their longest win streak was just three.

They set a number of club records during the season. Their 56 points were the fewest in franchise history, and also were the fewest in the league, the first time the Flyers finished at the bottom of the league standings.

Their 48 losses were the most in club history, and their 22 wins were the fewest since the 1969–1970 season. They posted six losing streaks of five games or more, topped by a club-record 10-game slide from December 8 through December 27.

They won just 10 times on home ice, their fewest ever in a season. Among their 31 home losses were skids of six and 13 consecutive games, shattering the previous club record of five straight. At one point between November 2 and February 8, the Flyers lost 19 of 20 home games, with the lone win coming against the Columbus Blue Jackets on November 24—ironically in Hitchcock's first game as Blue Jackets coach.

The 2006–2007 season was a historical one, for sure.

# THE UGLY

## BARRY ASHBEE

Barry Ashbee didn't need a nickname. He could have been called "Blood and Guts," but that didn't quite describe just how truly strong and tough a man and a player the Flyers defenseman was.

Ashbee toiled in various low-level hockey outposts before signing with the Hershey Bears of the American Hockey League in 1962. He spent four seasons in Hershey before finally making the big time with the Boston Bruins in the 1965–1966 season, for a whopping 14 games.

With expansion coming, the blueliner's NHL future seemed a reality, but a back injury led to surgery that kept him out for the entire 1966–1967 season, and he went unselected by the six new teams in the expansion draft.

"There was some disappointment when he didn't get picked in 1967," Donna Ashbee, Barry's widow, told Jim Jackson in his 2004 book *Walking Together Forever*. "However, especially after the back surgery, he was just determined to play again....He came to the conclusion that he still wanted to play hockey, and if it was going to be in the minors, we were in a good spot because Hershey was a great place to be."

The minor leagues was just where the Bruins, Hershey's parent club, saw him, and that's where he played the next three seasons.

On May 22, 1970, shortly after being named general manager of the Flyers, Keith Allen made one of the most important trades in franchise history, sending Darryl Edestrand and Larry McKillop to the Bruins in exchange for the 31-year-old Ashbee.

The *Philadelphia Bulletin*, in an unbylined story, termed the move "small and puzzling," but it didn't take long for fans and teammates to see just what kind of player, and person, Ashbee was.

"I have always said that he taught the younger players on our team about what it took to win," Allen said in *Walking Together Forever*. "He was the toughest, and as it turned out, bravest man I ever have seen."

Things nearly didn't work out between Ashbee and the Flyers. When the old-school defenseman showed up for training camp in 1972, he didn't like the laissez-faire attitude he saw from some teammates. He believed his fellow players should have a burning ache from the last-day loss that cost the team a spot in the previous spring's playoffs. Instead, what he saw when the 1972–1973 season started were teammates who didn't work hard enough in the offseason, didn't work hard enough in training camp, and who were staying out late and partying until all hours of the night.

To Ashbee, the personification of that lack of work ethic came in the form of promising young defenseman Rick Foley. Foley had what Ashbee didn't—great size, skating ability, and a high offensive skill level. But to Ashbee, Foley had no heart and no desire, and when he reported to camp at 243 pounds—28 pounds over what the team expected—Ashbee exploded, telling Allen he wanted out, that he was getting too old to waste his time with

## ASHBEE BULLIES THE REF

The Broad Street Bullies' brawling wasn't always limited to player-on-player violence.

During a game in Pittsburgh on January 25, 1973, defenseman Barry Ashbee protested a tripping call against him by punching referee Bryan Lewis in the face.

Ashbee was handed an eight-game suspension for his outburst.

players who had more interest in partying than working and winning. Allen talked Ashbee out of quitting, saying he would excise the malingerers, and as proof exiled Foley to the minors, never to be seen again in a Flyers sweater.

The players who remained shared Ashbee's work ethic and followed his lead when it came to grit, determination, and toughness. Young players like Bobby Clarke, Bill Barber, and Tom Bladon watched what Ashbee put himself through just to play, and it inspired them.

"He was the strongest guy mentally that I've ever seen," Clarke said in *Walking Together Forever*.

Ashbee played through torn knee ligaments in the 1972–1973 season, ligaments that needed to be surgically repaired but weren't fixed until season's end. The following season, a chipped vertebra in his neck caused shooting pain from his shoulder to his hand, and forced him to wear a horse-collar shaped brace on his neck. When the pain became too unbearable, he would tape his arm to his body and jam his stick into his glove.

Bladon recalled in *Walking Together Forever*, "I sat next to him in the [locker] room. I would pat him on the back as we got ready for a game or a period, forgetting about his cracked vertebra, and he would collapse to the floor on his knees in pain. The next

# BRUCE GAMBLE

Bruce Gamble was an overweight, 33-year-old chain-smoker, but he started in goal for the Flyers on February 6, 1972, in Vancouver.

Early in the first period, Gamble dropped to his knees to make a save. Barry Ashbee blocked the shot, but Gamble slumped over in pain. The referee blew the play dead, and Gamble got back to his feet as a trainer rushed onto the ice.

Gamble played the rest of the game, coming within 1:58 of a shutout in a 3–1 win, but felt lousy the whole time. He went to the hospital the next morning, and a doctor diagnosed the problem—the goalie had suffered a heart attack during the game.

period, he would be out there knocking people around into the boards. He was something."

He earned a second-team All-Star selection after the 1973–1974 season. That season, unfortunately, would be his last.

Game 4 of the Flyers' conference final series against the New York Rangers went to overtime tied 1–1. At 1:27 of the extra period, Rangers defenseman Dale Rolfe fired a shot from the point. Ashbee had moved into position to block the shot, but it rose faster than he expected, and the defenseman couldn't get his hands up in time to protect himself. The puck slammed into Ashbee's face, inches above his right eye.

"It was like a softball was stuck in my eye, and then there was just a big red ball of fire," Ashbee later told reporters.

He dropped to the ice in a pool of blood. He was rushed off the ice and taken directly to St. Clair Hospital, and then transferred to Wills Eye Institute in Philadelphia. Both eyes were patched as doctors waited for blood to drain out of the eye so the extent of the trauma could be assessed.

Tests showed damage to the retina, and while Ashbee's vision in general would be okay, he had lost almost all of his depth perception, meaning his playing career was over.

Publicly, Ashbee never showed any bitterness. In the press conference announcing his retirement, he said, "These things happen and you just have to accept them. The one good thing I've found out from this is that this old world isn't such a bad place after all. I can't begin to count the number of letters I've had from people offering to give me one of their eyes.

"I'm just happy that I was able to get my name on the Stanley Cup once. I look at it this way. I'm only 35. I've got a long time to live."

Unfortunately, that wasn't true.

After he retired, Ashbee was asked to stay on as an assistant coach to Fred Shero. Donna Ashbee said coaching wasn't something Barry was particularly interested in, and saw the offer as a pity gesture by the Flyers.

"I'm not sure if he had even given any thought to what he was going to do after he was done playing," she said in *Walking*

*Together Forever.* "Once he took the position, he grew to really enjoy it. He came to like the teaching aspect of the job, being able to answer questions the guys had and working with them."

He got to like the job so much that he told Donna that maybe there was a future for him as a head coach.

Before he could explore those options, though, he had something much worse to deal with.

On April 11, 1977, Ashbee noticed odd bruises on his arms and legs. He took his concerns to team doctor Edward Viner, and while Viner scheduled Ashbee for a follow-up visit, the physician already was certain what the grim diagnosis was. Tests the next day proved him tragically correct—Ashbee had acute leukemia.

On April 13 Ashbee called Clarke and told him, and said he would inform the team before practice. But when Ashbee hadn't arrived by the time the players were to take the ice, Clarke bolted the locker room door and told his teammates about Ashbee's illness.

"It was like getting hit with a brick," recalled Paul Holmgren.

Ashbee talked to the team after practice, and then checked himself into Hahnemann Hospital for treatment led by Dr. Isadore Brodsky, one of the country's leading oncologists.

A shaken Flyers bunch lost their playoff game to the Toronto Maple Leafs that night; the next day, Ashbee called a press conference in his hospital room. He told reporters, "I don't want everybody in town to think I'm lying up here dying. Heck, I'm lucky. The doctors are optimistic. They think they caught it in time.

"I don't want this to be written up as a 'Win One for the Gipper' story. The players know I'm sick, and I'm going to get better, that's all."

Despite two rounds of chemotherapy, Ashbee never got better. His kidneys became infected, and his body, overloaded with white blood cells, was incapable of fighting back. Players would visit, but Ashbee would drift in and out of consciousness.

"I saw him every day," Don Saleski recalled in *Full Spectrum.* "And to see a strong-willed guy like that wasting away was so hard."

**The gritty Barry Ashbee led by example on the ice, and during his losing battle with leukemia off the ice.**

Thirty days after he was diagnosed, on May 11, 1975, Barry Ashbee passed away.

The team flew to Toronto for the funeral, where Clarke gave the eulogy:

"It took an incurable blood disorder to quell a spirit that the loss of sight in one eye, a spinal fusion, torn ligaments in his knee, and a pinched nerve in his neck could not dampen. Barry never gave in to the luxury of exhaustion or pain. He always played the hand the way it was dealt.

"He may be gone from us physically, but he will never be forgotten because he left a little bit of himself with all of us."

Ashbee's place in Flyers history is indelible. His retired No. 4 hangs in the rafters of the Wachovia Center, the annual award given to the Flyers' best defenseman is aptly named the Barry Ashbee Trophy, and the biggest beneficiary of the annual Flyers' Wives Fight for Lives Carnival is the Barry Ashbee Research Laboratory at Hahnemann.

The best summation of Barry Ashbee's Flyers legacy was written by Bill Meltzer in a story on the Flyers' website:

"Barry Ashbee's retired number hangs in the rafters because he was the epitome of the type of hockey player that every team needs to win. He wasn't the most talented guy around, but no one was more dedicated to winning or persevered more tenaciously."

## BERNIE PARENT—BEATEN UP, BEATEN DOWN

Bernie Parent was on top of the world after winning the 1975 Stanley Cup. He had won back-to-back championships, back-to-back Conn Smythe Trophies as playoff MVP, and had been on the cover of *Time*. As Bernie himself likes to say, it was a beautiful thing.

But the beauty faded fast.

A week before the opener of the 1975–1976 season, Parent reported pain in his neck and elbow that nothing—not muscle relaxants, massage therapy, or a few days in traction—could cure.

While the Flyers started 3–0 with Wayne Stephenson in goal, Parent learned what had been causing him so much pain—a herniated cervical disc. On October 14, 1975, Parent had major surgery performed—a cervical laminectomy.

The original diagnosis was for Parent to miss just three to four weeks. But when the goalie tried practicing on November 27, he ended up back in the hospital, in traction.

On February 5, Parent put lingering pain in his arm aside and returned to practice. Three weeks later, February 24, 1976, in Washington, he suited up for his first game, surrendering five goals on 19 shots in a 5–5 tie with the Capitals.

He would go on to play just 11 games that season, going 6–2–3 with a 2.34 goals-against average.

When the playoffs opened, coach Fred Shero wanted to start Stephenson, but assistant coaches Mike Nykoluk and Barry Ashbee convinced Shero to go with Parent. And while Bernie

# HOLMGREN'S NEAR-DEATH EXPERIENCE

Today Paul Holmgren is the Flyers' general manager, but he nearly never made it through his rookie season.

On March 26, 1976, the day after his first NHL game, Holmgren reported to a team meeting in Boston with a swollen right eye. Barry Ashbee and Bobby Clarke took the youngster to the Massachusetts Eye and Ear Infirmary, where doctors found a puncture wound caused by a skate blade when Holmgren had been at the bottom of a pile during an AHL brawl several days earlier.

An emergency operation was performed to stop a fluid leak that was endangering Holmgren's eyesight, but he had a severe reaction to the anesthetic and nearly died on the operating table.

He survived, but didn't play again until the following season.

helped backstop a seven-game win over the Toronto Maple Leafs, he just wasn't the same Parent.

After an uneven performance in Game 1 of the second-round series against the Boston Bruins, Parent saved Shero the embarrassment by taking himself out of the lineup.

"I'm tired," Parent told reporters. "I'm not in playoff shape. I don't want to cost the team a game. Let's make the move before it happens."

Parent's neck felt better when the 1976–1977 season started, but he wasn't clear of injuries. A broken toe suffered during the preseason left him hobbled, but a special pad in his skate allowed him to play. He also missed time with a sprained knee, but played 61 games, going 35–13–12 with a 2.71 goals-against average. He was rusty in the playoff opener against the Toronto Maple Leafs, and was pulled after allowing four goals on 15 shots over the first two periods of Game 2. He came back in Game 1 against Boston in the next round, replacing Stephenson after the Flyers fell behind 3–0. The Flyers rallied to force overtime, but while trying to reach back and glove Rick Middleton's shot 2:57 into overtime, he knocked the puck into the net.

Parent didn't play again in the series, and the Flyers were swept out of the postseason for the second straight year.

In 1977 the Flyers brought Parent's idol, Jacques Plante, to training camp to help rebuild the netminder's confidence. Parent and Plante had played together during Parent's short stay with the Maple Leafs, and Parent credits Plante for turning him into the goalie he became.

"I went to the Leafs a pretty good goalie with a lot of talent but still very raw," Parent said in *Walking Together Forever*. "Plante worked with me on understanding the game, playing the angles, practicing properly, and all of those little things that I had been missing. Working with him really turned my career around."

It helped some—he won nine straight starts between Thanksgiving and Christmas—and finished 29–6–13, but Parent remained inconsistent, and Shero was splitting the goaltending chores nearly 50/50 with Stephenson.

When the playoffs started, Parent looked like the Bernie of old. He shut down the Colorado Rockies in a two-game preliminary-round sweep. In the quarterfinals against the Buffalo Sabres—a team that had gone 3–0–1 against the Flyers in the regular season—Parent held them to two or fewer goals in four of five games as the

# BAD VACATION

To keep some of his veterans fresh for the 1984 playoffs, coach Bob McCammon forced minivacations on some of his older players.

The players weren't in favor of them, especially Bill Barber, whose creaky knee was just starting to feel better when his time-out was ordered.

During four days in the Poconos, Barber was given a workout plan, which included modified squat thrusts—generally a bad idea for someone with chronic knee issues.

One morning while working out, Barber heard a crack in his leg like a gunshot, which was his femur snapping where it entered the knee joint. He never played again.

Flyers advanced with ease. Chants of "Bernie! Bernie!" again rained down from the Spectrum.

The dream, however, ended in the semifinals against Boston. The Bruins won Game 1 in overtime when Middleton knocked in a loose puck in front, and in Game 2 they turned Parent into *fromage* in a 7–5 victory. Parent rallied to hold the Bruins to just one goal in a 3–1 Flyers win in Game 3, but Boston closed out the series and the Flyers' season in five games.

At 33, Parent's best days clearly were behind him entering the 1978–1979 season. When the Flyers took to the Spectrum ice against the New York Rangers on February 17, 1979, Bernie was just 16–12–7 with four shutouts, but he hadn't won a game in nearly five weeks.

Midway through the first period, Jimmy Watson and Don Maloney were jostling in front of the net when Watson yanked on Maloney's arm and the Rangers' stick blade penetrated the tiny eye slit in Parent's mask. The goalie immediately yanked off his mask, clutched at his face, and skated off the ice.

Dr. David Pollock, the Flyers' team optometrist, found blood in the interior chamber of Parent's right eye, and he was rushed to Wills Eye Institute. There, Dr. James Tasman found Parent had suffered two conjunctival tears and admitted him to Pennsylvania Hospital. Both eyes were patched, and bed rest was ordered for at least a week.

"This is what happens to old goalies, I guess," Parent told *The Philadelphia Bulletin*'s Ray Didinger from his hospital room. "You forget to duck."

Three leading Philadelphia eye specialists all determined Parent should retire. His lens had been permanently subluxed, or pushed back, resulting in a build-up of pressure in the eye. Medication could control the condition, but his ability to focus and his depth perception never would be the same.

"He can't catch a ball his kids throw to him, let alone stop a puck," said Flyers team doctor Edward Viner.

"It was just one of those freak things," Parent says today. "The good Lord was saying to me that it was enough and it was time to move on with my life."

Parent played 486 games with the Flyers over 10 seasons (1967–1968 to 1970–1971, and 1973–1974 to 1978–1979), and remains the standard to which every Flyers goalie is compared.

He won 232 games as a Flyer (a mark since passed by Ron Hextall) and posted a 2.42 goals-against average, a .917 save percentage, and a remarkable 50 shutouts. He won a pair of Vezina Trophies and a pair of Conn Smythe Trophies. He was elected to the Hockey Hall of Fame in 1984, and was a charter member of the Flyers Hall of Fame in 1988.

Were it not for the injuries Parent suffered after the second Cup season, says team chairman Ed Snider, "I think Bernie would have gone down without question as the best goalie of all time."

# PELLE LINDBERGH

Sunday, November 10, 1985, is a date that still brings shudders and tears to Flyers fans. It was early that morning, on a sharp curve on Somerdale Road in the Gloucester County town of Somerdale that Pelle Lindbergh's souped-up Porsche 930 Turbo slammed into a three-and-a-half-foot-high concrete wall that was part of Somerdale Elementary School.

The goalie's car was pulverized, with the passenger side shorn away from the rest of what was left of the vehicle. Two passengers in the car with Lindbergh survived, but the goalie was left with a broken body and a dead brain.

It was a shocking turn for a player who seemed just to be reaching the prime of his life and his career. He was coming off a season with 40 wins and a 3.02 goals-against average, and won the first what was expected to be many Vezina Trophies. He was mere months removed from backstopping the Flyers to the Stanley Cup Finals, and at age 26, there seemed to be nothing but more winning on the horizon.

And then it all ended.

The night before, the Flyers had earned a 5–3 win over the Boston Bruins, ending a five-games-in-eight-nights stretch. With five days off before a finals rematch with the Edmonton Oilers, coach Mike Keenan gave the players Sunday and Monday off.

"He said, 'I don't want anybody at the rink the next two days. Everybody take the time off; you've earned it. Go and enjoy it, and we'll see you in a couple days,'" recalls Mark Howe.

Lindbergh didn't play that night against Boston, and with his mother and brother-in-law visiting from Sweden, Pelle and his fiancée, Kerstin, figured they would all just head home after the game. But with the extra time off, and in the midst of a 10-game win streak, the players were planning on celebrating, including a nice, long party at the Coliseum in Voorhees, which had an after-hours bar.

Lindbergh had no intentions of going out that night, but later told Kerstin he would make a social visit. She said she would stay home with his mom, and Pelle first met up with friends at the Bennigan's on Route 73.

The social visit turned into an all-night drinking session, and at about 2:30 AM, Pelle and a friend, Ed Parvin, drove to the Coliseum to continue the party, where they drank and enjoyed themselves until 5:00 AM.

Lindbergh told teammates Rick Tocchet and Murray Craven that he was going to drive Parvin home to Mount Ephraim, then return so they could get some breakfast. Kathy McNeal, a friend of Tocchet's, jumped into the Porsche with Lindbergh, and the three took off.

Tocchet and Craven, who shared a house within walking distance of the Coliseum, barely were inside when there was a knock on their door. Two fans who had been partying with the players at the Coliseum said Lindbergh's car had crashed.

Lindbergh was rushed to JFK Hospital in Stratford, where he was put on a respirator.

Lindbergh and Al Morganti, then the Flyers' beat writer for *The Philadelphia Inquirer*, were the same age and had grown close.

"He was my best friend on the team and in Philly," recalls Morganti. "I would go out with my then-girlfriend, and we would go out with him and his girlfriend a lot."

Morganti called Lindbergh a "whack job," but meant it in the nicest, most respectful way. Lindbergh always was aggressive, living on the edge. He didn't just drive fast. He loved physical hockey, loved to fight. Morganti said he and Pelle would watch hockey fight tapes for fun.

"I loved hanging out with him," says Morganti. "He had a condo on the water at the Moorings [a section of the Kings Grant development in Marlton]. "He had a big raft we'd go out in, we'd bring crossbows and shoot. It was cool."

Kerstin brought Morganti into Pelle's hospital room. It was Morganti who was given the awful assignment of explaining to Pelle's mother, Anna-Lisa, her son's condition.

"I remember I was the second one at the hospital. She [Kerstin] brought me in because his mom was over from Sweden, and [Kerstin] spoke English a little, but she asked me to help translate. The [doctor] went through the broken bones, and then she kind of asked, what about, can he play again. The guy just looked at her—'I'm the ortho [orthopedic] guy, and you had better talk to the neurologist.'"

The neurologist explained just how terrible Pelle's condition was. A CAT scan had shown that trauma to Pelle's brain stem had cut off the oxygen supply to the player's brain, making recovery impossible. He was brain-dead, and the only thing keeping him alive was a respirator.

"He explains brain-dead," says Morganti. "I'm in shock, and she's waiting for the translation. I had to tell her what it meant. It was awful."

Doctors said the only thing they could do was say good-bye, and their only remaining decision was whether surgeons would be allowed to harvest Lindbergh's organs for donation.

Two days later, after Sigge Lindbergh, Pelle's father, made the sad flight over from Sweden, he and Anna-Lisa made the decision to remove Pelle from life support. His heart, kidneys, and corneas were given to needy patients.

"Pelle's organs are going to save other lives," Keenan said. "It's appropriate. He died making one more save."

Players, some still hungover in the early Sunday morning hours, couldn't believe the phone calls they were getting. That grim task fell to team captain Dave Poulin, who had gotten the call from Craven.

"I was supposed to go down to Egg Harbor," recalls Howe. "I was anticipating buying a new boat, so I was going down to look at boats, and I got a call about 7:30 in the morning from Dave Poulin, and I couldn't believe what I heard."

"I was heading to the [Jersey] Shore," says Brian Propp. "I had a home I was going to do some work on."

One by one, they all received the call.

"You became numb to it," says Poulin. "You were just contacting them and trying to make it clear to them that they had to come down to the hospital."

Some of the players were bleary either from a night of partying or from the early hour of the call; Poulin said he had to do a little convincing.

"You had to explain," he said. "Some said 'We'll come down in a little while,' but I said, 'No, you have to come down now.'"

Team chairman Ed Snider got his own early phone call, from John Brogan, who was an assistant to team president Jay Snider.

"It was just awful," Snider recalls. "Poor kid. I felt a little guilty because everybody knew he loved his Porsche, loved to speed. I felt like I could have done more before it happened. Whether it would have worked or not, I don't know. He had that souped-up Porsche, and he loved to open it up."

Lindbergh had bought the 1983 Porsche 930 Turbo in Germany new for $52,000 and immediately sent it to the Stuttgart factory for another $41,000 of modifications.

The speedometer went to 190 mph, and Lindbergh told friends he revved it up to 150 on the Autobahn.

"He scared me," Clarke said in *Full Spectrum*. "We told Pelle he had to slow down."

Players met that Sunday morning at the hospital. Some saw Pelle, while others cried or sat like zombies. After a while, they went to Poulin's house to watch football, but mostly they sat and stared at the television for a few hours and then went home.

"It's something you can't believe is happening," said Dave Brown. "We were poised to go to the finals again that year, and he was the guy that was going to lead us there. There's no plan on how to get through things like that. Something like that happens, you lose your number one goalie, and most of all a friend. It sends the whole team into turmoil. What do you do? He was dead. You just try to cope with it after that."

The next day, on what was supposed to be their day off, Keenan got the players on the ice at the Coliseum.

"There was nothing else to do," said Tim Kerr. "Getting back out there on the ice was somewhat of a distraction at the time. It was the only place we could go where it wasn't an issue for a while."

Ed Snider and GM Bob Clarke had chosen to leave all decisions related to the team to Keenan, the 36-year-old, second-year coach.

"He was magnificent," Poulin said of Keenan. "He was stellar. His feel of the pulse of the team, and his decision-making process through that was just remarkable. He was at his best."

"Mike did an excellent job," agreed Howe. "He got the guys together at his house a couple times. If anybody watched Mike in practice, if the team made a bad pass or two bad passes, the whistle blew and you paid, because you weren't focused. We were practicing a few days later and we were as bad as a team can be, and Mike was patient with everybody. He kept everybody together."

On November 13, Lindbergh's funeral was held at the Gloria Dei (Old Swedes) Church on Delaware Avenue in Philadelphia.

Poulin delivered the eulogy: "We'll always carry him with us and draw from his energy.

"Pelle, we love. We all love you."

Clarke and Jay Snider had discussed playing the Edmonton game as they would any other, to help foster a sense of normalcy, of closure. But it was decided the proper thing to do for the fans, who had no other chance to bid farewell, was a pregame memorial service.

The boards were stripped of advertising, and fans were given wallet-sized pictures of Lindbergh with a message written on the back: "In loving memory of Pelle Lindbergh. Our friend. Our goalie."

By sheer coincidence, Lindbergh's picture had been preprinted on the tickets for that night's game. Rather than tear them, ushers put a black X on the back and returned them to fans.

## GRETZKY DONATION

Wayne Gretzky isn't called the Great One just for what he did on the ice.

In November 1985, Gretzky's Oilers were the first opponents for the Flyers following the death of star goalie Pelle Lindbergh. The Flyers asked that in lieu of flowers, and out of respect for Pelle's sister, Ann-Christine, who was fighting cancer, donations be made to a cancer research fund established in Pelle's name.

The only opposing player to make a donation was Gretzky.

Behind a wreath of flowers in the shape of Lindbergh's No. 31, Gene Hart led the service, saying the evening should be about "not the mourning of a death, but the celebration of a life."

After the service, the players were given a 15-minute chance to collect themselves. Then they returned to the ice for the game.

The Oilers had volunteered to postpone the game, but the Flyers players said the show must go on. In fact, it had to, it needed to. The ice was their safe haven from the horrors of reality.

"Once you step on the ice, everything else fades away," said Howe. "Just getting on the ice, your mind is on it, and your focus and your thoughts are there."

"The only thing Pelle would want us to do is go out and play great hockey," added Propp. "It was tough the first little while, then it was like someone got traded. You have to realize they're not going to be there anymore."

The game started tentatively, but once the skating, shooting, and hitting began, the sole focus became the next play, the next shift.

The Flyers took a 1–0 lead late in the first when Poulin beat Mike Krushelnyski on an offensive-zone faceoff. The puck went back to Howe, who shot a wrister that went off the glove of goalie Andy Moog and into the net.

"I came back to the bench and remember sitting down and almost crying," said Howe. "The emotions of losing a teammate like that."

Ilkka Sinisalo and Propp scored early in the third to break a 1–1 tie, and Rich Sutter and Brad McCrimmon added goals to cap an emotional 5–3 win, a victory that pushed their forgotten win streak to 11.

But no win streak, no matter how long, could soothe the pain of their tremendous loss.

"We lost a little invincibility there," says Poulin, who back then was the grizzled leader at the not-so-grizzled age of 26. "We had 19- and 20-year-olds, we had Tocchet, [Peter] Zezel, [Derrick] Smith, Craven, they were all so young. How could they not think they were invincible?"

"One thing that helped our team was the closeness of the team and leadership we had," says Propp. "We made sure we talked it out. We knew we had a job to do professionally. It was difficult. I still have a picture of Pelle in my office that I keep all the time. It's a shame."

## CHELIOS LAYS OUT PROPP

Those who know Ron Hextall say there is a thick line that separates the man from the player.

Currently the assistant general manager of the Los Angeles Kings, he's a devoted husband and father to four children. That's far removed from the player who hacked and whacked his way to more than 500 penalty minutes, including an NHL record for goalies of 113 in the 1988–1989 season.

"The only thing I think I can say was when I was on the ice, I had a job to do, and I took my job very seriously," he says now. "I'm opposite that off the ice, but on the ice I had a job to do, and I tried to do it to the best of my abilities. Sometimes my emotions got the best of me."

One of the most memorable of those moments occurred May 11, 1989, at the end of Game 6 of the Flyers' Wales Conference Finals loss to the Montreal Canadiens.

The bad blood had started in Game 1 of the series with spilled blood. Midway through the second period, Brian Propp skated into the left corner to clear the puck out of the Flyers' end.

# COOPERALLS

The Flyers' uniform generally hasn't changed much in 40-plus years, but there was one notable exception.

For two seasons, starting in 1981–1982, the Flyers wore Cooperalls, full-length pants that were supposed to be a more streamlined wardrobe. Instead, they looked like tuxedo pants and thankfully were banned by the league in 1983.

Montreal defenseman Chris Chelios skated toward Propp, and left his feet to deliver a crushing elbow to Propp's jaw. The blow drove Propp's head into one of the metal glass supports, knocking him unconscious. Propp dropped like a rock, with the back of his head bouncing off the ice like a basketball.

When teammates and medical personnel reached Propp and took off his helmet, blood began pouring from the back of the winger's head.

Referee Kerry Fraser made no call on the play, and Chelios told reporters after the game that Propp "was coming around the net and had just got rid of the puck when I hit him—I don't know how."

Propp was taken to Montreal General Hospital, where he was diagnosed with a concussion and a cut lip.

Two days later, Propp returned to the rink as the team skated. "These things happen in hockey," he said to reporters. "It's too important just to go out looking for revenge. We're looking for a win. That's the best way to get revenge."

While Chelios said he wasn't out to hurt anyone, Propp believes today that it was a deliberate cheap shot. His anger hasn't dulled one iota in the nearly two decades since the play.

"I know it was [a cheap shot]," he says. "If you want to take a look at it, it's on YouTube.

"At the time, I was the leading playoff scorer. There was no remorse, nothing....I have no respect for him."

Propp returned for Game 3 at the Spectrum, but that didn't stop the Canadiens from routing the Flyers and taking a 2–1 series lead. Game 4 also went to the Canadiens, with goalie Patrick Roy earning a 3–0 shutout that featured irate Flyers fans pelting the Canadiens' bench with all manner of debris.

The Flyers won Game 5 when Dave Poulin knocked in the rebound of Gord Murphy's point shot at 5:02 of overtime, setting up Game 6 back at the Spectrum.

Scott Mellanby gave the Flyers a 1–0 first-period lead, but Jeff Chycrun accidentally put the puck behind Hextall on a Montreal power play, tying the game.

In the second, Bobby Smith scored with Ron Sutter in the penalty box to give Montreal the lead, and then Chelios took a drop pass from Bob Gainey and fired through a screened Hextall to make it 3–1.

Ryan Walter capped it for Montreal in the third when he finished a two-on-one break.

Propp scored with 6:05 left to make it 4–2, but any Flyers momentum was stopped when Sutter took a head-high run at Chelios with 3:42 left. Chelios got his stick up in time to block

# THE HOLMGREN GATES

The Spectrum always had the feel of a zoo. And to separate the animals, there are two steel gates between the locker rooms, which are separated by about 90 feet down a narrow hallway.

But the gates weren't always there. They were installed to prevent another riot like the one between the Flyers and Bruins in a 1977 preseason game.

Paul Holmgren scrapped with Boston's Wayne Cashman, and the brawl spilled into the hallway. Holmgren, who thought Cashman had tried to gouge his eyes, charged after Cashman, who grabbed a stick out of the locker room to defend himself.

The next day, two steel gates, bolted to the floor and ceiling, were installed between the rooms. According to Pat Croce's book *I Feel Great*, they became known as the Holmgren Gates—something the current Flyers GM remains proud of.

Sutter's stick from crashing into his skull, and the Flyer was sent off for high-sticking.

"It wasn't planned," Sutter said in *Full Spectrum*. "I just saw who it was, remembered what he had gotten away with on Proppie, and did it."

Also remembering was Hextall. He had watched Game 1 from the stands due to an injury.

"It was just a dirty hit," he says. "I respect the hell out of Chris Chelios, but that was a dirty hit. And obviously it could have been a lot worst for Proppie than it was, but it was bad. I have an attack mentality, and someone did something to one of my foot soldiers. I felt like there had to be retribution."

That retribution came in the final two minutes. When Chelios brought the puck in offside, Hextall attacked. The goalie charged out of the net, waffled Chelios in the head with his blocker, and began whaling away at him in the corner. The referees tackled the two combatants to the ice, and Hextall emerged from the pile missing his sweater and still screaming at Chelios.

As the pair was separated, Hextall threw his blocker at Chelios. That's when Roy skated into the fray, and he and Hextall started jawing at each other. Were it not for a linesman fighting Hextall back to the Flyers' bench, the pair might have gone at it.

As Chelios was taken out through the Zamboni tunnel, fans pelted the ice with trash and chanted, "We want Chelios!" Chelios, though, stayed in the locker room during the post-game handshake line for fear of further antagonizing the situation.

"You never know what to expect with Hextall," Chelios said after the game. "But I saw him and was ready. I was fortunate I didn't get a skate in the head or anything."

Hextall was unrepentant for his action. "Did you see what he did to Brian Propp?" he said after the game. "Come on, I think we owed him something. God almighty, he just about took [Propp's] head off. I think that's good enough reason."

Flyers general manager Bob Clarke backed his goalie, saying, "I don't think you like to see a series end on that type of incident, but we like the fact that a player will stand up for one of his teammates."

For his outburst, Hextall was hit with a 12-game suspension, at the time the fourth-longest ban in league history, a decision which still rankles Propp.

"Chelios never got anything for [the hit]. Hextall threw his blocker and he gets suspended for 12 games at the beginning of the next year, which really hurt our club. That was the most ridiculous thing I've ever seen the league do."

Years later, a far more mature Hextall admits that perhaps he went a bit too far.

"I look back and think, 'How could I be so into it to do that?'...The guy almost killed my teammate. Did I overreact? I don't know. Would I like to take it back? I don't know."

## ROGER NEILSON'S PAINFUL ADMISSION

During his tenure as Flyers coach, Roger Neilson had pulled off the amazing task of achieving détente at the height of the Cold War between Bob Clarke and Eric Lindros. Clarke considered Neilson a good friend, while Lindros knew Neilson was his biggest supporter in the organization.

"As a person, you always know you've got someone to trust," Lindros told reporters. "Roger means a lot to me—coming to the rink every day and knowing someone is there who is honest with you. He knows when to kick you in the butt to get you going and when to pat you on the back when you need it. Never too high, never too low. And he always keeps things humorous."

Neilson even made cancer a joke.

The coach had fought a persistent sinus infection through the early part of the 1999–2000 season; he eventually beat that bug, but never felt right. Further tests diagnosed multiple myeloma, a form of bone cancer; the announcement was made December 10, 1999.

Neilson, known for his goofy ties and even goofier personality, told his players in a manner consistent with his persona—he showed them a video which featured Chris Therien's embarrassing attempt to fight from the previous game, which included the defenseman flopping and flailing, and at one point having his back to the player he was trying to slug it out with. Interspersed were scenes of the famed Black Knight losing his arms and legs from the film *Monty Python and the Holy Grail*. Laughter could be heard echoing throughout the Flyers' practice facility.

When it was over, Neilson told his players about his cancer.

"Everyone is laughing and then, all of a sudden, Roger tells us," Craig Berube said to reporters that day.

While doctors believed Neilson could be cured, the players, and the club in general, were devastated.

"I couldn't believe how positive and upbeat he was," said Lindros then.

A visibly shaken Clarke added, "He's such a good man, a good person."

Neilson was put on a regimen of chemotherapy and decided to coach through the pain. The plan was for the treatments to go on for three months; if after that time they weren't working, Neilson then would need a bone-marrow transplant. That plan, though, was shelved, and it was determined that Neilson would have to leave the team in late February to have the transplant procedure.

"He should be able to make it back for the playoffs," Dr. Isadore Brodsky, chief of oncology hematology at Hahnemann University Hospital, told reporters.

It also was decided that assistant coach Craig Ramsay would stand in for Neilson during the coach's absence.

Neilson's last game was February 19, 2000, a 4–2 win over the Washington Capitals. He told his players that morning that it would be his last regular-season game.

"I think it was Mark Recchi who said in the locker room before we went out, to win this one for Roger," goalie Brian Boucher told reporters. "It'll be his last game for a long time. I think we were really inspired by that."

The Flyers didn't miss a beat when Ramsay took over, going 16–6–1–2 to end the regular season.

Unfortunately, this is where the real ugliness comes into play.

On April 10, the day after the end of the regular season, Neilson told Clarke he felt healthy enough to resume his coaching duties. Clarke and the doctors weren't so sure. Neilson spent Game 1 of the first-round series against the Buffalo Sabres advising Ramsay and

## LAUREN HART'S CANCER

On January 5, 2000, six months after watching her father succumb to cancer, Lauren Hart was told she had non-Hodgkin's lymphoma.

Lauren, who has sung the national anthem before Flyers home games since 1997, vowed to stay on, and on January 15, 2000, she received a louder ovation than normal when she sang before a game against the Devils.

As she walked off the ice, there to greet her was coach Roger Neilson, who had just a month earlier been diagnosed with cancer.

fellow assistant Wayne Cashman via headset from the press box. But after Game 1, Neilson left for his home in Dallas, saying he didn't want to be a distraction to the team.

The Flyers walked through the Sabres in five games, setting up a semifinal match with the Pittsburgh Penguins.

Neilson again said he felt strong enough to return, but Clarke didn't want to make a big change during what looked to be a long playoff run, so he made the decision to keep things status quo for the remainder of the postseason. In other words, Ramsay now was the head coach for the rest of the playoffs, and Neilson would continue to advise from the rafters.

"You can't make a change when the team is going good," Clarke told reporters. "Roger knows that."

It wasn't a scenario Neilson had foreseen, or one he was overly pleased by. He had intimated to reporters that during a meeting with Clarke after the regular season that a new two-year contract had been verbally agreed to. Neilson's original deal, signed when he was hired in March 1998, was set to end after the 2000 play-offs. Clarke, though, said that no deal had been made, and that nothing would be discussed until the season was over.

The next day, April 25, 2000, Neilson was asked about his job status on a Toronto radio station. He replied, "I don't think they want a cancer patient who's a friend of Eric Lindros behind the bench right now."

All through Neilson's illness, the battles had restarted between Lindros and his family and Clarke and the Flyers. Lindros was suffering through another concussion, and in early March had started a firestorm when he criticized the club's training and medical staff. Neilson's past loyalty to the player apparently pushed him onto the Lindros side in the war, and the coach viewed his diminished status within the club as a punishment.

Clarke said Neilson's relationship with Lindros and his coaching status were completely unrelated. Neilson himself said the statement was meant as a joke that just didn't go over well. Clarke and team CEO Ron Ryan accepted Neilson's response, but the peace wouldn't last long.

Neilson watched from the press box as the Flyers beat Pittsburgh and then fell apart after taking a 3–1 series lead over the New Jersey Devils in the Eastern Conference Finals.

After the series ended, Neilson said he either wanted his old job back with the Flyers or an early release from his contract so he could seek work elsewhere.

"I still want to be a head coach," Neilson told reporters. "If not here, then somewhere else."

The Flyers made Ramsay the full-time coach, and Neilson left the club and signed on as an assistant with the Ottawa Senators. He substituted for Jacques Martin for two games in the 2001–2002 season to reach the milestone of 1,000 career games coached.

But Neilson's cancer returned, this time as skin cancer, and the great coach, a pioneer in his field, passed away June 21, 2003.

## THE BARBER REVOLT

Bill Barber was the epitome of a team-first person. As a player, coach, or front-office staffer, Barber always saw the crest on the front of his sweater as far more important than the name on the back.

Barber's Hall of Fame career ended after a serious knee injury in 1984, but that only started his second life as a Flyer.

"I said to Clarkie [GM Bob Clarke], put me where you need me. It doesn't matter," he says. And that's what Clarke did, utilizing Barber's hockey mind first as coach of the team's AHL affiliate, the Hershey Bears, than as an NHL assistant coach and director of pro scouting. When the Philadelphia Phantoms were born in 1996, Barber was the first head coach of the Flyers-owned AHL team. In four seasons the Phantoms never won fewer than 44 games, and won the Calder Cup in 1998.

When the Flyers started slowly in the 2000–2001 season, coach Craig Ramsay was let go, and Barber stepped into the breach. Barber inspired the team to a 31–13–7–3 finish (after a 12–12–4 start under Ramsay), a 100-point season, and a second-place finish in the Atlantic Division, and he won the Jack Adams Award as the NHL's best coach.

The playoffs, though, were a different story. The Flyers couldn't solve nemesis Dominik Hasek and the Buffalo Sabres, losing twice in overtime and suffering an embarrassing Game 6 8–0 loss in Buffalo.

As bad as things were on the ice, it was nothing compared to what was going on at the Barber home. Barber's wife, Jenny, had been diagnosed with lung cancer in April 2001. Bill told few people—and almost none of his players—because he didn't want to cause a distraction. Instead, he came to work every day.

Bill and Jenny Barber had met when both were teenagers, when Bill played for Jenny's hometown Kitchener Rangers of the Ontario Hockey League. They were married when Bill was 21 and Jenny was 20. They bought a house in Cherry Hill shortly after Bill began playing for the Flyers in 1972.

"It was a high school–type romance," former Flyer Orest Kindrachuk, who roomed with Barber when they were in the minors, told the *Courier Post*. "Nowadays those romances don't last. This one did."

"We knew his wife was not doing well," said Chuck Gormley, the longtime Flyers reporter for the *Courier Post*, "but we didn't know how bad she was doing. He let us in a couple times. He let us in on how she was feeling, [but] not very often. He wanted to keep it business."

Jenny's condition worsened early in the fall of 2001, but Bill stayed with the team, never missing a game and rarely skipping a practice. He always said that's what Jenny wanted.

At 12:05 PM, on Saturday, December 8, 2001, Jenny Barber, Bill Barber's wife of 28 years and mother of two, lost her battle with cancer. She was just 48 years old.

That afternoon, the Flyers had a game against the Minnesota Wild. For Bill Barber, the only place he could have been, should have been, was behind the bench. And when the puck dropped at 3:00 PM, there he was, coaching his team.

"We heard that morning in the press box before the game that she had passed away," recalls Gormley. "When I saw him on the bench, I couldn't believe it. How you coach in those circumstances is beyond me. Especially when you know he's a good husband and father."

After the game, Barber allowed people to see into his emotionally ravaged soul.

"She was a champion," he said. "I'll miss her more than anyone knows."

Few players knew Jenny had died that morning, but Barber's late arrival that afternoon clued them in.

"He was a little late to the game, and we knew what the situation was, but we didn't know the finality of it," winger Paul Ranheim told reporters. "After the game Keith [Primeau] gave him the team puck. Billy said a couple words. It was very emotional."

"We can't even imagine or fathom the intense stress this caused him," Primeau said that afternoon. As team captain, he was one of a handful of players who knew of Jenny's passing before the game. "His only release was to come to the rink. Bill Barber has two passions, his family and the Philadelphia Flyers."

"After that game I walked down to the coaches' room, and it's the only time I've ever walked down to the coaches' room, to offer my condolences," said Gormley. "He showed me a ring that his wife had given him, and he had it around his neck on a chain, and he said something like, I'm never going to take this off. It was something that you could see how much he was impacted by this."

Barber was encouraged to take time off from the stress of his job, but instead he did what he always did. He showed up for work.

"It's not like this was a sudden thing," he says today. "This was going on for a long, long time. As a family, we stood tall for what we believed and we prepared ourselves right to the very end. We were all mentally stable and understood what really happened here. It's not like it was happening that day. This was going on for around seven months. The family prepared, I was prepared. I didn't let anything family-wise intrude on the team.

"Time off? Where would it lead? My honest opinion is it would have went worse."

At the time, Gormley was one of the people who believed time away was the right thing. Years later, he can understand why Barber chose to stay.

"When we asked him why you would coach, he said, 'My wife understands how much this team means to me, and this is my way of dealing with stress.'...She gave him her blessing to do whatever he wanted to and whatever he needed to do. How can you take that away from somebody? It's easy to criticize somebody for that, but until you've been through that situation, you can't. He did what he felt was right."

Barber did as best he could to keep his personal issues out of the locker room. The team finished 42–27–10–3 (29–19–5–2 after Jenny's death), and captured the Atlantic Division title. The Ottawa Senators were the first-round playoff opponent, but that's where things fell apart.

After scoring 234 goals, fifth-most in the conference, the Flyers started handling the puck like it was a concrete block. They scored just once on the incredibly underwhelming Patrick Lalime through the first four games of the series—an overtime marker by Ruslan Fedotenko in Game 1.

The Flyers scored just one other goal in the five-game series, and were shut out for a remarkable 243:53 in regulation. Dan McGillis's goal at 3:53 of the first period of Game 5 was the only time the Flyers scored in regulation.

Between Game 1 and Game 5, the Flyers lost three straight 3–0 decisions, with Game 4 marred by goalie Roman Cechmanek skating to center ice and screaming at his teammates on the bench.

Brian Boucher started Game 5, and after McGillis gave the Flyers the 1–0 lead, Daniel Alfredsson scored late in the first, and Martin Havlat netted the overtime winner.

The series was over, but the Flyers still were firing shots.

A group of disgruntled players first complained about Barber to Clarke and team chairman Ed Snider, then took their issues public.

"There were a lot of problems," Boucher told reporters. "Not only in the playoffs, but in the last two, two and a half months. There were meetings about meetings...and it seemed like nothing ever got solved.

"Everybody made suggestions, what we felt we needed, and I think for the most part we felt we didn't get it. I know that people are saying that the players are crybabies. But we're players, and we needed to be led in the direction that the players suggested. It was frustrating because it wasn't just something that popped up at the end."

The players said the problems went back as far as October, and that in the final two months of the season, Primeau said he and Rick Tocchet, rather than the coaching staff, began making in-game adjustments between periods.

"You can't have 20 guys coaching," said Mark Recchi. "You have to have one guy take charge. It was very tough....It's been a very tough year for him. I know that, we all know that. And that's probably why we left it as long as we did. You have to respect the man for what he went through and how he handled it. But, ultimately, things didn't get done at the end."

Primeau had a number of meetings with Barber about what the players felt needed to be done.

"[The power play] was one issue," Primeau told reporters. "We had the worst power play in the league; why are we not practicing it?

"Then there were the systems, and the tirades on the bench. All season long we said we know when we make mistakes out there, and we're getting yelled at. We say when we come to the bench, make the adjustment, and he wants the players to make the adjustments. Well, our job is to play."

# COACHING CAROUSEL

When Fred Shero was hired as Flyers coach in 1971, *Philadelphia Inquirer* columnist Frank Dolson called Ed Snider the "Charlie Finley of the Atlantic Seaboard," for changing coaches so often.

Shero was the third coach in the first five seasons of the franchise.

That's nothing compared to what Bob Clarke accomplished between 1997 and 2002, when he went through five head coaches.

After 61 games in 1997–1998, Wayne Cashman was replaced by Roger Neilson. Neilson's illness ended his Flyers tenure in favor of Craig Ramsay 57 games into the 1999–2000 season. Ramsay was fired 28 games into the 2000–2001 campaign, replaced by Bill Barber. Barber was fired at the end of the 2001–2002 season, replaced by Ken Hitchcock.

According to Primeau, any time he brought ideas from the locker room, Barber's response was, "Don't make suggestions. Work harder."

"All season long we tried to be on the same page and get the situation addressed," Primeau said. "So that's why everyone is so discouraged, because our thoughts weren't accepted.

"We go in there and say, 'Look, we'll do whatever is asked, we just want to be led, just lead us in the right direction. Do the things that will make us successful.' Then we hope that occurs, and we felt we were spinning our wheels."

When asked why he went public with his complaints, Primeau said, "I'm sticking up on behalf of my teammates because I want to walk out of here with my pride intact."

"The fact that the captain did that showed everyone there was a real problem," says Gormley. "That would not ordinarily be addressed like that. That he addressed it like that spoke volumes that Barber wouldn't be back if everyone felt that way."

Barber refused to comment on his players' biting barbs, and days later, he was fired. The loyal soldier, the player who took below-market contracts to stay with the team, the man who said put me anywhere, let me help, I just want this organization to win, was dumped at the curb after 30 years of faithful service.

Barber always has taken the high road. He still lives in South Jersey and remains a regular presence at Flyers home games.

"I had a year and a half here [as coach] from the NHL standpoint, but it was good. I enjoyed it," he says, looking back. "Times were tough, expectations were high, and we fell short. There's no secret to it. As a coach you have to take responsibility for that, and as a coach I had no problem understanding the direction they were going. I was on a different page at the time, to be honest. I know what it takes to win, and I'll stand my ground on that. It was unfortunate that I had to go, but it was time to move on."

For his part, Primeau says today he'd like to have a mulligan on his public tirade against Barber.

"I grew up in Toronto and I was a huge Darryl Stitler fan," Primeau says. "He was captain of the Maple Leafs and a Hall of Famer and all those things that I loved about the Toronto Maple Leafs. [My dad] said to picture somebody coming out and saying something about Darryl Stitler, and that really put it into perspective for me.

"My thought process when all of that was taking place, I was going to let people on the outside see exactly what was going on in our locker room, and that was probably the wrong thing to do. As a player, you don't want to be called out on the carpet by your coach, and that's basically what happened, and it was now public knowledge. And whether I was defending teammates or speaking the truth because I was the leader in the locker room, it could have been handled differently."

Boucher, 25 at the time, also believes he should have handled the situation differently.

"I answered the questions honestly," he says. "But as an athlete you should know better how to handle questions and whether you want to answer questions honestly or be politically correct.

"I have regrets about how I answered those questions. Looking back on it now, being an older guy, it was unprofessional how I handled it."

For Barber, there are no hard feelings. He said he still speaks to Clarke and holds Ed Snider in the highest regard.

"There's no peace factor involved," Barber says now. "It was time for me to move on. I did my 30 years, and it was time to move on. I have no complaints."

## FIGHT NIGHT IN PHILLY

Old-style, bench-clearing brawls don't happen very often anymore, but on March 5, 2004, fans got a memorable throwback affair.

The Ottawa Senators were in Philadelphia for the first time since Martin Havlat cross-checked Mark Recchi in the face a few weeks earlier. Havlat was suspended for his stick work, but the Flyers believed that wasn't nearly enough punishment.

Days before Ottawa came to town, coach Ken Hitchcock said someone was going to make Havlat "eat his lunch."

Serving as waiter would be the Flyers' chief enforcer, Donald Brashear. He, as well as his partner in fisticuffs, Todd Fedoruk, had missed the previous Flyers-Senators game with knee injuries, which allowed the Senators to hit the Flyers with impunity.

"Guys get a little braver and play a little chippier when Brash and me aren't in the lineup," Fedoruk told reporters the day before the game. "You'll see how some guys shy away and are quiet."

There was little quiet on this night. In the first period, Ottawa's Shaun Van Allen drove Flyers rookie defenseman Joni Pitkanen into the boards, knocking him out with a concussion. Later in the first, the Sens' Marian Hossa rode the Flyers' Chris Therien hard into the boards, knocking the defenseman out of the game with a strained left shoulder.

While the Flyers may have been losing the war of attrition, they were in firm control on the scoreboard, and when Alexei Zhamnov scored with 6:54 left in the third period, they held a 5–2 advantage.

But with 1:45 left in regulation, a time warp hit Philadelphia, and suddenly the game turned into a typical Broad Street Bullies donnybrook.

The brawling started with the teams' two veteran enforcers, Brashear and Rob Ray, tangling in front of the Flyers' net. Brashear shoved Ray, who at first seemed uninterested, but then elbowed Brashear in the head. That set off the volatile Brashear, who began raining left hands down on Ray's face, and then a nasty right cross opened a vicious gash over Ray's right eye.

While Brashear watched Ray skate off, two Senators—Todd Simpson and Brian Pothier—jumped Brashear from behind, with Pothier throwing punches over a linesman. When Patrick Sharp tried to intervene, Simpson knocked him down and began pounding him. Danny Markov jumped in and began scrapping with Simpson.

While this was going on, Senators goalie Patrick Lalime began shedding his gear and skated into the fray, heading right for Flyers netminder Robert Esche, who provided a more than willing combatant. Lalime tore Esche's jersey off, but Esche kept throwing punches.

Meanwhile, Branko Radivojevic was tossing Van Allen around. The Flyers' winger lost his sweater, but won the battle. With Markov and Brashear already off the ice, the 6'3", 220-pound Simpson showed his courage by taking pokes at the Flyers' 5'10", 185-pound Sami Kapanen, who had been forced back onto defense after Pitkanen and Therien had been knocked out.

When officials finally got things settled down, and the players were sent off the ice, Brashear, Markov, Esche, and Radivojevic stood in the tunnel leading to the locker room, watching the replays on the center-ice scoreboard, and Brashear continued to jaw at the Senators as they skated off.

Round 2 began at the drop of the next puck, when Senators tough guy Chris Neil first speared Radovan Somik, then began throwing punches at the Flyers' soft second-year Czech winger. Neil easily buried Somik, who at least got in one good punch, but Neil got at least one cheap shot in after he knocked Somik down.

Meanwhile, Sens gargantuan defenseman Zdeno Chara, all 6'9" of him, made a bee-line for another non-fighting Flyer, 6'1" defenseman Mattias Timander. Chara rag-dolled Timander for a bit before officials broke it up.

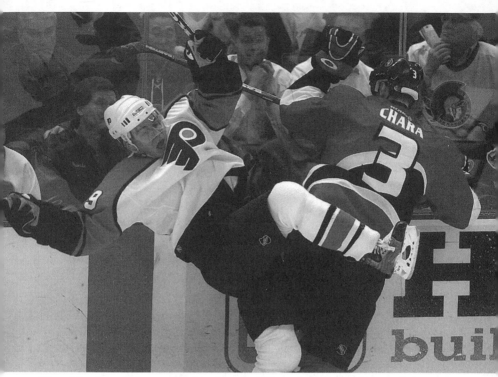

**The chippiness between the Senators and Flyers boiled over into a vintage hockey brawl in March 2004.** *Photo courtesy AP Images.*

Only three seconds had dripped off the game clock.

Once that was settled, another brawl broke out between centers Michal Handzus and Mike Fisher. The bigger Handzus, though, got a little overzealous and allowed Fisher to use his leverage to flip Handzus down onto his back in what could have been a scary scene. Instead, the Flyers' Czech ironman skated off as part of the seventh fighting major of the night.

After all that, another three seconds had dribbled away.

Finally, a hockey game interrupted the fights, which caused the fans to boo lustily. Only in Philadelphia. But they wouldn't have to wait long for Round 4.

After a Flyers dump-in, Recchi laid a solid hit on Senators defenseman Wade Redden, who responded by grabbing the nearest Flyer, who happened to be John LeClair.

While the two big bulls wrestled around in the Ottawa end, back at center ice Recchi and Bryan Smolinski threw down their gloves and went at it, with the tenacious Recchi pounding Smolinski with right hands before Smolinski landed a right cross and both players ran out of gas. This time, 24 seconds had elapsed, leaving 1:15 of game action remaining, which was just enough time for one more throwdown.

At the next drop of the puck, Ottawa center Jason Spezza went after Sharp, which ended badly for Spezza. As Spezza came forward, Sharp caught him and threw a few right-hands, and when Spezza went down, Sharp landed on top of him and got in another good shot before the officials could separate them.

After Sharp and Spezza were sent off, and the teams lined up for the faceoff, there were as many players—Zhamnov, John Slaney, and Tony Amonte—left on the Flyers bench as there were coaches. There were just two players left on the Ottawa bench, Hossa and Antoine Vermette.

All the while, the player around whom all the venom centered, Havlat, sat safely in the penalty box, sent there by coach Jacques Martin to serve a penalty.

The night the Wachovia Center became the Blue Horizon turned into a record-setter. In all, there were an NHL-record 413 penalty minutes assessed, breaking the former league record of 406 from a 1981 game between Boston and Minnesota. The 409 penalty minutes in the third period also was a record, as was the 213 penalty minutes given to the Flyers for the game, and the 209 given them in the third period alone.

The previous Flyers record for penalty minutes in a game was 380 against the Los Angeles Kings on March 11, 1979. Of that 380, 194 of them were whistled on the Flyers.

There were 21 fighting majors called, two on Brashear. The Flyers' enforcer ended the night with 34 minutes in penalties to lead the home team, but his total was topped by Spezza, who not only got pounded by Sharp, but was flagged for a double game misconduct, and finished with 35 PIM.

Oddly enough, there were non-fighting related milestones as well that night. Markov's first-period goal was the 10,000th in

Flyers history, making the club the fifth in league history—and the first expansion team—to reach that mark. Also, the game was the 1,000[th] of Amonte's career.

There nearly was one more brawl after the game. Flyers general manager Bob Clarke, who was part of similar full-scale fracases as a player, attempted to get into the Ottawa dressing room to get a piece of Martin, but was restrained by Flyers staffers.

"I would not have hit him. I am not that stupid," Clarke said a day later. "But I would have confronted him. I understand Rob Ray fighting Donald Brashear. That's okay. Even Mark Recchi and Patrick Sharp, they can fight. But don't go after guys who don't know how to defend themselves like Somik and Timander.

"I don't think a guy like that [Martin] should send players out to beat the crap out of players who can't fight. I wanted to say something. It's not like [Martin] is a big, tough bugger whose teams play that way and stuff.

"What Neil did is not something to be proud of....I'm ticked off that a player like Neil would go after a player like Somik....If Martin says it's not his responsibility, then he doesn't have control of his bench."

Days later, Comcast SportsNet (CSN) showed a replay of the game, which drew a 1.0 rating—higher than many regular Flyers telecasts. The league, unhappy with the right hook to its public image, demanded CSN never replay the game again.

And for the record, the only player fined or suspended was Markov, who got a one-game ban for being hit with his third game misconduct of the season.

## TERTYSHNY AND HART—TRAGEDY TIMES TWO

In 40-plus years of Flyers hockey, no single time period could have been worst than the month of July 1999.

In a nine-day double-barrel shotgun blast of tragedy, the club lost a giant piece of its past and a potential piece of the future.

Gene Hart, 68, the team's broadcaster from the club's inception until his retirement in 1995, passed away from liver cancer and kidney failure on July 14, 1999.

Nine days later, on July 23, defenseman Dmitri Tertyshny was killed in a boating accident at the far-too-young age of 22.

Hart was a hockey minstrel, spreading the gospel of the sport throughout the Delaware Valley. His voice was the one coming through the transistor radio as children huddled in their beds, staying up far too late to listen to games. His voice was the one that filled smoky bars and living rooms from Allentown to Cape May, from Cherry Hill to Conshohocken. His voice provides the soundtrack to fans' personal highlight reels.

"I would fall asleep with Flyers games," said the one-named Eklund, the anonymous proprietor of the popular hockey Web site Hockeybuzz.com. Eklund was a hockey fanatic growing up in Cherry Hill in the early 1970s. "I would put the [radio] underneath my pillow. The old AM dials would give off heat, and my parents would worry that I would start a fire."

Joe Watson remembered a Flyers fan who told him that when he went to college in South Carolina during the heyday of the Broad Street Bullies, the student would try to find the highest point in the area to pick up the games on WCAU radio. That was the length people would go to hear Gene Hart's voice.

"We used to turn the television down and put the radio on," said Al Piazza, a life-long South Philadelphia resident and 40-year Flyers fan, of the days when Hart was shifted to radio. "You didn't want to hear anybody else."

Hart was hired in 1967 only because the team didn't have enough money to employ a better-known Canadian broadcaster.

"And," Hart said in a 1992 interview, "they needed someone who wasn't too concerned with how much money he made or didn't make."

He got the job for $50 a game that first season, and went on to call every Flyers game, either on TV or radio, between 1967 and 1995. Along the way, his calls became synonymous with Flyers hockey, whether it was joyously counting down the seconds to the Flyers' first Stanley Cup in 1974, or his signature sign-off, "Good night, and good hockey."

"When they went to the finals against Edmonton [in 1987], I remember saying to my parents, we have to listen to Gene tonight," said Eklund. "Because if the Flyers win the Stanley Cup tonight, I have to hear Gene Hart call it. It's got to be Gene Hart calling it."

Hart's most memorable call came May 19, 1974, when he proclaimed over and over: "The Flyers win the Stanley Cup! The Flyers win the Stanley Cup!"

"His voice kept getting stronger and louder," Flyers chairman Ed Snider said in a story accompanying Hart's death, "And to this day, I think it remains one of the greatest calls in sports I've ever heard."

As the voice of the Flyers, everyone became Gene Hart's friend. He was their link to the Flyers family, making him a kind of wizened old uncle to the masses.

"We didn't know hockey. It was a foreign sport," says Eklund. "The fact that he had this passion for it and made you love it, that's what Gene Hart did for the city. He taught us to love hockey, and that taught us to learn everything about it. I think Hart should be up there with Clarke and Parent and Snider. If there were four pillars that made hockey work in Philadelphia, he should be there."

And when he died, a part of them died with him.

"There's not a single game where someone doesn't come up to me and say I loved your father," says Lauren Hart, a Wachovia Center staple since she began singing the national anthem before every game during the 1997–1998 season. "He became a friend to people in a way that sportscasters don't do anymore. People always come to me and say, 'I hope you don't mind but...' It's my fear when people stop and forget him. It's especially exciting when a younger fan comes up and is informed and knows, because their parents or brother or sister has passed it on.

"It's really moving. When I'm in the building, especially this year [the 40th anniversary season], they're playing the clips, to hear him, his great voice. Inevitably someone will come up to me and say, 'When I was a little boy, my dad and I would watch together.' It was a coming of age, a passing of time. The birth of the Flyers, having a championship so early in their history, really cemented [the relationship] in a way that is so unusual. It doesn't happen with lots of teams. Because it happened during the time my father was teaching everybody the game, people feel such an amazing connection."

Players also were fond of Hart.

"He would bring up games that you played in that you wouldn't even remember," Eric Lindros told reporters at the time of Hart's death. "He remembered every little detail."

Lindros was so fond of Hart that he drove two hours from his lakeside cottage to Toronto to fly back to Philadelphia for the funeral.

And Hart was as devoted to the club as any player who ever wore the sweater.

"What convinced me to hire him was that Gene had a tremendous amount of enthusiasm, even though he didn't have a major background in the sport," Snider told reporters. "We knew he'd do a fabulous job for us. A lot of people don't realize that for about 10 years, he would do games on the road and then take a red-eye back to New Jersey to teach school the next day."

For years the Flyers simulcast Hart's radio call on television, but eventually added a separate TV broadcast, pushing Hart and partner Bob Taylor to radio in 1988. In response to a survey the club sent to season-ticket holders, fans said the one thing they would change is for Gene Hart to be back on television; their wish was granted when he worked on the telecasts from 1993 to 1995.

Hart called more than 2,000 Flyers games, including six Stanley Cup Finals; he was inducted into the Flyers Hall of Fame in 1992 and the Hockey Hall of Fame in 1997. Also, the press box at the Wachovia Center is named in his honor.

He retired from the broadcast booth after the 1994–1995 season, but worked in various capacities for the team, including as the man at the microphone when the Philadelphia Phantoms won the Calder Cup in 1998.

That would be the last call he would make; fittingly, the champion broadcaster went out with a championship call.

A memorial service was held days after his death, attended by more than 2,000 fans, not to mention present and former Flyers, the club's front office, media members, and friends from Gene's other loves—members of the Opera Company of Philadelphia and the Philadelphia Orchestra performed throughout the service.

"When you think of Gene Hart," Snider told the audience, "you think Flyers."

The team chairman then used Hart's own words from years earlier, when Hart had led Pelle Lindbergh's memorial service, as a reminder of the true purpose of the ceremonies.

"Rather than mourn," Snider said, quoting Hart, "we are here to celebrate the life that enriched all of us."

Where Gene Hart was a legend in Philadelphia and beyond, Dmitri Tertyshny was a little-known Russian-born defenseman.

Taken in the sixth round of the 1995 draft by the Flyers, Tertyshny stayed in Russia for three more seasons, playing for his hometown team, Chelyabinsk. He played 62 games for the Flyers in 1998–1999, totaling two goals, 10 points, and 30 penalty minutes. At 6'2" and 180 pounds, the only thing that stood out about Tertyshny was his stringy, collar-length black hair. His teammates called him Tree, more as a play on his name, but apt enough to describe his frame.

While not considered one of their prime prospects, the Flyers were interested enough to send him on a retreat to Kelowna, British Columbia, with other players and prospects for a two-week skating and conditioning camp run by strength coach Jim McCrossin and skating coach David Roy.

On the final day of the camp, Tertyshny and two teammates, Francis Belanger and Mikhail Chernov, rented a 17-foot boat for a ride around Okanagan Lake. Belanger was driving the boat when it hit a wake. Tertyshny was thrown over the front of the boat, which then went right over top of him. Tertyshny was mangled by the motor's propeller; he made it back to the boat, but the blades had, among other gruesome damage, sliced both his carotid artery and jugular vein. He bled to death on the boat in Chernov's arms.

Many of Tertyshny's teammates were at John LeClair's golf tournament in Vermont when they got the news. The grim task of informing them fell to Eric Lindros and Rod Brind'Amour. As team captain, it also was Lindros's unenviable job of expressing the players' condolences, with the help of a Russian interpreter, to Tertyshny's family, including his wife Polina, now a far-too-young widow, who at the time was pregnant with the couple's first child.

Lindros described the young Russian, as "a real gamer. Consistent. A terrific person. Kind of quiet, with a great sense of humor. He was outgoing; his wife was just wonderful. He'll certainly be missed....He always put the team first, always worked extra hard. He was going to be an All-Star one day."

# ERIC LINDROS

## WELCOME TO PHILADELPHIA

No one personifies the title of this book—the good, the bad, and the ugly of the Philadelphia Flyers—more than Eric Lindros.

At 6'4" and 240 pounds, he had attributes that left scouts drooling—Wayne Gretzky's skills packed into Mario Lemieux's body, with Mark Messier's temperament and physicality. He was the next great Canadian hockey player, destined to lead whatever team lucky enough to land him to championships well into the 21$^{st}$ century.

Heading into the 1991 NHL Draft, that team looked to be the Quebec Nordiques, who finished the 1990–1991 season last in the league.

There was just one problem: Lindros and his parents, Bonnie and Carl, publicly—and repeatedly—stated that Eric never would play in Quebec. The Lindroses believed going to Quebec would stifle Eric's earning potential. They also believed Nordiques owner Marcel Aubut wouldn't have enough money to pay Lindros what he was worth and build a winning team around him.

The Nordiques still took Lindros first overall, but soon realized Lindros would stick to his threat to sit out two seasons and re-enter the draft in 1993. Aubut and general manager Pierre Page then let it be known that Lindros was available for the best offer.

"Marcel Aubut was trying to run not a trade but an auction," says Russ Farwell, who was the Flyers' general manager at the time.

According to Farwell, the Nordiques were looking for certain players, but Aubut demanded a minimum of $15 million in any deal.

"They would always talk whatever the cash was going to be in addition [to the players]," says Farwell. "We had a number of meetings, and we met with [team president] Jay [Snider] and his dad [owner Ed Snider] one time, and we kind of worked it out, and there were very few teams that could meet what Quebec was looking for. We were down, we were motivated, and yet we had a little more depth than other teams in the market. And teams that had players couldn't satisfy them from a cash standpoint. We thought at the end of the day we would be one of the only one or two available contenders."

The day before the 1992 draft in Montreal. Aubut and the Nordiques bunkered down in a Montreal hotel suite, where they would host their own version of *Let's Make a Deal*. According to Tim Whartensby in the (Toronto) Globe and Mail, the list of possible trade partners had been whittled down from 14 to four: the Flyers, the New York Rangers, the Toronto Maple Leafs, and the Chicago Blackhawks.

# FLYERS SHOW SOME INTEREST

A year before it happened, the seeds were planted for Eric Lindros to bloom in Philadelphia.

The Flyers held the sixth overall choice in the 1991 draft, giving them no shot of landing Lindros. Still curious, **Courier Post** writer Chuck Gormley asked GM Russ Farwell about him.

"I asked the question, what about this kid Lindros, what will he bring to any team," said Gormley. "He [Farwell] was so excited about Lindros. He said he was the type of player who is going to make kids want to play hockey. Kids in the playground are going to say they want to be Eric Lindros.

"I thought to myself, Russ really likes this guy. I wonder if he'll try to create something for him."

# MUSICAL LAWYERS

If the Lindros arbitration case had been a hockey game, the Flyers would have been skating shorthanded.

Club attorney Phil Weinberg wasn't sure he could get to Montreal for the case—his pregnant wife's delivery date was the first day of the hearing. Weinberg flew to Montreal anyway, arriving Sunday evening. Monday morning, before the hearing started, his wife called and said the baby was coming, and Weinberg left.

"We borrowed an attorney from the Blackhawks to start the proceedings," recalls Russ Farwell. "Our guy flew in from Philly, got there that night, his wife went into labor, and he had to fly home. A day and a half with the Chicago guy, and then our guy came back and picked it up and was excellent."

Farwell and team president Jay Snider did most of the negotiating for the Flyers, dealing directly with Aubut and Page. The Nords first asked for forwards Rod Brind'Amour and Mark Recchi, but Farwell said that wasn't going to happen. But when Snider dangled the Flyers' first-round pick from 1991, a young Swedish center who the club had taken five spots after Lindros—Peter Forsberg—the tide turned in the Flyers' favor.

"Brind'Amour and Recchi weren't two guys we were prepared to trade," says Farwell. "When we put Forsberg in and gave them [defenseman] Steve Duchesne…"

After a marathon negotiating session, Snider returned to his hotel room for the night. But shortly after 1:00 AM, Aubut called and asked if he could come up. Aubut had written on a sheet of paper a list of players and picks—forwards Mike Ricci and Chris Simon, defensemen Duchesne and Kerry Huffman, goalie Ron Hextall, the rights to Forsberg, the Flyers' first-round pick the next day and in 1993, and $15 million. According to Whartenby's story, Aubut tossed the piece of paper at Snider and said, "Give us these players and conditions, and you have got yourself Eric Lindros."

While Snider told Aubut he would give him a decision in the morning, Aubut wasn't done for the night. After meeting with

Snider, he spoke with delegations from the Maple Leafs and the Blackhawks. At 4:30 AM, Toronto GM Cliff Fletcher offered a package that included center Doug Gilmour, goaltending prospect Felix Potvin, wingers Wendell Clark and Craig Berube, defenseman Dave Ellet, multiple first-round picks, and $15 million. Fletcher, though, immediately had buyer's remorse—mostly due to having to include Gilmour—and pulled out of the deal.

Later that morning, Blackhawks general manager Mike Keenan offered a package that included goalie Ed Belfour, forward Steve Larmer, and defenseman Steve Smith in a five-player, seven-pick deal, and by 10:00 AM, it looked as if Lindros was headed to Chicago. The trade was scuttled, however, when Blackhawks owner Bill Wirtz refused to pay the Nordiques an additional $5 million.

At 10:30 AM Saturday, Snider called Aubut and said the Flyers had agreed to the Nordiques' terms.

"Jay handled it pretty well," recalls Farwell. "He said 'Marcel, do we have a deal?' And in order to get the deal, he had to say yes, not thinking that it could come back to bite him, and that's how it happened. He told us we had a deal, he gave us the phone number. We called Eric and talked to him."

Even with a deal in hand, Aubut wasn't done. He took the Flyers' deal to Rangers GM Neil Smith and Stanley Jaffe, president of Paramount Corp., which owned the Rangers. New York offered forwards Doug Weight, Tony Amonte, and Alexei Kovalev, defenseman James Patrick, goalie John Vanbiesbrouck, three first-round picks, and $12 million. At 11:50 AM, 10 minutes before the start of the draft, the Nordiques and Rangers agreed on a deal for Lindros.

And that's when the circus started.

"I left to go to the draft floor, and Jay comes in and says here's what happened," remembers Farwell. "[Aubut] came into our room, changed his mind, and said they're going in a different direction."

A fuming Snider went directly to NHL President John Ziegler, who immediately convened a meeting in a back room with Aubut, Smith, Snider, and NHL chief counsel Gil Stein. A decision was made to allow an independent arbitrator, Toronto lawyer Larry Bertuzzi, to have the final decision. And while Bertuzzi lived just a half-block from the Lindros family in North Toronto and had played football with Carl Lindros at the University of Western Ontario, the two former teammates had not seen each other in years.

The lawyer flew to Montreal to begin meeting with all parties on Sunday, June 21, 1992. Nine days later, Bertuzzi rendered his decision.

"It was the natural thought that the NHL is going to take care of the Rangers because they're New York," recalled prominent Philadelphia sports-radio personality Howard Eskin. "[Philadelphia fans] always have that defeatist attitude that thinks New York gets everything. [Fans] were waiting, but the only thought they had was, it's New York and there was no way the Flyers would get him."

But the Flyers did get him. Bertuzzi ruled that the 1:00 AM meeting between Aubut and Jay Snider, and the Flyers' subsequent acceptance of the deal, made for an oral contract and a valid trade agreement. And when the Flyers were given permission to speak with Lindros—Quebec had many times stated that no other club could speak to anyone associated with the Lindros family until a deal had been finalized—that clinched it for the Flyers.

Eskin said the fan response over the ensuing days was overwhelmingly positive.

"They had already put him up on that pedestal," he said of Lindros. "The fans thought the Flyers had the next Wayne Gretzky. It wasn't just they were going to win one Cup, it was they were going to win multiple Cups. They had put the Flyers in the same realm as the Edmonton Oilers when Gretzky was there and they won all those Cups."

# OFF-ICE ISSUES

Eric Lindros's troubles weren't limited to on-ice injuries and bad losses. At 6'4" and 240 pounds, with Hollywood-star looks and a load of money, he was easy to find and made a ready target.

In November 1992 Lindros strained ligaments in his left knee. During his rehab, Lindros flew home to Toronto—with the team's permission—to see his own doctor and work himself back to health.

When Eric Lindros arrived in Philadelphia in 1992, the eyes of the hockey world were upon him. *Photo courtesy AP Images.*

During his time at home, Lindros and friends visited a night-club in Whitby, Ontario, called Koo Koo Bananas. While partying with friends, he was accused of spitting on a woman and pouring beer on her. The woman further alleged that when she confronted Lindros in the club's parking lot to ask for an apology, he said, "I make $3.5 million a year. What are you going to do?"

Lindros was cleared of all charges in February after three independent defense witnesses all said no one saw the player pour beer on anyone.

Things got uglier in May 1996. In a report in *The Fan* magazine, a short-lived Delaware Valley sports publication, a story was published linking Lindros to Philadelphia mob boss Joseph "Skinny Joey" Merlino. The story also was broadcast on WIP (610 AM), the

# THE LINDROS CASE INTRIGUE

The Lindros arbitration case had all the machinations of an episode of *Law and Order*.

In making their case, Flyers CEO Ron Ryan wanted to obtain a copy of the phone bill from the Flyers' hotel suite from the day before the draft, which would include Jay Snider's call to the Lindros cottage in Ontario.

But when he got the bill, the phone call mysteriously was missing. When Ryan pressed the issue with hotel management, he learned that someone had gotten into the closet where the telephone computer was and deleted the record of the call.

Ryan subsequently got phone records from Bell Canada to prove that the Flyers had spoken to Lindros the day before the draft.

Philadelphia-based sports-talk radio station that also was the team's radio broadcast rights holder.

The publisher of the magazine and the radio host who broke the story was Mike Missanelli, at the time one of WIP's most popular hosts.

The genesis of the report was a *Philadelphia Daily News* story that had reported Merlino had sat in Lindros's complimentary seats during a game at the Spectrum.

Lindros downplayed any "relationship" with the local mafia icon, saying he had been introduced to Merlino a handful of times during his first four seasons with the Flyers. And while the seats in question were Lindros's, he claimed he had returned them to the team for resale, a common practice among players. That Merlino got them was only a coincidence.

"That was such [expletive]," Lindros told the *Philadelphia Daily News* in August 1996. "That was just one person [Missanelli], coming up with...they were nothing comments, wanting to publicize his radio show."

One of the ways Lindros and Merlino met could have been through a relationship Lindros was having with one of Merlino's sisters. In a story in late February 2006 in *City Paper*, a free

Philadelphia daily, a former girlfriend of Joey Merlino said Lindros went on a number of dates with one of Merlino's sisters.

Merlino himself said he never used any relationship with Lindros for any illegal activity. Merlino said he was a fan of the team—and of Lindros. He also admitted to losing a significant amount of money betting on the Flyers—something he said never would have happened if he had inside information.

The NHL investigated and apparently agreed. Carl Lindros said he and Eric discussed suing Missanelli, the magazine, and the radio station, but decided it wasn't worth pursuing.

In 1997 WIP became the source of more frustration for Lindros and the Flyers.

There's a bit of irony that the local all-sports talk station could cause so much agita for the club. When WIP shifted into an all-sports format in 1987, the station was owned by Ed Snider (he sold it to Infinity Broadcasting in 1994).

On February 28, 1997, WIP host Craig Carton reported Lindros had missed a game against the Pittsburgh Penguins on February 15 because he had been suspended by the team for being drunk the night before and hungover the day of the game.

The story immediately became front-page news across the Delaware Valley.

"There is only so much I can take," an emotional Lindros said on March 4 of that year. "I haven't done anything at all. I'm innocent."

That same day, club president and GM Bob Clarke was incensed, telling reporters, "You know where Lindros was the night before that Pittsburgh game? He was sitting in a hyperbaric oxygen chamber with our trainer [John Worley]."

Carl Lindros, still smarting from the embarrassing publicity surrounding the Merlino report less than a year earlier, said from his suburban Toronto home, "Eric is very upset about this. This is unbelievable to us. It's sad. It's sick....These things wear you down."

The Flyers said Lindros missed two games—February 15 and 16—due to what the team called a lower back strain. Newspaper reports said Lindros injured himself in a game against the Ottawa

Senators on February 13, when he leaped to avoid a check and landed hard on his back.

Carton, who cited four unnamed sources for his information, including two within the Flyers' organization, stood by his story, and WIP stood by Carton.

In response, Snider and the Flyers filed a libel suit against Carton, WIP, and Infinity Broadcasting in Philadelphia Common Pleas Court.

"We're seeking damages for libeling of this organization and to Eric Lindros," Snider said on March 5 in announcing the suit.

Asked why he took these actions now, and not during the Merlino brouhaha, Snider said, "Because this is one step too many. They finally went over the ledge. We were willing to give them the benefit of the doubt last time, but we're not willing to do it any longer. We're not going to sit back and take it. We understand that they have the power of the airwaves, but we have the power of our integrity and our pride, and we're not going to sit back and take this garbage."

Clarke said the organization had to make this move to show its support for the shoddy treatment given to Lindros.

"If management and ownership won't support their players, then you don't really have a team, you have a bunch of people playing hockey," Clarke said. "It happens to be Eric this time, but if it was any other player, we'd do the same."

Carl Lindros also threatened a lawsuit on behalf of his son, saying he had evidence to document Eric's whereabouts on February 14 and 15, including a video rental receipt and phone bills that show Eric making long-distance calls from his South Jersey home.

After first backing Carton, WIP changed course and didn't renew his contract in July of that year. About a year after suit was filed, WIP settled with the Flyers and Lindros, giving the player an on-air and written apology and making a donation to a charity of Lindros's choosing. Also, hosts and callers were barred from discussing the settlement.

After Snider's threats to take his team's radio rights elsewhere, WIP continues to broadcast Flyers games.

# THE LEGION OF DOOM

When Bob Clarke returned to the Flyers in 1994, he took one look at his team and realized there was a certain element missing.

"[Eric] Lindros was going against the biggest players from the other teams, and he needed help," he said in a June 1995 interview with the *Philadelphia Inquirer*. "His line had to have more size. And we knew we had to have a veteran defenseman."

With one transaction, he managed to fill both holes.

Clarke had a chip in Mark Recchi, who was coming off his second-straight 100-point season. Knowing the Montreal Canadiens needed scoring help, he first tried to acquire 25-year-old defenseman Mathieu Schneider, but was rebuffed. Instead, Clarke turned his attention to another 25-year-old blueliner, Eric Desjardins.

He also inquired about a giant forward who had taken up residence in the Montreal doghouse. John LeClair had scored a pair of overtime goals in the Canadiens' 1993 Stanley Cup run, but he was flip-flopping between center and left wing, with no success at either spot.

"We thought we could try him with Lindros," Clarke said in *Full Spectrum*.

## LINDROS CHANGES HOW DEALS ARE DONE

In the aftermath of the Eric Lindros trade debacle, many things changed about the NHL.

Most importantly, it altered the way trades were made. Previously, deals were worked out over cocktails and written down on restaurant napkins until they officially could be called into the NHL Central Registry during normal business hours.

"The Lindros deal changed how deals were made," said Farwell. "Every deal was a handshake or a napkin and you just worked it out. But that deal went sideways and now it wasn't a deal until everything was on paper and a league person saw it."

On February 9, 1995, Clarke sent Recchi and a draft pick to the Canadiens for Desjardins, LeClair, and forward Gilbert Dionne.

"That trade changed the whole atmosphere and confidence level of our entire organization," Clarke said in a 2005 interview on the Flyers' website. "Desjardins was an All-Star, and LeClair was about to turn into one. We had no idea that LeClair was going to be that good. But that deal turned out pretty good."

That's certainly an understatement.

With Mikael Renberg completing the threesome, a new day had dawned in Flyers history.

In their second game together, against the New Jersey Devils, Lindros chased a Desjardins rebound into the corner in the first period, looked up and found LeClair all but blotting out Devils goalie Chris Terreri, an immovable object the Devils' defense couldn't handle. Lindros fed a pass in front that LeClair stuffed into the net, which started the Flyers on their way to a 3–1 win.

"That was the game where things started to go with Renny and Eric," says LeClair. "We had a game with lots of chances. I scored my first goal as a Flyer, and you could tell there was some good chemistry there."

## THE FIRST CONTRACT

Future problems were foreshadowed by the first meeting between the Flyers and Carl Lindros.

The first meeting was held at a hotel in Syracuse, New York, about halfway between Philadelphia and the Lindros home in Toronto.

Says Russ Farwell, then the Flyers' general manager: "Prior to meeting with Eric, we [he and team president Jay Snider] met with [agent] Rick Curran and Eric's dad [Carl]. It didn't go well."

An angry Carl Lindros left the meeting, presumably to get some air and cool off. Instead, he got in his car and drove home.

"It was Jay's first dealings with the family, and he reported back to me," remembers Ed Snider. "It was, 'Oh my god, what did we get into?'"

Watching Lindros (6'4", 240), LeClair (6'3", 233), and Renberg (6'2", 235) run over, around, and through their Devils counterparts, Flyers fourth-line center Jim Montgomery said, "They look like the Legion of Doom out there."

With their size, speed, and a bruising, crushing forecheck, there was no Superman around to stop this Legion.

"Nobody could get the puck off them," says Chuck Gormley, the Flyers beat writer for the *Courier Post*. "Once they dumped the puck into the corner, regardless of which corner it was, no defenseman was strong enough to stop that line. Nobody in the league. Even if you had a big, tough defenseman, there was only one of them out there, and there were three of these guys."

The threesome rained doom down on teams throughout the league. Lindros had 25 goals and 34 assists in 36 games after the trade, while LeClair had 25 goals in 37 games with the Flyers. Renberg scored 25 times in the final 37 games of the season.

The Flyers, 3–6–1 the day of the trade, finished 25–10–3, including separate eight- and nine-game win streaks.

The Flyers marauded their way into the playoffs, making it to the 1995 Eastern Conference Finals. Two years later, it would be more Doom for the East as the Flyers topped the Rangers to take the conference title and were the heavy favorites against the Detroit Red Wings in the Stanley Cup Finals.

In the first three rounds of the playoffs, Lindros racked up 11 goals and 11 assists; LeClair had seven goals and 10 assists; Renberg had four goals and five assists.

It was thought the Red Wings didn't have the size to handle the Flyers, especially down low in the offensive zone, and over time the Flyers would push the Wings right off the ice.

Instead, the Wings used a combination of skill, finesse, and grit to frustrate the Flyers.

"It was incredibly frustrating," says LeClair. "Both those guys [Detroit defensemen Nicklas Lidstrom and Larry Murphy] are very skilled, especially with their sticks. Those guys are also very talented defensemen; they just used a different tactic. They definitely stayed away from our strength, trying to outmuscle guys in the corner and stuff."

Lindros finished with a pair of assists in Game 1 and scored the final Flyers goal of the series, which came with 15 seconds left in regulation in Game 4, with the Flyers already down 2–0. He finished a minus-5 in the series, as did LeClair, who added two goals and an assist. Renberg had one assist and was a minus-2.

"They confused the Flyers with the left wing lock," says Gormley. "The Flyers had never seen that and I think that they were baffled by it. They [the Red Wings] were more ready. They had veteran guys who were willing to pay the price and understood the glare of the spotlight. The Flyers, they looked like deer in headlights."

Two months after the finals, Renberg was traded to Tampa Bay to get back the four first-round picks the team lost as compensation for the signing of Chris Gratton. The Legion of Doom was no more, but in three seasons together, they had accomplished much.

Renberg had three straight 20-goal seasons. LeClair had the first two of his three straight 50-goal seasons and wrote the definition for an NHL power forward. Lindros won his only Hart Trophy as league MVP in 1995, and in 1995–1996 had the best season of his career, finishing with professional-bests of 47 goals, 68 assists, and 115 points.

"I turned into a different player," says LeClair. "Being able to play with them [Lindros and Renberg], confidence is a big thing. You play with them, you have some success and your confidence grows.

"When I came to the Flyers, I got the confidence in me as a player. Playing with Eric and Mikael, I had some success and built that confidence."

Adds Gormley, simply, "In my opinion, they changed the game."

## THE COLLAPSED LUNG

When the Flyers took the ice against the Nashville Predators on April 1, 1999, Eric Lindros was in the midst of his best season as a Flyer.

It was Lindros's 71st game of the season, and he had 40 goals, 53 assists, and 93 points, the third-highest total in the league. The

# "MORE SASKATCHEWAN THAN SASKATCHEWAN GUYS"

In 1991—the year of the heralded Eric Lindros draft—the Flyers held the sixth overall choice. Atop their list were two players, one a defenseman from the Saskatoon Blades of the Western Hockey League named Richard Matvichuk, the other a center who played like he was from the rough-and-tumble WHL. But actually he was from a small village in eastern Sweden—Peter Forsberg.

At the time, Swedes were considered soft players, not worthy of a top-10 draft pick, least of all for a team like the fearsome Philadelphia Flyers.

"We just felt he may have been born in Sweden, but he's more Saskatchewan than Saskatchewan guys," said Russ Farwell. "They can hardly handle him in his hockey league because he plays so hard and so tough. We felt he was the ideal guy."

A year after passing on Jaromir Jagr with the number four pick because they didn't want the stigma of spending such a high pick on a European player, the Flyers tabbed Forsberg.

Farwell wanted Forsberg to come over the following season, but he said no, which gave Farwell the reluctant encouragement to include him in the Lindros blockbuster a year later.

71 games already was a personal career best, and he was evolving into the captain and leader the Flyers had hoped for.

The Flyers slogged their way to a 2–1 win as the Predators, like most teams, targeted Lindros physically and held him to just two shots in 21:16 of ice time. The big center looked slow, which was chalked up to it being his first night back after a two-game suspension for high-sticking the New York Rangers' Petr Nedved.

During the game, Lindros complained to teammates and trainers of soreness in his side and chest, but never missed a shift. He received ice and electrical stimulation on his upper body after the game, and left the arena for a late dinner and drinks with teammates. Still not feeling right, he made it an early night and returned to his room at the Renaissance Hotel.

# THE HOUSE THAT ERIC BUILT

The Wachovia Center is a lot of things to Ed Snider, but it's absolutely not The House That Eric Built.

"That's bullshit. That's pure, unadulterated bullshit," fumes Snider. "There's no role he [Eric Lindros] had in building this building. I can tell you that unequivocally. The lender couldn't care less who was on the team at a given time....That's an old wives' tale by sportswriters who don't understand finance. Eric Lindros had nothing to do with this building being built. It's absolutely untrue. I don't think our lenders even knew who Eric Lindros was."

When Keith Jones returned to the room he shared with Lindros, he found Lindros awake, watching a movie, and still complaining of soreness in his chest area. Jones said in his autobiography *Jonesy: Put Your Head Down and Skate*, that he got Lindros some Advil and went to sleep.

A few times during the night Jones said he heard the bathtub running, but that didn't concern him.

"I don't think much of it, because when you play hockey sometimes guys will hop in the tub and try to give the body some relief, so I just assumed that's what Eric is doing," Jones wrote.

Early the next morning, Jones said Lindros still was in pain, and Jones noticed he looked pale. He called trainer John Worley, but he had taken Mark Recchi to the hospital the previous evening with concussion-like symptoms.

Jones wrote that at about 7:30 am he finally reached Worley, who was just returning from a sleepless night at the hospital with Recchi. Jones explained Lindros's situation, and Worley said he would come up to their room after he cleaned himself up.

Jones then went for breakfast, but when he returned, Lindros looked worse than ever.

"I come back up and Eric is back in the tub, pale and in even worse shape than he had been," Jones wrote. "I say to him, 'Something is wrong here. Maybe it's something internal. I'll go get John right now. I think we got to get you to the hospital.'"

As Jones approached the elevator, Worley stepped out, and the two went back to see Lindros. With Worley on hand, Jones gathered both his things and Lindros's to catch the team's flight to Boston for their game against the Bruins the next night.

Worley considered having Lindros fly back to Philadelphia so Flyers doctors could see him. He quickly reconsidered, though, and called Rick Garman, the Predators' team physician, and an ambulance. Paramedics rushed Lindros to Baptist Hospital in Nashville, where Garman met them. Lindros was admitted at 9:44 AM on April 2.

When he arrived at the hospital, Lindros said he was having more pain in his chest and shortness of breath. X-rays showed a collapsed lung due to the loss of three liters of blood—half of Lindros's total blood volume. The blood had filled his chest cavity, collapsing the lung.

Doctors performed emergency surgery in the intensive care unit out of fear Lindros wouldn't survive long enough to get to an operating room. A chest tube was inserted between two ribs, and as blood began draining out, Lindros's breathing returned to normal.

Teammates had no idea of the drama unfolding back in Tennessee. About the time doctors were cracking open Lindros's chest, the team was practicing in Boston.

"It's incredible," gasped teammate Sandy McCarthy. "No one knows what happened."

Not even Lindros. Jones said Lindros told him during the game that he had been cross-checked in the upper body in the third period, while Rod Brind'Amour said he heard Lindros complain of sore ribs during the first period. Garman said Lindros told him he had been cross-checked hard during the Rangers game and felt back pain for a day or two after that.

Regardless of what caused it, Lindros's life was in serious jeopardy. Garman said that Worley's decision to not send Lindros back to Philadelphia kept a severe injury from turning into a fatality.

After Lindros's injury, the Flyers immediately ruled him out for the remainder of the regular season, but wouldn't close the door on a playoff return.

# THE 1998 OLYMPICS

When Bob Clarke named Eric Lindros the captain of the 1998 Canadian Olympic hockey team, the first to include NHL players, the criticism was unyielding.

Hall of Fame Edmonton Journal columnist Jim Matheson wrote, "He's wearing the 'C' and that's a heavy letter of the alphabet....Most wonder why he was given the 'C' over more established players."

Jack Todd of the *Montreal Gazette* was even blunter, writing that Lindros would be "the worst captain since Ahab."

Carl Lindros, though, thought otherwise.

"It's premature right now to be even contemplating this," he told the *Philadelphia Daily News*. "It's going to take a couple of doctors to convince me that common sense shouldn't apply. I'm not a doctor, but as a parent and as an agent, we've got to see the rationale that it makes sense for him to be back this spring. I'm not saying that there won't be a good argument. But probably it will take more than a couple of doctors to convince me."

Carl also told the *Philadelphia Inquirer* he had trouble getting in touch with Flyers doctors, and had yet to speak to general manager Bob Clarke. He added that when Eric returned home, he would be placed in the care of Larry Kaiser, the director of thoracic surgery at the Hospital of the University of Pennsylvania—and a doctor unaffiliated with the Flyers.

A day later, Ed Snider responded, and agreed with the elder Lindros.

"We are operating on the assumption that we are not going to have Eric for the rest of the season or the playoffs," he told the *Philadelphia Inquirer*. "We have to figure out a way to win without him."

Lindros returned home April 12, and within a few days he was able to visit with teammates, ride an exercise bike, even jump on the ice for a few minutes at a time. His blood count and stamina seemingly rising each day, he practiced in pads and remained steadfast that he would return for the second round of the play-offs if the Flyers made it that far.

Doctors and Carl Lindros said otherwise, and were worried that members of the organization were pressuring Eric to return sooner than safety should allow. *Toronto Star* columnist Damien Cox wrote as much in a May 1, 1999 column: "Within the Philly organization...there exists the ludicrous sentiment that Lindros should...courageously shake off the lingering effects of the collapsed lung he suffered exactly 30 days ago and leap back into the fray like a comic-book hero."

Cox wrote that in the days following Lindros's ordeal, Eric was pressed into considering having a blood transfusion in order to speed along his recovery. He also wrote that Lindros met with Clarke, during which time Eric asked Clarke why he was being "overtly challenged to rush back."

Clarke, Snider, and Lindros all denied any undue pressure ever was placed on Eric.

It all became a moot point when the Flyers' season ended with a six-game first-round playoff loss to the Toronto Maple Leafs.

## MOMMA AND POPPA LINDROS

Carl and Bonnie Lindros will be remembered as polarizing figures in hockey circles. Some see them as fine people who doggedly defended the health and welfare of their oldest son and refused to allow him to be exploited for the financial gain of others.

"Carl's an extremely meticulous, extremely thorough person," says Rick Curran, Eric's first agent, who added that he found his work with the family to be "a worthwhile experience."

There are others, though, who saw them as paranoid, over-protective pains in the butt who did more to hurt their son's career than help it.

"The big interference came from his mom and dad," says Terry Murray, who coached Eric from 1994 to 1997. "When they came into town and were staying with him for several days at a time, you could always see a different Eric coming to the rink every day. He had different questions, he had a lot of concerns on his mind, he was a little more distracted. When everybody was away and he was there and just playing hockey, he was a real good player."

In Lindros's early days in Philadelphia, Al Morganti was covering the NHL for ESPN, putting him on the receiving end of frequent phone calls from Carl Lindros.

"Carl could be oppressive," he says. "Because I was with ESPN, I was one of the key media people, and Carl would call...and suggest it would be a good story on how bad our GM, [Bob] Clarke, [was].

"They had this agenda—they wanted Clarke gone. I remember I went into the Coliseum to see Clarke with [assistant GM Paul] Holmgren, and said you've got a big problem here. They're trying to engineer stories, and I'm just telling you this, what's going on with this guy.·

"They said, 'We already know.'"

Chuck Gormley, who covers the Flyers for the *Courier Post*, also got his fair share of phone calls from Carl Lindros:

"[Carl] would call me and say, 'Chuck, I was on vacation last week, and I'm going through all my stacks of newspapers, and I saw here you wrote on Wednesday such and such, that's not true. And I want to make it a point that that's not true.' He would try to let you know what was fact and what was not fact. And the real challenge in covering Lindros was that he would not give you a lot of information. And so a lot of things were left to speculation, and as soon as you speculated, they would call and say that's not what happened. So you would ask what happened, and they would say, 'I'm not going to get into that.' They would profess to take the high road, and we would be left to guess. And so often you would lose their respect, and they would lose yours, because no one was telling you the truth. Lies were getting in the paper, in their opinion. It became an untenable situation because you couldn't distinguish between who was telling the truth and who wasn't. And that became an everyday issue. The Flyers would say one thing, his agent would say another."

Morganti said he tried to prod Lindros into finding a new agent.

# CURRAN DISMISSED

To the Lindros family, loyalty is an honor above all else. And if you go against the family, you get whacked—figuratively, of course. They're the Lindroses, not the Sopranos.

Rick Curran, Lindros's agent since he was about 14, learned that after negotiating Eric's first Flyers contract.

"The day that I completed the negotiation for his first contract, there was a press conference," Curran recalls. "We all went out and had lunch together, the family and myself, [attorney] Gord Kirke. And we've never spoken since."

Curran's offense? Moving his office from Canada to Devon, Pennsylvania, near his wife's family.

"I liked Eric," he says. "I told Eric to get another agent, and he'd listen to you and then he'd hear from Toronto."

Morganti wasn't the only person to suggest Lindros needed new representation. In a July 31, 1998, story in the *Philadelphia Inquirer*, Clarke said upcoming negotiations for a new contract might go smoother if it wasn't Carl Lindros he was dealing with.

"I don't know if it would make it easier, but it probably would," Clarke said. "But that's the way it is. I get along with Carl. I like Carl. I have no problems with Carl. But certainly, having a father as an agent..." Clarke never finished the thought, but the story served as a public glimpse into the growing canyon between the team and its star player.

The chasm only would grow bigger over the ensuing years. What had been limited to private spats became public brawls, played out daily in the newspapers. Lindros accepted a one-year contract for the 1999–2000 season rather than the security of a long-term deal, and rumors swirled that Carl Lindros wouldn't let Eric sign a multiyear deal as long as Clarke was general manager. The Lindros family believed signing one-year deals was their only assurance Eric would not get traded.

As the situation continued to devolve, the best solution looked like a complete divorce, and trade rumors started to run rampant.

"There is no basis for trust anymore in the relationship between Flyers management and the Lindros [family]," an anonymous source told the *Philadelphia Inquirer*. "And because there is no ability to have honesty in that relationship, neither side believes each other's intentions are sincere. That's the reality."

The story went on to describe unnamed teammates who were pushing for Lindros to find a new agent, believing Carl Lindros's acrimony with the Flyers' front office was affecting Eric's play.

"My agent does what I say, whether it is my father or anyone else," Eric Lindros replied. "It shouldn't matter who the agent is."

The 1999–2000 season was Eric Lindros's last with the Flyers, but it certainly was a memorable one.

He suffered four concussions, none bigger than the violent shoulder to the head thrown by the New Jersey Devils' Scott Stevens in the first period of Game 7 of the Eastern Conference Finals.

In the aftermath of the Flyers' season coming to a premature end, and with yet another contract negotiation on the horizon, Snider received a letter from the Lindros camp outlining where they felt they had been the aggrieved party in the relationship.

The jump-off-the-page line came from the events surrounding Eric's treatment in Nashville regarding his near-fatal collapsed lung in April 1999. It was an accusation worthy of a daytime soap opera.

"We did everything right," Snider says today, "and the mother said that Bob Clarke tried to kill her son."

A frustrated Clarke lashed back, torching whatever remained of the bridge between him and the Lindros family. In a sit-down with the team's beat writers and columnists, he said, "It's pretty hard to believe that [trainer] John Worley wouldn't treat Eric properly [or that] I would put him on a plane and try to kill him.

"This is the kind of stuff that just never ends, and it's hard on a hockey club. It's disruptive. And as hard as it's been on all of us on this team, it's been a lot harder on Eric.

"You can't tell me how a 27-year-old man can have his dad speaking for him, taking him to the doctor, showing up in the darn locker room....You do that to a 14-year-old kid, he'd be embarrassed."

Clarke said that after years of meddling from Carl Lindros, he was done with it, and said Eric, who was going to be a restricted free agent in the summer of 2000 could return to the Flyers, but only Eric—not his family.

"We want to retain his rights," Clarke said. "We want him back. If he comes back, it's going to be his own self. We don't want his mom and dad back. We've had enough of them."

Carl Lindros's reply came a few days later, when he said, "It's somewhere between humor and tragedy, sort of like a play from Shakespeare."

Things only would get more tragic for both player and club. Lindros sat out the 2000–2001 season, recovering from his injuries, and then declared he never would play for the Flyers again.

Clarke replied that he was done letting the Lindroses dictate where Eric might play, and that his responsibility was to make the best trade possible for the Philadelphia Flyers. That finally happened on August 20, 2001, when Eric was dealt to the New York Rangers for forwards Jan Hlavac and Pavel Brendl, defenseman Kim Johnsson, and a draft pick.

According to Ed Snider, the move was a long time coming.

"He and his parents are the most difficult people I've ever dealt with in any field, in any business," says Snider. "In my entire life I've never met people like this. We always thought he would grow up and speak for himself, but whatever gene that family has, it's everywhere. Everyone is guilty until proven innocent, and Eric is never guilty. They would take facts that we had and say they aren't the facts."

Attempts were made to speak with Carl Lindros, but he refused to return phone messages left at his office or emails. Attempts to reach Eric Lindros were equally unsuccessful.


# THE END

When Eric Lindros took the ice on the last day of May in 1997, the day of Game 1 of the Stanley Cup Finals, it was high point of his career with the Flyers.

And from a peak, there's only one way to go—down.

It started March 8, 1998, in Pittsburgh. Lindros had played in 59 of 60 games to that point of the season, and scored his 28th goal about eight minutes into the second period.

Forty-nine seconds of game time later, Lindros' life, and the course of Flyers history, would be changed forever.

Pittsburgh's Jiri Slegr scored moments after Lindros. On the ensuing faceoff, Lindros grabbed a loose puck at center ice and cut toward the right-wing boards. As he moved around one Penguin, he lost the puck and kicked it ahead of himself, toward the Pittsburgh blue line. Lindros looked down to find the disk, which was within inches of his stick as he skated through the neutral zone.

Lindros had developed an awful habit, going to back to his youth hockey days, of skating with his head down. Growing up, he was so much bigger and stronger than other kids that anyone who dared venture into his path would bounce off him like tennis balls off a concrete wall.

NHL foes don't bounce as well.

And it wasn't a tennis ball that night in Pittsburgh—it was a wrecking ball.

Lindros skated directly into the path of Pens defenseman Darius Kasparaitis, who drove his right shoulder into Lindros's jaw.

The hit separated Lindros from the puck and his senses. The force of the blow snapped his head back and dislodged his helmet. Lindros landed on his back and immediately put his hands up to his head. He rolled onto his knees and twice tried to get up with help from the Flyers' medical staff, but twice fell back down. On his third try, he found his feet and was helped off the ice by teammates.

"He wasn't himself as I was helping him off the ice," recalls John LeClair. "For me, that was the disturbing part, to see him like that."

Lindros walked to an ambulance under his own power, but was diagnosed at a Pittsburgh hospital with the first concussion of his career.

According to an *ESPN The Magazine* story, during the ride to the hospital, Lindros got a call on his cell phone from his mother,

Bonnie, a nurse. The story, as related to writer Tom Friend, said GM Bob Clarke, riding with Lindros, rolled his eyes and said, "Isn't that nice—Mommy called."

He missed the last five weeks of the regular season, and his return for the playoffs didn't help as the Flyers were eliminated in five games by the Buffalo Sabres.

The summer featured Lindros passing on a five-year contract that would have paid him $45 to $50 million, and he reported to training camp in 1998 free of any distractions, on or off the ice.

"He's looked dominant the whole preseason," goalie John Vanbiesbrouck remarked. "He's using his body, playing strong at both ends of the ice. We feed off his intensity, and it's fun to watch."

Lindros played the first 35 games of the season, a personal best, but that's where the streak would end. On December 29, 1998, Calgary's Jason Wiemer waylaid Lindros, giving him the second concussion of his career. He sat out two games, and when he came back, he went on an 18-game scoring streak, tying Clarke's team record.

# TEAMMATES

Those who played with Eric Lindros hold him in high regard, but temper it with a bit of wistfulness—a what-if sense pervading their opinions.

"I always got along great with Eric," says Rod Brind'Amour. "I thought he cared, I thought he played hard and I always supported him."

"[Eric] is one of the guys that [my son] Brett thinks back on that I played with that was the nicest guys to him," adds Ron Hextall.

Keith Primeau said when he came to the Flyers in 2000, Lindros invited he and his wife to stay at his home.

"Eric was a very nice person, a really nice guy. I think he's another one of those guys that because of his stature and because of his ability was always front and center, and I don't know if he necessarily wanted to be front and center."

That season ended prematurely after his near-fatal lung injury in April, and after signing a one-year contract, he started the 1999–2000 season healthy—again—but it wouldn't last—again.

On January 14, Atlanta's Darryl Shannon elbowed Lindros in the head, and he was diagnosed with a "mild" concussion—number three, if you're counting—but Lindros said he felt worse after concussion number three than he did after number two.

The forth concussion came March 4, when 6'7", 240-pound Bruins defenseman Hal Gill elbowed Lindros in the head. Despite feeling less than 100 percent, he played the next four games before getting pulled from the lineup prior to a game in Phoenix.

"This is not a concussion injury," team doctor Jeff Hartzell told the press. "We don't believe it has anything to do with that." He said the headaches could be the result of a sinus problem, muscle contractions, or teeth grinding when Lindros was asleep or chewing gum.

Days later, though, Hartzell changed course, ruling the Gill hit a Grade I concussion—the most mild on the scale, and less severe than the Grade II injury Lindros had suffered in Atlanta.

But in a report in the *Philadelphia Inquirer*, an unnamed member of the organization said Lindros actually had a Grade II concussion from the Gill shot, which includes memory loss. The source added the team knew about Lindros's headaches and treated him with over-the-counter headache medication and massages, despite Lindros having suffered his second concussion of the season and fourth in three years.

Clarke defended his medical and training staff and said Lindros never let on to the extent of his injuries.

"We're very confident that our trainers did the right thing, that our doctors are the best doctors you can get, that our trainers are the best trainers you can get," he said. "The speculation against our doctors and trainers is very offensive....If Eric has a problem, he can bring it up."

The Flyers sent Lindros to visit Dr. Stephen Silberstein, a headache specialist at Thomas Jefferson University Hospital, who agreed with Hartzell and said Lindros had a Grade I concussion.

The Lindros family felt differently, though, and sent Eric to see concussion expert Dr. Larry Kelly in Chicago, who diagnosed a Grade II concussion, which would shelf Lindros through the first round of the playoffs.

The difference in the diagnoses could be chalked up to two reasons. One is the difference in expertise, while the other is slightly more sinister—Silberstein was recommended by the Flyers, while Kelly was an independent practitioner.

Days after returning from Chicago, the tenuous strings binding the Flyers and Lindros were irreparably torn.

During a press conference, Lindros described the culture around the organization as "wacky," ripped the team for its handling of his latest concussion issues, and said Clarke had insulted his father/agent. He added that neither Clarke nor Snider had called him since his latest injury, saying the only Comcast-Spectacor representative he had heard from was Pat Croce, the 76ers president and a minority partner in the Flyers.

A sampling of Lindros's statements, taken from the March 24, 2000, edition of the *Philadelphia Inquirer*:

"I tried to explain my symptoms and that things were not real good, but I was not going to pull myself out of the game....John Worley knew what I had. I was clear in what I told him. I was not concealing it. I might not have been up front with the doctor in Boston [after suffering the injury there]....I knew what would happen [if I had requested to sit out]....It's a wacky situation around here.

"I was hoping the team would take me out—knowing what went on and expressing to them for days about my headaches. Another reason I kept playing is this environment here. The last time I had a concussion, I didn't talk to Clarke for three weeks. What he would say off the record was that my agent was a fool and disruptive for insisting the team follow the [league's] return-to-play guidelines [for concussions]."

The team issued a bland, political statement later that day, but a different statement was made days later. Clarke convened a meeting with coach Craig Ramsay and alternate captains Eric Desjardins, Mark Recchi, and John LeClair, during which Clarke said he was stripping Lindros of the captaincy and handing the role to Desjardins.

"He criticizes our trainers, criticizes our doctors, criticizes our organization," Clarke told reporters. "If he's that unhappy with us all, he shouldn't be the captain of our team."

Clarke today says he had no choice.

"When our organization, our team, our other players were being hurt by what was going on," he says, "I guess it just had to change. I didn't want this organization to be hurt by things that Eric and his family were trying to accuse us of, so we started to fight back. I only saw Eric as a hockey player who was responsible to his teammates, like any other hockey player.

"Our doctors never tried to do anything to hurt Eric, or our trainers, the team didn't, but we were accused of it."

On May 4, 2000, while his teammates were in Pittsburgh, about to engage in the longest playoff game in modern history, Lindros suffered concussion number five when he collided with Phantoms forward Francis Lessard during a four-on-four scrimmage in Philadelphia.

The hope was Lindros could return for the Eastern Conference Finals, but his father said, "We're shutting everything down. We're all the way back to where we were before," meaning when the early March hit first took place.

Despite Carl's proclamation, Eric received clearance on the day between Games 5 and 6 of the conference finals against the New Jersey Devils. With one day to practice, Lindros was a surprise addition to the lineup for Game 6.

"I still think it was a foolish decision," says Chuck Gormley, who chronicled the Lindros saga for the *Courier Post*. "I remember standing in the parking lot at the Coliseum, and I remember saying to myself, you can't [let him play]. You can't do that because of all the animosity."

It was animosity, Gormley said, that had developed because Lindros had set himself apart from the team one time too many.

"I remember Rick Tocchet saying all hands on deck. Whether we have Lindros or not, we don't care. We don't have time for individuals. That's what I sensed from that team. Eric became an individual, and they would not allow that. As an organization, they had to take a stand. I don't think it had as much to do with criticizing John Worley as it did, we have an individual on this team, and we're not going to stand for it."

Keith Jones said Lindros's return, "changed the entire dynamic, because we had played as a team. Then your superstar comes back, and everyone settles in and says, 'Okay, take over.' And it wasn't about the team as much as it was about him coming back into the lineup and everyone taking a breath of fresh air and saying, 'Okay, now he's going to take it.'"

For one night, though, he did take it. In his first game in two and a half months, he was the Flyers' best player. He played 14:47 at center and right wing, and scored their lone goal, even thought it came with 30.1 seconds left in the third period and with the Flyers trailing 2–0. He also had a goal disallowed because it came after the buzzer to end the second period.

And the few cheers coming Lindros's way in a raucous Continental Airlines Arena came from a surprising source— Clarke.

Recalls Gormley, "I sat there in the press box for Game 6 right next to Clarke. I never saw Clarke root harder for somebody than for Lindros that night. He was just, 'Come on Eric, come on Eric.'"

Despite the loss that night, there was hope that if Lindros could play Game 7 the way he played Game 6, the Flyers could survive what was shaping up as a monumental collapse. Those hopes were dashed quickly and painfully. The video proof is readily available online.

On May 26, 2000, on his fourth shift of the game, with 12:10 left in the first period, Lindros comes across the Devils blue line, his head down. He never sees Devils defenseman Scott Stevens skating in from his right. Two Brahma bulls moving at top speed collide; Stevens drives his left shoulder and upper arm into the side of Lindros's head and jaw. The force of the blow spins Lindros 180 degrees, his stick pinwheeling out of his hands. Lindros lands hard on his back, the back of his helmeted head snapping violently off the ice, and he bounce-rolls onto his left shoulder. His legs wrap around him, nearly curling him into the fetal position.

Eric Lindros lies on the ice after getting hit in the first period of Game 7 of the Eastern Conference Finals against the New Jersey Devils in Philadelphia, Friday, May 26, 2000. Lindros was skating up the ice with the puck when the Devils' Scott Stevens blindsided him with an elbow. Lindros left the game. No penalty was called. *Photo courtesy AP Images.*

"When that hit occurred, when they say the air went out of the building, the air went out of that building," recalls Gormley. "It was very frightening."

Lindros was taken by ambulance to Pennsylvania Hospital, where he was kept overnight for observation. He was diagnosed with concussion number six, and his fourth in four months.

"Once that [Stevens hit] happened," says Gormley, "everyone knew his career was over. I thought his career as a Flyer was over the second that hit happened."

Gormley was right. Lindros remained silent while home in Toronto recovering from his injuries.

On November 16, he declared he was done playing for the Flyers.

"I made it clear when I turned down $8.5 million [qualifying offer] that I would not play there again. It's time to move on," he told reporters. "Moving on with a trade is the best thing for that organization, and the best thing for me," he added. "I'm open to meeting with [Clarke] with regard to trade possibilities, but not for any other reason."

A fuming Clarke fired back, "I don't give a crap whether he ever plays again or if I ever see him again. All he ever did was cause aggravation to our team. If he wants to play, he might have to come back [to the Flyers] if no one else wants him in the NHL."

Lindros later said the only team he would play for is the Toronto Maple Leafs, but Clarke was non-plussed.

"My responsibility is to the Philadelphia Flyers, not to Eric Lindros, and we're going to do what's right for the Flyers," Clarke told reporters. "Eric may want to play in Toronto, but that may not happen....We want the best compensation we can get for this player."

The story dragged on throughout the 2000–2001 season, with the Flyers unable to work out a deal with the Leafs, while Lindros scotched any trade possibilities with other clubs by threatening not to report.

The stalemate continued into the summer of 2001, but a bit of daylight came through the dark skies on July 4—ironically, Independence Day—when Lindros family attorney Gord Kirke told Clarke Eric would consider a trade to the New York Rangers. Eric Lindros finally received his independence from the Flyers on August 20, 2001, when he was dealt to the Rangers. In return, the Flyers received forward Jan Hlavac, defenseman Kim Johnsson, prospect winger Pavel Brendl, and a 2003 draft pick.

In announcing the deal, Clarke took the high road, saying to reporters, "No point in rehashing old stuff."

But later he couldn't help himself, saying of Lindros, "He hurt this organization. I couldn't care less about him."

Snider said if he had to do it all over again, he said he would have cut the cord much sooner than 2001: "I really regret my own role in all this because I put up with it for too long. We put up with a lot of crap that we shouldn't have put up with, hoping. It was always the hope that Eric would step up to the plate and be accountable."

That never happened.

## FEELINGS TODAY

Years removed from day-to-day dealings with the Lindros family, Bob Clarke says today he holds no grudges.

"I liked Eric," Clarke says. "I liked Eric, and through most of all the messes that went on, I liked Eric. I liked his dad. I wish it had worked differently."

Clarke says he's unsure where the breakdown first started, but says, "It got a life of its own, and I'm not quite sure how to describe it all.

"I don't know or understand so much that went on. Everybody had the right intent, but the results were different."

While Clarke is content to let the past stay in the past—"That was a long time ago, and it turned out okay for everybody in the end," he says now—Snider isn't as delicate.

The chairman's loyalty to former players is well-known throughout the league, and when he had a more active daily role, he made it a point to thank players traded away for their service to the club.

"I have a special affection for most players," he says. "The only player that we ever traded up until the last couple years...that I didn't call was Eric Lindros. The only guy."

# REBIRTH

## SOLD!

In 1996, after 30 years of owning the Flyers pretty much by himself, Ed Snider no longer was the rambunctious young executive who was as willing to drop the gloves as his players.

Times had changed, and the Ed Snider of 1996 was a sports mogul, one of the longest-tenured owners in the NHL, the owner of one arena with another, his hockey pleasure palace, going up across the parking lot. Spectacor, the arena management company he had started to run the Spectrum, had become incredibly successful.

"I'm one of the few guys who made his money in sports," he says.

Heading a major corporation as well as a major sports team had taken its toll. His contentious dealings with 76ers owner Harold Katz and the city of Philadelphia over the construction of what would become the Wachovia Center had worn him out.

But as Snider was slowing down, one of his former employees had made the jump from a 33 RPM record to a 78.

Pat Croce had been the strength and conditioning coach for the Flyers and 76ers in the 1980s. He had turned a physical fitness and therapy center in Broomall, Pennsylvania, into a 40-franchise chain before selling out in 1993.

Looking for a new challenge, Croce took Katz to lunch in November 1995. Croce knew Katz had grown weary of the negative press surrounding his ownership of the NBA team and asked

Despite the ownership shakeup in the 1990s that brought Comcast into the fold, Ed Snider remains at the center of the Flyers organization as shown here in a January 2008 press conference.

if he could become Katz's partner. Katz rejected the overtures, saying the team wasn't for sale; if he would sell, he told Croce, he would get out completely.

Croce, never one to take no for an answer, pounded away at Katz. With Philadelphia real estate magnate Ron Rubin in tow—Rubin had developed the Bellevue Hotel complex and the Suburban Station building, among others—Croce finally wore Katz down. On February 5, 1995, the 76ers owner gave Croce and Rubin 30 days to make a formal offer.

Rubin told Snider, an old friend, that he planned on speaking with Comcast Corp., the Philadelphia-based cable television behemoth, about financing their deal to buy the 76ers. Rubin had watched media companies like ITT/Cablevision buy the New York Knicks and Rangers, as well as Madison Square Garden and the MSG television network, and thought that was the way of the future. To Rubin, that future needed to involve Comcast. At the time, Comcast was the nation's third-largest cable television provider, with more than nine million subscribers.

Comcast chairman Ralph Roberts and his son Brian, the company's president, shared Rubin's belief that media companies owning sports teams—which would provide relatively inexpensive, easy programming—was a good direction in which to head.

"Ron Rubin was in the shower one day and came up with the idea that it would be fantastic if Comcast got involved in buying the Sixers and buying me and all the other stuff [the two buildings]," says Snider.

"I was starting to think about having some exit strategy sometime in the future," he adds.

Snider and Rubin met the Robertses on February 24 at the Comcast offices in Philadelphia. When the meeting started, Snider was unsure of where it would go. But by the end, he says, he was completely on board. And on March 19 the deal was finalized.

"I wouldn't have made the deal if I had had doubts," says Snider. "It made sense for everybody. I really like the Robertses."

It helped that Snider had an extra ace in his pocket. The Flyers' boss had agreements in place with the 76ers and Phillies to start a new all-sports television network.

"It was the most important part to Comcast," he says.

In 1976 Snider had created PRISM, a pay-cable channel built around Flyers, 76ers, and Phillies games, plus first-run movies. He sold the channel in 1989 to a company owned by Cablevision founder Charles Dolan.

"I was very unhappy with the job Dolan was doing, so I worked the job with the Phillies, and when all of our contracts would end, I would start a new channel. I was in the process of starting the channel when I made the deal with Comcast. They have never really wanted to own teams, per se, but they felt the ownership would be an advantage if they were going to come into partners with the channel."

The deal saw the Robertses and Snider merge to form Comcast-Spectacor. The newly created company purchased the Flyers, 76ers, the new network (later named Comcast SportsNet), the Spectrum, and the under-construction CoreStates Center. Comcast owned 66 percent of the new venture, with Snider retaining the other 34 percent. He was named chairman of the new company and held full control over the Flyers and 76ers, as well as the management of the two buildings. Croce held a minority interest in the company and was named president of the 76ers.

"They wouldn't do the deal if I didn't stay in," Snider told *The Philadelphia Daily News*. "The management contract gives us complete control."

Snider relished the fact that he maintained control of the Flyers while being relieved of the financial burdens that came with sole ownership.

"I didn't need a partner in what I'm doing now," he told the media that day. "There are no financial problems. But I felt what Comcast brings into the fold will be very important to our future.

"I have no financial worries at all. There's been an awful lot written in the press that's erroneous....I just feel that this was an incredible opportunity for a synergy with people who don't really want to get involved in the operations. It gives us control of the whole operation, including the Sixers, and we'll be in control of our own destiny. We have a tremendous partner that has far-reaching tentacles, particularly in the media, and we hope to grow in those areas and make a whole lot more money."

That partnership has gone even better than Snider could have foreseen.

"I have to almost beg them to give input," he says. "They're just wonderful people in the sense that when they have a partner or an executive, they let them run with it. In sports, everybody knows better than the owner or the GM. When you think of a two-thirds partner, you'd think you'd have problems because things aren't always done the right way all the time. I've never heard a bad thing from Brian and Ralph Roberts. They're great partners."

And the success of that partnership is the only reason Snider continues to come to work every day.

"I didn't think I'd be here 12 years later," he says. "The relationship with Comcast and Brian and Ralph has been positive for me, not just from a partnership point of view, but it's really fun being around a company like Comcast that has grown in 12 years from 4 million subscribers to 25 million subscribers. It's been fun to be on that end, too, to watch what they've done and be in the inner circle. It's expanded my view. It's expanded my horizon."

# REBUILDING

Sunday, October 22, 2006—the Flyers' version of Black Sunday—the team was 1–6–1, the worst start in franchise history. That morning, team chairman Ed Snider replaced Bob Clarke as general manager with assistant Paul Holmgren; Holmgren's first move was to fire coach Ken Hitchcock and replace him with assistant John Stevens.

The change was an attempt to spark a struggling team that, at least on paper, looked like a playoff squad. Instead, it was a band-aid on a sliced artery.

The Flyers continued to hemorrhage losses while Holmgren, along with Comcast-Spectacor president Peter Luukko, formulated a plan.

"As we got into the season, we saw the team wasn't heading in the right direction," said Luukko. "And we said, 'What are we going to do to make this team better long-term?'"

Ahead of the Flyers were two paths.

"There were two courses we could take," says Luukko. "One was trade away some of our youth to get some older veterans and maybe just make the playoffs, but probably knowing that you don't know how much better you'd be the next year. That could have been Plan A, but Plan B was the better one. In sports, if you build short-term, you're in trouble. We said, don't give up on young players, maybe they're in situations that you wouldn't really want them in at that time, but they're gaining in experience.

The coe of the team would be their rich crop of youngsters—Jeff Carter, Mike Richards, R.J. Umberger, Joni Pitkanen, Antero Niittymaki—and complement them with high-character veterans.

Snider game his blessing, but as Luukko said, "It's one thing to have a plan; it's another to execute it."

Holmgren's first moves, though, looked like he was reverting back to Plan A. Out went young defenseman Freddy Meyer to the New York Islanders for veteran blueliner Alexei Zhitnik. Not long after, winger Randy Robitaille went to the Islanders for center Mike York.

While on the surface those moves looked like a desperate grab for a postseason that seemed farther away by the day, Luukko said there was more to it.

"He said to me, 'Peter, I'm going to do this, but this is what I'm thinking. These guys will make our team better if we start going, but if we don't, they're also assets that teams are going to want at the trade deadline. I can move these guys at the trade deadline.'"

Holmgren's biggest decision, though, centered on what to do with Peter Forsberg. The sublimely talented Swede had spent more time in doctor's waiting rooms than the locker room. Besides his chronically sore feet, there was his impending unrestricted free agency.

It became a daily soap opera. What would Peter do? Re-sign? Retire? Accept a trade to a contending club? It all added another drag to a team plummeting to new depths by the day.

"We all took turns trying to convince Peter to re-sign," says Holmgren. "The players, myself, even Mr. Snider. To Peter's credit, he couldn't commit due to his own personal health issues. Once we were able to begrudgingly make that trade, we were able to move forward."

Forsberg eventually waived his no-trade clause, and on February 15, he was sent to Nashville. Coming back from the Predators were forward Scottie Upshall, highly regarded defense prospect Ryan Parent, and first- and third-round picks in the upcoming draft.

"Peter helped us because he wouldn't commit because of his health issues," says Holmgren. "That really got the ball rolling to retooling. He was a strong asset we were able to parlay into different assets along the way."

While Parent was the major defense prospect the Flyers needed, Upshall had an immediate impact. He had six goals and 13 points in 18 games, and his speed, energy, and exuberance almost single-handedly fueled some strong, late-season play.

The sixth pick in the 2002 draft, Upshall had yo-yoed between Nashville and the Preds' AHL club in Milwaukee. Some may have given up on Upshall, but not Holmgren. Holmgren had long been an admirer of Upshall's, and says the Flyers debated using the fourth choice in that 2002 draft on him, but instead opted for Pitkanen.

"The reason Scottie couldn't crack the lineup was he always seemed to come down with an injury," says Holmgren. "The last few times he was down there, it seemed like he was too good for that league.

"We had a knowledge of Scottie. I felt he couldn't crack that lineup [in Nashville] because they were too good. In the new NHL, he was going to be a good player for someone."

Holmgren continued to retool his team at the trade deadline. Out went Zhitnik, to the Atlanta Thrashers for defense prospect Braydon Coburn, a 6'5", 220-pounder who could skate like a greyhound. Out went disappointing winger Kyle Calder to Detroit as part of a three-way trade which landed the Flyers young shot-blocking defenseman Lasse Kukkonen from Chicago.

"When we acquired Alexei, we had no intention of moving him on at any point," recalled Holmgren. "We liked the player, we liked the fact that he had two years more remaining on his contract at a fairly reasonable [salary cap] number for a player of that caliber. When Braydon Coburn's name came into the equation, it was something we felt we couldn't pass up."

Holmgren liked Kukkonen after seeing him play against the Phantoms with the Blackhawks' AHL team, and thought he was stuck behind fellow Chicago youngsters Duncan Keith, Brent Seabrook, and Cam Barker.

"I think they have a lot of young players," Holmgren said, "but at the end of the day, you can't play them all. He just became available."

Also coming available was goaltender Martin Biron.

Biron had spent most of the last decade on the Sabres' bench, first backing up Dominik Hasek, and then caddying for Ryan Miller. He had opportunities at the starter's spot before, but injuries usually seemed to sidetrack him.

"The Marty Biron thing came about over a month of conversations back and forth trying to work that out," said Holmgren. "I think Marty was a sought-after guy by a couple other teams."

The Flyers bid the highest, surrendering a second-round draft pick. It was a gamble, as Biron was due to become an unrestricted free agent that summer.

"Giving up a high pick to get him, it's a little bit of a gamble," said Holmgren. "You know he's going to be an unrestricted free agent, you have no idea whether you can sign him. You have no idea whether he's going to like Philadelphia. We all liked the goalie, had a lot of good knowledge because of Donnie Luce. [The Flyers' director of player development had served a similar role for years in Buffalo.] His character, what type of guy he was. You're giving up the 31$^{st}$ pick in the draft, and you have to talk him into staying."

The Flyers, though, gave Biron the chance he always had wanted—to be the unquestioned starter. He played well enough—and liked his time in black and orange enough—that he signed a two-year contract extension just before the season ended.

"Personally, this is very big for me," Biron said the day he signed the new deal. "It was big that they came in and got me at the trade deadline, to be able to know more about me and introduce me to this organization and move forward. I want to move forward, too. That was a big part of my decision."

The decisions made by Holmgren at the trade deadline put an end to any lingering doubts that he was the right man for the job. Holmgren had been installed as the full-time GM months earlier, but it came after the embarrassing news broke in early November that Snider had previously offered the post to NHL vice president Colin Campbell. Shortly after Campbell rejected the deal, Snider removed Holmgren's interim tag.

"I thought he was very steady and calm during the process," says Luukko. "Also, he acted like that job was definitely going to be his. He didn't panic—make this move or that move and they'll give me the job. He was very comfortable in doing what was right for the team long-term, which I thought was very impressive."

"Once the initial thing with Colin Campbell was put to rest, I just went about doing what I was going to do anyway," says Holmgren.

But he couldn't rest on his successful trade-deadline moves. Part of the plan he had put into place was clearing cap room to make a big splash in free agency.

"We knew we were going to have some money to spend in the summertime, and we knew there would be free agents," says Holmgren. "It would be a pretty good market, and there would be players that could plug holes in the areas we needed."

Those needs included scoring depth on the wings, a top-line center, and a stronger leadership core. In a two-week span, all his wishes were granted.

His first step on the road back to success was for the GM at the southern point of the standings to turn his gaze south on the map. In June Nashville Predators owner Craig Leipold, claiming he was tired of losing money, put the team up for sale. To cut liabilities and make the team more buyer-friendly, GM David Poile was told to cut payroll. That meant impending unrestricted free agents like forwards Forsberg, Paul Kariya, and Scott Hartnell, and defenseman Kimmo Timonen would not be re-signed.

"I called David a little bit after they had lost out in the playoffs, and we talked for quite a while that first time," recalls Holmgren. "There was a lot going on about Nashville, with their team's status, and he had the pending free agents—Kariya, Timonen, Hartnell, and Forsberg—and I asked him the question, are you going to try to get any of your guys signed. He said, 'We're going to try, but I don't know how successful we'll be.' I raised the idea of, 'Maybe there's something we can do where you don't just lose the players for nothing.'"

# ONE FINAL LOSS

Even after the disastrous 2006–2007 season ended in April, the Flyers still suffered one more loss.

Finishing with the worst record in the league, the club had a better than 50-percent chance of winning the draft lottery. But when the Ping-Pong balls were pulled, the Flyers slid down to the number two spot, one position after the Chicago Blackhawks.

Holmgren was focused on Timonen and Hartnell. Timonen is considered one of the best all-around players in the game at his position. Hartnell brought size at 6'2" and 210 pounds, and skill, shown by his consecutive 20-goal seasons.

Holmgren and Poile spoke a few more times, and in late June, Poile gave Holmgren a 48-hour window to negotiate deals with Timonen and Hartnell.

"We agreed to a timeframe where I could talk to the players themselves, and if we came to an agreement with those players, there would be a return for Nashville. If we could only sign Timonen, it was a certain price; if we could only sign Hartnell, it was a certain price; and if we could sign both, it was the first-round pick." That first-round pick would be the one the Predators had given the Flyers in the Forsberg deal months earlier.

Hartnell agreed to a six-year, $24 million deal before the deadline. Getting Timonen inked proved a bit harder.

"As the time was ticking down, I had to call [Poile] for a half-hour extra," recalls Holmgren. "We just had to finalize a few things with Timonen."

The blueliner eventually agreed to a six-year, $37.5 million pact. Drawing assists on the signing were Kimmo's brother Jussi, a defenseman playing for the Phantoms, and Sami Kapanen, a long-time friend from Finland.

"I talked to my brother and I talked to Sami right away," said Kimmo after the trade. "There were so many positive things about this city of Philadelphia and the Flyers.

"They had a bad year last year, but I believe that we can turn it around and have a really good team next year. The one big thing was maybe getting a couple of more players before the start of the season, and talking to Holmgren, he said he was going to do everything he can to get a couple more guys."

Holmgren lived up to his words. On July 1, the first day of free agency, he went fishing for the biggest catches. He put hooks in the water for centers Daniel Briere, Chris Drury, and Scott Gomez, as well as power forward Ryan Smyth.

All the offers went out about noon. Then, like any other fishing trip, it became all about patience.

Daniel Briere (third from left) is shown with coach John Stevens (left), team general manager Paul Holmgren, and Peter Luukko, president and C.O.O. of Comcast-Spectacor (right) after a news conference at the Philadelphia Flyers offices in Voorhees, New Jersey, July 12, 2007. *Photo courtesy AP Images.*

"To me, that was more nerve-wracking than the trade deadline," recalls Holmgren. "It was the first time I ever went through that as a manger. You're just waiting. There's nothing you can do but wait."

Holmgren's patience paid off when Briere took the Flyers' bait.

"We talked again, it was 3:30, and we were able to get it done by 4:15," says Holmgren. "There was a lot of excitement in my office that day."

For sure, there was a lot of excitement in the Briere household, as well. The league's 10th-leading scorer with 95 points, Briere inked an eight-year, $52 million contract that was front-loaded to pay him $10 million in the 2007–2008 season.

While Holmgren was celebrating reeling in Briere, another fish jumped in his boat.

The Flyers' GM had been talking to his Edmonton counterpart, Kevin Lowe, for months regarding winger Joffrey Lupul. The 24-year-old forward had dropped from 28 goals to 16 in his first season in Edmonton and was in desperate need of a fresh start after a disappointing season in his hometown. In return, Lowe demanded Pitkanen.

Holmgren had long been holding out hope Pitkanen would live up to his vast potential, but the enigmatic Finn would flash one moment of brilliance for three moments of mind-boggling ineptitude.

"I had a hard time even talking about moving Joni," recalls Holmgren. "But when Jason Smith's name came up that morning, I think something just said I better think about that one."

The defenseman had served as Edmonton's captain longer than either Wayne Gretzky or Mark Messier, and his toughness and dependability were unquestioned. Once Smith's name was added to the equation along with Lupul, Holmgren added winger Geoff Sanderson to complete the transaction.

Timonen and Hartnell also officially signed their deals, making July 1, 2007, one of the most productive days in Flyers history.

"That was the first time in our 40 years that we ended with the worst record in the league and, not only was it embarrassing, it was unacceptable, and I certainly hope that the moves that we've made will fix that problem," Snider told reporters that day.

Briere was the big catch, turning down more money from other teams to come to Philadelphia.

"They were the best fit, the best organization, and the team that committed to winning the most," he said days after he signed. "I don't think money was an issue at all."

But it certainly helped, as did having a few familiar faces in the locker room. Briere's best friend and road roommate from Buffalo was Biron, and defenseman Denis Gauthier was a teammate in junior hockey.

"Having some friends on the team, playing with Marty, being his roommate in Buffalo [helped]," he says. "I played with Denis

Gauthier in junior. [Defenseman] Alex Picard is from my hometown. And Simon [Gagne], knowing him from here and there. There were a lot of guys I knew in the dressing room that I felt very comfortable with."

And while he signed on the first day possible, Briere didn't just jump at the first big-money contract thrown his way.

"I'd been watching [the Flyers] since the trade deadline," he says. "What they did at the trade deadline, what they did before July 1, it was something that was very interesting. They're committed to winning. And they showed everybody they were serious about turning things around. A lot of teams will say that, but here we had a team that was doing it, acting it, as well."

"I never want to go through this again as long as I live," says Luukko. "But there is something to be said that things need to get worse before they get better. We had a chance to take a core of guys we believe in and really build for the future. And now we can see where that goes."

# STADIUMS

## THE SPECTRUM

In 1965 Ed Snider was putting together his bid for a professional hockey team. On the top of his to-do list was finding a home for his club.

Owning a pro hockey team was a second job for Snider, who in his day job was treasurer and part owner of the Philadelphia Eagles. One of his major roles with the football team at the time was developing a new multipurpose stadium on the south end of Broad Street, near the Philadelphia Navy Yards, which would be the new home of the Eagles and the Philadelphia Phillies.

While struggling to move the project through the Philadelphia city machinery, Snider was approached by Ike Richman, who owned the Philadelphia 76ers. Richman wanted to move his team out of the Philadelphia Convention Center and wanted to know if Snider thought Eagles majority owner Jerry Wolman could help him build a new arena.

"I said we're not in the business of building arenas," said Snider, "but let me think about it."

Snider still was thinking about it as he was completing his bid for an expansion NHL team. In the plan for what would become Veterans Stadium, he saw room for not just one, but two buildings.

"I thought to have it in South Philly because I always thought this was the best location because of the roads all converging here, from New Jersey, from Northeast Philadelphia, the

Schuylkill, from Delaware," he said. "I thought this was the [perfect] location."

Snider met with Philadelphia City Councilman Paul D'Ortona, with whom he had been working on the Vet Stadium project. Snider proposed that since the city owned the land where the new stadium was being constructed, as well as the surrounding parking lots, an arena could be built in one of the lots between the new building and JFK Stadium. Snider said his group would lease the land and parking lots from the city, but the arena would be privately built and owned. The building would house the Flyers and the 76ers, as well as all sorts of concerts and other events.

"You have to understand, I was talking to a guy who had been involved with a stadium project that had been delayed 10 years in haggling over the use of city funds," Snider said in *Full Spectrum*. "It had become a huge political football. And I'm talking about putting down an arena at no cost to the city that would generate all kinds of revenues to help pay off the [stadium] debt."

D'Ortona loved the idea, and he and Snider took their plan to Mayor James Tate, who didn't need much convincing. According to Snider, "They all agreed to it, and we made a deal in 15 minutes."

Snider, in *Full Spectrum*, said, "Tate turned to the city solicitor and said, 'I want you to do everything humanly possible to cut through all the garbage so that they can get this thing done.'"

On February 9, 1966, the NHL announced Philadelphia would be home to one of six new expansion franchises. That afternoon, Snider and Tate announced plans for the new 15,000-seat South Philadelphia indoor arena.

On April 4, 1966, team president Bill Putnam announced the highly respected architectural firm of Skidmore, Owings and Merrill had been hired to develop the new arena. Ground was broken on June 1. A two-tier design was planned, which would seat 15,000 for hockey and 16,500 for basketball. The tiers were tapered sharply to provide the best sight lines, and there would be no obstructed views.

"The guidelines the architects used was that if you were sitting in the last row, you could see the goalies," Hal Freeman, first president of the new arena, said in *Full Spectrum*.

Finding a name for the new building fell to team vice-president Lou Scheinfeld, who Snider had hired off *The Philadelphia Daily News'* city hall beat.

Scheinfeld didn't know what name to use, but he knew what he didn't want—no use of the "A" word: arena. Scheinfeld and Bill Becker, an executive for the company designing the Flyers' uniforms, donned hard hats and walked around the construction site, hoping an idea and not a steel beam would hit them.

"I'm thinking about how this building will host a number of different events," Becker recalled in *Full Spectrum.* "I thought of color and this being a stadium or auditorium, and 'Spectrum' popped into my head and out my mouth.

"I remember Lou saying, 'Doesn't that sound a little pharmaceutical?' I told Lou no, that it suggested blocks of colors which would be great for a billboard and a logo."

The pair came up with a proposal to take to Snider and Wolman. They turned Spectrum into an acronym—SP for sports, E for entertainment, C for concerts, T for theatrics, R for recreation, and UM for stadium.

Snider and Wolman thought it was a grand idea, and the new building would be named the Spectrum.

In making the announcement, Freeman said, "Spectrum is a series of images which form a display of colors. We have the only Spectrum in the whole world. It sounds like spectacle and spectacular."

Not everyone, though, was on board with the idea.

"It sounds like they've reached too far in groping for something unique," wrote *Philadelphia Daily News* columnist Stan Hochman.

Snider recalled other dissenting opinions.

"People were coming up to me and saying, 'It sounds like a doctor's instrument,'" he recalled in *Full Spectrum.*

The original plan was for the seats to play off the "display of colors" motif, with the chairs to come in four colors—blue, apple green, magenta, and orange—that would be arranged in concentric circles throughout the building. That plan was scrapped,

# BROKEN WINDOW

The large windows that ring the Spectrum concourse aren't supposed to open. But they did March 13, 1993.

During the first period of a game against the Los Angeles Kings, a vicious wind and snow storm—which dropped two feet of snow in some parts of the Delaware Valley—blew out one of the windows, sending shards of glass through the concourse and down to the ice.

The teams finished the first period tied 1–1, and the game was canceled, much to the chagrin of the 2,000 or so hearty souls who braved the elements to see it.

though, when the fabric company couldn't get all the right shades in time for an August installation. Instead, a uniform dark red was chosen.

The Spectrum opened for business September 30, 1967—less than 16 months after ground was broken, and at a cost of just $6.5 million. For the record, the first event at the building was the two-night Quaker City Jazz Festival.

The Flyers took their first laps around the new ice October 15. The doors were opened to the public to watch practice, but the fans said a hearty no thanks, as there only were about 10 people in the building. Those that stayed away missed little, as shooting was kept to a minimum due to the boards having not yet been delivered due to a manufacturers' strike. Snider allegedly had to bribe a union worker to open the gate so his trucks could come in and get the boards out.

The first official sporting event at the Spectrum was held October 17, a boxing card headlined by Philadelphia native Joe Frazier. The building's official dedication came the next day, prior to the Philadelphia 76ers' home opener.

The pundits weighed in on the arena, with one calling it the "Fish Can on the Delaware Flats," while another wondered why a building named for an array of colors would have such a bland, brown brick exterior.

The interior, though, was a different story, as the ushers wore blue suits and the usherettes were attired in burnt-orange blazers and hot pink miniskirts.

Finally, the first Flyers home game arrived, on October 19, 1967. A curious crowd of 7,812 paid between $2 and $5.50 for tickets. The high prices were blamed for the poor turnout—7,812, to be exact—but NHL president Clarence Campbell, on hand to drop the ceremonial first puck, said the league had to "charge luxury prices for a luxury product."

# SPECTRUM II

In November 1989 the Spectrum was just 22 years old—not ancient by any means, but in the world of sports arenas, 22 is the new 62. And with just 14 lucrative luxury suites to sell and player salaries ever on the rise, the Flyers had just about maxed out their building revenues.

Sixers owner Harold Katz was in a similar boat, but his was a little leakier. He shared the Spectrum with the Flyers, but believed he was just a lowly tenant in Snider's hockey home. He paid about $1.5 million yearly in rent and shared in none of the money the building raised in suite sales or concessions.

In 1988 Katz opened talks with Robert Mulcahy, the chairman of the New Jersey Sports and Exposition Authority, about moving the team to an arena on the Camden waterfront.

At a Police Athletic League event on a November night in 1989, Snider, seated next to Philadelphia Mayor Wilson Goode, mentioned Katz's talks with Mulcahy. Goode replied that a deal for a new arena in Philadelphia could be done in five days.

With Goode's assurances in hand, Snider told Katz that building a single-tenant arena was a bad idea. Katz agreed, and the pair formed a partnership to construct a new arena, ostensibly in Philadelphia. Spectacor, the company Snider had created to manage the Spectrum, would take the lead role in negotiations.

Katz signed a 30-year lease agreement with Spectacor to have the 76ers play in the new building. In return, Katz was given a $1 million reduction in yearly game-night costs, and he would receive a share of parking, concession, luxury box, and advertising revenue generated by the new building.

Goode suggested JFK Stadium, which had fallen into disrepair and had been shut down in July 1989, as the best site. Spectacor agreed.

Despite promises from the state of New Jersey to pay for nearly two-thirds of the projected $100 million Camden arena cost, Snider and Spectacor's first choice was to stay in Philadelphia. There was no way the city, nearly bankrupt at the time, could equal New Jersey's offer, but Snider was committed to staying where he was, even if it meant privately financing the building in a similar way to how the Spectrum was built.

That Spectrum deal—a trade of city land for a privately financed building that paid no property taxes—was under serious political scrutiny. Regardless, all Snider needed to do was look at a map.

"We were in the best location in the Delaware Valley," Snider recalled in *Full Spectrum*. "The subway and I-95 are right there. I was reluctant to go to another location that I thought was less desirable."

In late 1990 Spectacor and the city of Philadelphia reached an understanding on a 21,000-seat arena to be built in place of JFK Stadium. Nothing could be announced, though, until the state of Pennsylvania was able to provide a financial bail-out for the city.

# PHANTOMS

When the Flyers moved across the parking lot from the Spectrum to the CoreStates Center, the club wanted a new tenant for the old building.

Enter the Philadelphia Phantoms, the Flyers' new American Hockey League affiliate.

Since debuting in the 1996–1997 season, the team has been a hit on the ice and at the box office. The Phantoms generally rank near the top of the league in attendance, averaging 6,000 to 7,000 fans per game. And on the ice, the club has won a pair of AHL championships and developed a number of players and coaches for the Flyers.

**Interior view of the Wachovia Spectrum in July 2008. The Spectrum will close in 2009 and be demolished to make way for a new entertainment development.** *Photo courtesy AP Images.*

New Jersey, though, learned of the offer and countered with a proposal to pay for as much as 80 percent of the new project.

With a solid deal in hand from New Jersey, a push was made by Katz and members of Spectacor to move across the Delaware. Snider, though, held firm and continued to negotiate with Philadelphia.

Part of the preliminary deal would see the city give a $6.5 million gift to Spectacor, which would pay for half of a multilevel parking garage, from which the city would receive no money. Frank Rizzo, running for reelection as mayor, used that part of the deal as a bullet point in his campaign, forcing Spectacor and the city back to the bargaining table.

The sides agreed to make the payment a low-interest loan, repayable by Spectacor over a 24-year period, and make it the only money laid out by the city. On June 10, 1991, at the Hershey Hotel, schematics were unveiled for the new arena, tentatively titled Spectrum II. The design called for 19,000 seats for hockey and included 78 luxury boxes. Included in the original design was a store-lined concourse that would connect the new building with the original Spectrum. Total cost was approximated at $200 million.

The land for the building would be leased from the city at a cost of $100,000 per year, with the cost rising by $5,000 a year through 2057. In return, Spectacor received a five-year tax abatement; starting in the sixth year, the property tax would be $2 million per year until 2024, and from that point it would go up $100,000 per year, until it maxed out at $4 million per annum. The state of Pennsylvania also agreed to pay $5 million to demolish JFK.

City councilwoman Anna Verna, who represented the stadium district, wasn't pleased by the deal, but when the contract went up for approval, the vote was unanimous, and on July 7, 1991, the contract was ratified.

Meanwhile, there was another deal, nearly just as big, happening a few thousand miles away. In Montreal, at the 1991 draft, the Quebec Nordiques used the first choice on an 18-year-old phenom who was going to lead the NHL into the 21st century. Eric Lindros was the Nordiques' pick, despite his and his parents' promise to never play for the team.

The Flyers were floundering. Russ Farwell, Bob Clarke's replacement as general manager, had made a number of deft moves, including obtaining defenseman Steve Duchesne and forwards Kevin Dineen, Mark Recchi, and Rod Brind'Amour. The work went for naught, though, as the Flyers were forced to watch the 1992 playoffs on television, making it an unprecedented three-year drought.

Even in the pre-Internet days, Lindros was a name on the lips of even casual hockey fans. The legend of the hockey prodigy with gargantuan size and Gretzky-like touch had spread throughout the hockey portion of the lower 48 states.

## SAME BUILDING, DIFFERENT NAMES

The Flyers' new home may have taken five years to go from conception to completion, but the building has changed names like the team changes coaches.

In September 1994 CoreStates Financial Corp. spent $40 million to buy the naming rights to the Flyers' home, as well as the Spectrum. The contract with CoreStates was for 29 years. The name lasted four. First Union merged with CoreStates, and on September 1, 1998, the buildings were renamed for First Union.

On July 28, 2003, Wachovia Security's purchase of First Union meant another new name for the buildings.

The price of doing business was steep, but the price of not making the move was even worse. The club sent Mike Ricci, Duchesne, Kerry Huffman, Ron Hextall, Chris Simon, the rights to the unsigned Peter Forsberg, two first-round draft picks, and $15 million to the Nordiques for Lindros. Then the two sides negotiated a six-year, $20.5 million contract.

In the days following the trade, fans swamped the Flyers' ticket office with requests.

"I've never seen anything like it in my 10 years here," recalled Jack Betson, then the team's vice president of sales, in *Full Spectrum*. "Some people who had canceled their season tickets called to say they want them back." Larry Rubin, a Spectacor spokesman, said calls regarding luxury boxes were running 60 percent higher than normal.

Snider had his star to put on the marquee of his new home. What he didn't have, though, was progress. More than a year after the city council had approved the deal, ground had yet to be broken.

Still without financing on November 28, 1993, Snider scotched the deal with Katz and started all over. Katz, freed from the constraints of the Spectrum, nearly secured his own deal from New Jersey governor Jim Florio for an arena on the Camden waterfront near the state aquarium. But when Florio lost his reelection bid to Christine Todd Whitman, the new governor flushed the deal.

Eventually, Snider received $140 million from Prudential Power Funding Associates, and he and Katz made a tenuous peace. On February 1, 1994, Spectrum II again was announced, and on June 23, the new contact was ratified by Philadelphia City Council. On September 13, 1994—five years after Wilson Goode told Ed Snider the city could approve a new arena in five days—ground was broken.

"From the time I had the idea to build the Spectrum to the time it was completed was 16 months," recalls Snider "Construction was 11 months. On the same parking lot, that building cost $6.5 million to build. This one cost $200 and something [actually $210 million]. The agreements with the city and everybody else for [the Spectrum] was about [3 or 4 inches] thick; the agreements for this building filled a whole conference room. Same city, same parking lot, same circumstances.

"Just the workmen's compensation for this building [the Wachovia Center] cost more than that building [the Spectrum] to build."

On August 31, 1996, the Flyers' new home, named the CoreStates Center, finally opened.

# NUMBERS DON'T LIE

## THE STREAK

The 1979–1980 season started with Pat Quinn in his first full season as coach. Quinn had replaced Bob McCammon 50 games into the previous campaign, and worked hard to rebuild relationships with players that had soured during McCammon's tenure.

Quinn also installed an up-tempo style of play, encouraging defensemen to join the rush and allowing forwards to move freely through the offensive zone. Helping install the new plan was Quinn's new assistant, player/coach Bobby Clarke.

Flyers GM Keith Allen also drafted well, tabbing Brian Propp with the 14th choice of the 1979 draft. The left wing had scored a remarkable 94 goals in 71 games the previous season for the Brandon Wheat Kings in the Western Hockey League. The quiet 20-year-old meshed well with the remaining Broad Street Bullies— Clarke, Bill Barber, Reggie Leach, Rick MacLeish, Bob Kelly, Jimmy Watson, and Moose Dupont.

"I think I looked at it as I was going to help any team I could get to," Propp says today. "Going later in that first round helped me to be with a more competitive team. I was just happy to contribute, but I knew I would really be able to help them out."

The rookie impressed early in camp and earned a prime opening-night assignment.

"My first linemates were Bobby Clarke and Reggie Leach," says Propp in amazement more than 25 years later. "They helped me to adjust pretty quickly."

The season opened with a tribute to the retired Bernie Parent. The great goalie's eye injury suffered the previous season would never heal enough for him to get back in net, so the Flyers wanted to send him off in style.

Parent's No. 1 was raised to the rafters, never again to be worn. In a sense of irony, teammates presented their teammate with a hunting rifle.

The Flyers won opening night as Paul Holmgren, Propp, and Al Hill all scored in a 1:41 span in the second period, and the Flyers cruised to a 5–2 victory against the New York Islanders.

Two nights later, though, the team was thoroughly outclassed by the Atlanta Flames, 9–2.

Quinn was confused as to how his team could beat the high-flying Islanders one night, then get embarrassed in Atlanta the next. But he would have time to get over the loss, because it would be a while before he had to worry about another one.

Al Morganti was in Atlanta for that defeat. It was the young reporter's first year on the Flyers beat for *The Philadelphia Inquirer*. At the time, the press was viewed as seeing the team through rose-colored—or orange—glasses. When Morganti was given his new assignment, he was told to be extra critical.

"I was brought in to be a little rough on them," he says today. "They said, 'Al, we need a little more critical coverage.' But I got to cover one loss, then it's like, how am I going to criticize this?"

"This" started with a home game against the Toronto Maple Leafs on October 14, 1979. Holmgren, Leach, and Propp scored 4:29 apart in the first period. After the Leafs pulled within one on goals by Lanny McDonald late in the first and Darryl Stitler 33 seconds into the second, Kelly scored an insurance goal with 3:16 left in regulation, making McDonald's last-minute penalty-shot goal irrelevant.

Next, Leach scored twice as the Flyers beat visiting Atlanta 6–2. Two nights later, the Flyers made their last visit to Detroit's

Olympia Stadium a victorious one, as Holmgren, Propp, and Leach all scored twice as the Flyers took home a 7–3 win.

The next night, the Flyers jumped to a 6–2 lead midway through the second period against the Montreal Canadiens before hanging on for a 6–6 tie.

Barber scored twice that night and said after the game, "We have the speed, we have the movement now. Pat's system is letting us go where we want to go. Sure, it's contributing to some mistakes, but hopefully we'll cut down on them. I have this feeling we're coming on, just like my first year here."

His first year also was the Flyers' first Cup championship season.

Their unbeaten streak at four after the tie with Montreal, the Flyers would only know victory in their next nine games. New players stepped up nightly. It was Propp and Leach scoring 12 seconds apart in the third period against the Rangers, capping a rally from a 2–0 first-period hole en route to a 5–2 victory. Propp, Dennis Ververgaert, and Leach scored third-period goals to turn a 2–1 deficit against the Red Wings into a 4–2 lead, then used Leach's goal with 60 seconds left to win it 5–4.

Barber scored early in the third period to break a 3–3 tie and send the Flyers to a 5–3 win over Montreal, as the Flyers snapped a 16–game winless streak against the Canadiens.

The unbeaten streak reached 11 on November 10 when the Flyers traveled to Nassau Coliseum to play the New York Islanders. Barber scored twice, sandwiching goals by Leach and MacLeish, and Clarke added a goal late as the Flyers skated away with a 5–2 win.

It was notable that members of the old Bullies team had scored all the goals. "[The Islanders] said something in the papers last year, that we aren't the Flyers and just don't have it anymore," MacLeish told reporters with a we'll-show-you joy.

Wins against Vancouver and Edmonton pushed the unbeaten streak to 13, and the winning streak to nine in a row, five short of the NHL record, when the team arrived in St. Louis. The Blues scored twice in the first period and led 2–0 before Norm Barnes, Barber, and Leach scored 7:29 apart in the third to put the Flyers ahead. But a Barnes giveaway led to a Blair Chapman game-tying goal with 2:32 left. The win streak was over, but the team won four of its next five to enter December unbeaten in 19 straight.

At this point, more people outside the locker room began to take notice of what was going on. Mentions of the NHL record of 28 in a row, set by the 1977–1978 Montreal Canadiens, began popping up in more and more newspapers.

"It was around 18 or 19 games into it [that] we started getting more and more press," says Propp. "And we were getting closer to Montreal's record. When we hit 18 or 19 games, everyone was out to beat us. But it was just fun."

But wearing a bull's-eye and getting every team's best effort just because they wanted to be the ones to say they stopped the streak didn't make things easy.

"Every night someone became a hero," says Morganti. "It was an astonishing thing. The longer it got, you got really immersed in it."

Three straight ties, capped by a two-goal second-period rally to tie the Boston Bruins, pushed the streak to 22. That game against the Bruins saw Leach score his 19th goal, and just 1:08 later, Holmgren added his 10th. Two nights later, the Flyers spotted the Los Angeles Kings a 3–0 first-period lead at the Spectrum, but then scored the next nine in a 9–4 victory. After a tie with the Chicago Blackhawks, the Flyers spotted the Quebec Nordiques a 3–1 lead 7:52 into the third period. The Flyers scored the next four en route to a 6–4 victory, and the streak reached 25.

"They can put on the tap when they want to," Quebec coach Jacques Demers told reporters.

The scoring was flowing from everywhere.

"It wasn't like it was one or two guys contributing," recalls Propp. "It was all four lines contributing when it counted."

Twenty-five games into the streak (now the second-longest in NHL history), Leach had 24 goals despite missing two games. MacLeish, demoted to a fourth-line role, still had 16 goals. Barber had 15, and Propp 13. Ken Linseman had 29 points, Clarke had 26 assists, and Holmgren had 18 points.

"Somebody stepped up every night," says Propp. "That's why we had such a good team. We had four solid lines, and everybody knew their role. It was a total team effort."

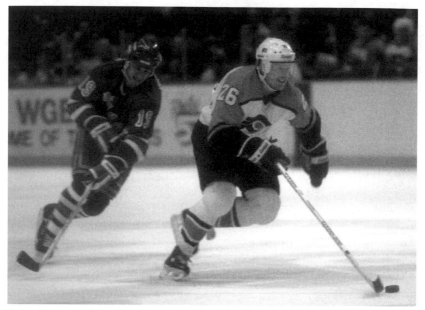

**Brian Propp and the Flyers separated themselves from the rest of the league in the 1979–1980 season by going on an astounding 35-game unbeaten streak.**

MacLeish had the game-winner in a 3–2 defeat of Buffalo, and the next night, at Madison Square Garden against the Rangers, Flyers goalie Phil Myre stopped 34 shots, including a glove save on Ron Greschner late, to preserve a 1–1 tie and push the Flyers within one game of the Canadiens' record.

With a spot in the history book at hand, Quinn told reporters, "We've been saying it's not affecting us, but you know that's a crock. This is a once-in-a-lifetime opportunity. You might play 100 years and never get another chance at something like this."

They almost missed their opportunity on December 20, 1979, against the Pittsburgh Penguins. The Flyers played like a team trying not to lose, but they were on their way to doing just that, trailing 1–0 entering the final five minutes of the game, in front of 17,077 fans at the Spectrum yearning to witness history.

With 4:39 left, the Penguins' Bob Stewart was sent off for hooking Hill. On the ensuing power play, Behn Wilson slipped behind Pittsburgh's Gregg Sheppard in front of the Penguins goal and knocked Ververgaert's pass through the crease into the goal with just 4:08 left.

The game ended tied, and balloons fell from the ceiling along with coupons that read "You Were There."

The team headed to Boston with a chance to break the record against their old nemesis.

The names may have changed, but the Bruins remained a tough, talented team. They were led by rookie defenseman Raymond Bourque and featured aging but still-talented Jean Ratelle, and tough guys Terry O'Reilly and Stan Jonathan.

It was that toughness that Quinn hoped would enliven his team.

Five minutes into the first period, Clarke lifted Al Secord's stick deep in the Bruins' end and took the puck away. Taking two strides into the right faceoff circle, his wrist shot went between Kelly's legs and into the Bruins net for a 1–0 lead.

An extra roughing penalty on the Bruins' John Wensink after a fight with Holmgren put the Flyers on the power play, and a slashing penalty assessed to Bobby Lalonde a little over a minute later put the Flyers on a five-on-three advantage. Twelve seconds later, Barber's slap shot from the point went through traffic and past Gilles Gilbert to make it 2–0.

In the first minute of the second, Jimmy Watson started a rush out of the Flyers end, and as he crossed the Boston blue line, he dropped a pass for Linseman. Linseman made a nifty move to pull the puck out of the reach of Mike Milbury and cut to the outside. When Gilbert failed to come out to cut down the angle, Linseman wristed a shot inside the far post to make it 3–0.

The Bruins got on the board when Tom Songin banked a shot off Bob Dailey's skate at 3:03, and just 67 seconds later, Milbury's point shot bounced off Myre's stick and into the net.

After the ensuing faceoff, the Bruins' Dwight Foster intercepted Linseman's pass to Mel Bridgman, but hurried his clearing attempt was stolen back by Mike Busniak. Busniak slid the puck to Watson at the left point, and the defenseman rifled a low shot past a surprised Gilbert at 4:40 of the second to restore a two-goal lead.

Busniak made another nice play midway through the third period, when he knocked down Brad McCrimmon's pass behind

# A STREAK OF TRAGEDY

When people think of Flyers streaks, they think of the 1980 team.

That team, though, doesn't hold the longest win streak in club history. While their 35–game unbeaten run remains the North American professional sports standard, the most consecutive wins they ran off was nine.

Rather, it was the tragedy-laced 1985–1986 team that set the club mark with a 13-game win streak, from October 19, 1985 to November 17, 1985.

The numbers the Flyers put up during their 13-game win streak were nothing short of amazing. They scored at least five goals in 12 of the contests, and Tim Kerr scored 16 goals in the 13 games.

Above all else, though, they pushed the streak three games higher while being little more than skating zombies following the death of their friend and teammate, Pelle Lindbergh.

the Bruins net and Kelly scored to make it 5–2. The win earned not only earned the Flyers a spot in the record book, but a standing ovation from the Boston Garden crowd.

"There's a tremendous feeling of relief," Clarke told reporters. "Nobody can say we came in the back door. We set the record against one of the top teams and we did it in their building."

The record was broken exactly 70 days after their last loss. Remarked Linseman, "I've almost forgotten what it feels like to lose."

The Flyers returned to Philadelphia the next night to start a home-and-home set with the Hartford Whalers. The Spectrum crowd rewarded the Flyers with a thunderous ovation.

"The fans were always tremendous," says Propp. "They knew what was going on. And the support was awesome."

Propp rewarded them by scoring the first two goals of the game in a 4–2 victory. The Whalers played better three nights later at their temporary home in Springfield, Massachusetts. Propp scored twice, and Mel Bridgman's goal early in the third put the Flyers up 4–2, but Mark Howe, set up by his father, Gordie, pulled the Whalers within a goal, and then Brian Hill tied it. The Flyers held on over the last 13 minutes to preserve the 4–4 tie as the streak reached 31.

Wilson, Leach, and Kelly scored third-period goals as the Flyers held off the Winnipeg Jets 5–3, and after an overnight flight from Winnipeg to Denver, they jumped to a 3–0 lead against the Colorado Rockies on goals by Propp, MacLeish, and Dailey, but had to hold on late for a 3–2 victory.

After a six-day break, the Flyers opened 1980 by jumping to a 5–0 lead over the Rangers at Madison Square Garden en route to a 5–3 victory that pushed the streak to 34. It also broke the North American all-sports record of 33 straight games without a loss set by the Los Angeles Lakers.

Joked Rangers defenseman Carol Vadnais, "We play them again the last day of the season. We'll break their streak then."

January 6, 1980, saw the streak carry the Flyers into Buffalo for a game against the second-place Sabres. Al Hill scored to put the Flyers up 1–0 midway through the first, but they trailed 2–1 midway through the second after the home team got scores from Rick Martin and Danny Gare.

Ververgaert scored with 3:14 left in the second to tie the game, and Barber and MacLeish tallied goals in the third as the Flyers shuffled off with a 4–2 win and more stunned amazement in both locker rooms.

"You look at the travel, the schedule, the balance of the league, and it's impossible," said Sabres coach Scotty Bowman. "But it's not impossible. They've done it."

The streak was at 35 when the Flyers arrived in Minnesota on January 7, 1980. The hockey hotbed had 15,962 screaming fans, as well as 20 skaters dying to end the streak.

"We were like every team waiting to play them," said Craig Hartsburg, then a North Stars defenseman, in *Full Spectrum*. "We hoped they would keep winning so we could be the ones to end the streak."

Early on, it looked like that opportunity would fall to someone else. Barber scored just 3:49 into the game, but Minnesota came back to take a 3–1 lead after one period.

Holmgren, a St. Paul native, scored midway through the second period, but the goal was wiped out as the Flyers were whistled for having too many men on the ice. Just 63 seconds later, Hartsburg cashed in the power play to make it 4–1, and 21 seconds later Mike Polich scored to make it 5–1.

The North Stars added two more goals, and finally, after 35 games spanning 81 days, the streak was over in a thudding 7–1 defeat.

The final numbers on the streak are as mind-boggling now as they were then. The Flyers won 25 of the 35 games. They won six one-goal games, and 11 two-goal games. They beat second-overall Buffalo three times. They rallied from a two-goal deficit eight times and a three-goal hole once; they came from behind in the third period to prolong the streak on six occasions.

"It was a magical ride," Quinn recalled in *Full Spectrum*. "With that team, with that defense, there was no reason to think we could even put a 10-game streak together."

The 1979–1980 Flyers team is remembered almost as much for what it did—the 35–game unbeaten streak—as for what it didn't—win the Stanley Cup.

"We knew they either would be the streak team or the Cup winner," said Morganti. "It became their whole headline. It's their whole identity, it's the streak team."

Propp, though, disagrees.

"That's going to be looked at as one of the longest streaks in sports history," he said. "We still made it to the [Stanley Cup] Finals that year, and unfortunately lost in Game 6. We could have won it all that year. But it didn't take away at all from what we did during the season. I think if you ask most of the players, it's an accomplishment that will be there for years and years, and everyone on our team has to be very proud of it."

## MR. PLUS, MARK HOWE

In 40 years the Flyers have had a number of really good defensemen pull on the sweater, from original Flyer Joe Watson straight through to classy, consistent Eric Desjardins.

None, though, were better than Mark Howe.

The son of hockey legend Gordie Howe, Mark Howe is viewed by many as the greatest defenseman never to win the Norris Trophy. But on August 20, 1982, when the Flyers traded for him, he was the greatest member of the Hartford Whalers' doghouse.

Howe's problems dated to December 27, 1980. In a game against the Islanders, Howe fell into the goalpost and one of the metal spikes used at the time to anchor the post to the ice pierced his buttocks.

Howe was taken to the hospital, where doctors told him, "an inch one way, and [the metal] could have gone into my spinal cord; an inch the other way, it would have pierced my sphincter muscle, and I would have been walking around with a colostomy bag."

He lost nearly three and a half pints of blood, developed an infection which led to a second surgery to drain an abscess that had formed at the injury site, and his weight plummeted from 192 pounds to 176.

Howe should have sat out the rest of the season, but rushed back after 17 games despite feeling less than 100 percent. Promised he would be worked back into the lineup slowly, he wound up playing 26 minutes a night. He was in the top 10 in league scoring when he got hurt, so his final numbers for the 1980–1981 season (19 goals, 65 points, plus-10 rating) don't show just how much he struggled when he returned.

"Things were different then," he says today. "You didn't have the same workout facilities they do now. That made a difference."

The next season Howe's numbers plummeted—eight goals and 53 points in 76 games—as did his desire to stay in Hartford.

He said a trade was something both parties needed.

"They were a little disgruntled with me, and I was getting a little disgruntled with them," he says. "The people that were running the team then, they were unhappy with me, they thought I was underachieving, not playing well, and I was not playing well."

Howe had a no-trade clause in his contract, but told GM Larry Pleau he would waive it to go to one of four teams—Boston, the

Rangers, the Islanders, or the Flyers. Philadelphia, though, was his first choice.

The reason? Simple. "They won," Howe said.

"I had always played on winning teams, championship teams, my whole life," he said. "Hartford went a couple years, they didn't make the playoffs. I'm not a guy who so much loves to win as I hate to lose. And to me, they [Hartford] weren't making strides to get better at that time."

The Flyers were, and they sent forwards Ken Linseman and Greg Adams, plus two draft picks, to Hartford for Howe.

"I was something they didn't have," says Howe. "They had a big, strong, tough defense, but they didn't have a guy with a lot of mobility. I think they were looking for a guy to play the point on the power play. I'm in the business now of scouting, and you look for certain players for certain roles and I think I was a guy—I was young, I was 28 at the time—I could fill a role they needed at the time."

Howe immediately made the Flyers a better team and raised the caliber of play of any defense partner to career-best levels.

His first partner was Glen Cochrane, an heir to the tough-guy mantle previously held by Dave Schultz and Paul Holmgren. Cochrane had rung up 200-plus penalty minutes in his first four Flyers seasons.

"Before the [1982–1983] season, [coach] Bob [McCammon] calls [Cochrane] and me into his office," Howe recalled in a story on the Flyers' website. "He says, 'Mark, your job is to move the puck and run the power play. Cocher, make sure no one touches him.' When we left, Glen put this big arm around me and said, 'Don't worry. No one's gonna lay a hand on you.' That was music to my ears. In Hartford I used to get run 20 to 25 times a game. In Philly, I could just do my thing."

With the extra room, Howe had 20 goals, 67 points, a plus-47 rating. He won the first of his four Barry Ashbee Trophies as the team's top defenseman, also earned a spot as an NHL First-Team All-Star and helped Cochrane to a plus-42 rating.

In 1984–1985 Howe skated with Brad McCrimmon, and it wasn't long before the pair was ranked the best defense pairing in the league. Howe had 18 goals, 57 points, and a plus-51 rating,

**Though others are worthy of consideration, Mark Howe is the greatest defenseman in Flyers history.**

while McCrimmon added 43 points was a plus-52 as the Flyers reached the Stanley Cup Finals.

The next year the duo was even better—Howe finished a remarkable league-best plus-85, while McCrimmon was a plus-83. Even more amazing was that, besides Howe and McCrimmon, the Flyers did not have another plus defenseman on their roster. Howe also had his best offensive season, pocketing 24 goals and 82 points. He finished as a finalist for the Hart and Norris trophies, but won neither (Wayne Gretzky took the Hart, Paul

Coffey the Norris). He did, though, earn his first Bobby Clarke Trophy as team MVP as well as another Barry Ashbee Trophy.

The 1986–1987 season marked the final stretch of a three-year arc for the Howe-McCrimmon pairing. Playing through a bad back, Howe finished with just 15 goals and 58 points, but he put up a plus-57 rating, while McCrimmon was a plus-45.

Howe again won the Ashbee Trophy and again was a finalist for the Norris, this time losing out to Boston's Ray Bourque.

After the season, McCrimmon was traded to Calgary; in three seasons together the pair helped the Flyers reach two Stanley Cup Finals and made life easier for goaltenders Pelle Lindbergh, who won the Vezina Trophy in 1985, and Ron Hextall, who won the Vezina and Conn Smythe Trophy as playoff MVP in 1987.

In their three seasons together, Howe was a plus-193, while McCrimmon was a plus-180.

"We were plus-200 in three years [actually, plus-373]," Howe says of his time with McCrimmon. "I don't think Brad ever got the credit he deserved. Brad was a very quality hockey player, but just because players are great players doesn't mean they play well together. We had a great chemistry, we roomed together, we basically did everything together. It was great. You never had to think of the game; everything was instinct. We knew where each other was going to be. And even though we'd both screw up, have bad nights, nobody ever pointed the finger at each other. We'd always take the blame even if maybe the other guy deserved it. We were true teammates in every sense of the word. And we had the abilities to go along with it, and we had the team to go along with it.

"It's not to say the other guys were bad, and the stats sometimes work in your favor, but it's hard to deny the fact that when over three years you're [plus-373], they can take away 10 percent but they can't take away them all."

## HEXTALL SHOOTS…HE SCORES!

Most goalies use their sticks to deflect shots on net, or to make short outlet passes.

Ron Hextall, though, changed all that. The grandson of Hall of Fame forward Bryan Hextall and the son of former Rangers forward Bryan Hextall Jr., Ron inherited his family's skating ability, but not their position. Instead, he redefined how a goaltender plays the game.

Hextall had size (6′3″, 192 pounds) and athleticism unseen at his position. He also had intensity to spare, and certain peculiarities, like slamming his stick off the goalposts like a Keith Moon on ice.

"Sitting in between periods, he was so intense, he would sit and rock the whole intermission," says Kjell Samuelsson. "Then he would put his gear on and go out. It's like every period he walked into a fight. That was his thing. Every time he stepped on the ice, he was full out."

Adds Dave Poulin, "He played to the edge of what he had to to get out of him what he had. When he was at his best, he could play at that edge without going over."

Toeing that edge on the slippery ice wasn't always possible. Hextall often would slide from the sublime to the violently ridiculous. Ask Kent Nilsson what happened to those who strayed too close to the Flyers' goal.

"He was extremely intense, a lot more than most people," says Dave Brown. "He's an easygoing guy away from the ice, but that's how he played. To me, it's all the emotion of the game, and sometimes things like that happen. I don't think it's such a bad thing, in my opinion. Everyone goes off once in a while."

He nearly went off in his first NHL game. The 22-year-old rookie was handed the starting job to open the 1986–1987 season, and his first game came against the Edmonton Oilers.

When Wayne Gretzky came in on a breakaway, Hextall dragged a pad to stone the Great One. Gretzky said to Hextall, "Who the hell are you?"

Hextall shouted right back, "Who the hell are *you*?"

Hextall backstopped a 2–1 win that night, and cruised to a 37–21–6 record in 66 games, with a 3.00 goals-against average and a .902 save percentage. He won the Vezina Trophy and finished second (to the Los Angeles Kings' Luc Robitaille) for the Calder Trophy as league rookie of the year.

He was even better in the playoffs, starting all 26 games and going 15–11 with a 2.77 GAA and .908 save percentage. For nearly singlehandedly carrying the Flyers to Game 7 of the Stanley Cup Finals, he was awarded the Conn Smythe Trophy as playoff MVP. He was the first losing netminder, and the second rookie goalie, to ever win the award.

"For a full 80-game schedule, that was the best goaltending I've ever seen," says Mark Howe. "He was incredible his first year. For the most part, especially in the [Stanley Cup] Finals, as good as we played and as close as we came, we wouldn't have been that close without Ron Hextall, there's no doubt about it."

"There was a kid in Edmonton who was a stick boy," recalls Hextall today. "He said, 'I love the way you play, but you'll only be able to keep it up for five years.' I said I wanted to play for 20 years or 30 years if I could, and I'd still want to be the best."

He certainly didn't play his best in the 1987–1988 season. He rejoined the team after his eight-game suspension for slashing Nilsson across the legs during the Cup Finals, but they didn't play like a team expected to battle for a Stanley Cup.

When the Boston Bruins arrived at the Spectrum on December 8, 1987, the Flyers were limping along at 9–13–4, and they were wracked by a growing hatred for coach Mike Keenan.

Hextall, who had just signed a new eight-year contract, was an abysmal 4–9–3.

"We're a disgrace to the uniform," he told reporters after a game in November. "And I'm a lot of what's going wrong right now."

Things started going right that December night.

With the Flyers leading 4–2 with 1:43 left, Boston pulled goalie Reggie Lemelin for an extra attacker.

"The media kept asking me, 'Are you going to score?' and I said, 'Yeah, I'll score at some point,'" Hextall recalls. "It wasn't something I thought about. I felt like I was going to, [but] it's not like it was high on my priority list. It wasn't like it was something I was going out to do."

Only once had an NHL netminder been credited with a goal— the Islanders' Billy Smith in 1979, because he was the last Islander to touch a puck a Colorado player shot into his own net.

In 1971 Michel Plasse of the Central Hockey League's Kansas City Blues became the first goalie ever to shoot and score a goal, and Darcy Wakaluk of the American Hockey League's Rochester Americans had turned the trick just three days before the Flyers and Bruins took to the ice.

But when the Bruins' Gord Kluzak dumped the puck into the Flyers' end, Hextall saw his opportunity. He played the puck off the backboards just to the left of the cage, and with the closest Bruin more than 15 feet away, he wristed the puck down the ice, 20 feet in the air. It dropped a foot from the Bruins' blue line and skidded into history just inside the right post.

As Derrick Smith dug out the puck, teammates jumped off the bench to mob Hextall.

"I remember when I scored, the whole team came off the bench, it was like we were kids in a candy store," says Hextall. "The fact the whole team was excited was a thrill to me."

Another thrill would come a season later. The Flyers faced the Washington Capitals in the Patrick Division semifinals and were looking for revenge for Washington knocking them out of the playoffs the previous season.

The series was tied 2–2 when the teams met at the Cap Center in Landover, Maryland, on April 11, 1989. The Flyers scored three times in the third period to turn a 5–4 deficit into a 7–5 lead with 4:28 left to play.

When Jeff Chychrun was whistled for cross-checking Dino Ciccarelli, the Caps went on a power play with 2:33 remaining. Caps goalie Pete Peeters was pulled to make it a six-on-four advantage.

When Scott Stevens dumped the puck into the Flyers' end, Hextall saw another shot at history. He moved behind his goal to play the puck, took a step toward the goal line, and from next to the left post, let fly. The puck landed on the Washington side of the red line and slid inside the right post.

With 1:02 left to play, Hextall became the first goalie to shoot and score a goal in an NHL playoff game.

"Somebody told me the other day that it had been over 100 games since I had scored," Hextall joked after the game. "I guess it was time."

The Flyers rode the momentum of Hextall's historic goal to a series-clinching win two days later at the Spectrum, and advanced to the Wales Conference Finals.

That was the last hurrah for Hextall. Injuries limited him to just eight games the following season, and he was traded to the Quebec Nordiques in the blockbuster Eric Lindros deal in June 1992.

He came back to the Flyers in 1994, but the temper and talent both had diminished. He backstopped the Flyers to the 1995 Eastern Conference Finals, and split time with Garth Snow as the Flyers went to the Stanley Cup Finals in 1997.

When he retired after the 1998–1999 season, Hextall left as the Flyers' all-time leader in games played by a goalie (489) and wins (240), and his 18 shutouts are more than only Bernie Parent (50) and Roman Cechmanek (20). He's also the team's all-time leader in playoff games (84) and playoff wins (45). Besides the numbers, Hextall embodied all that Philadelphia hockey stood for.

"He was not a lunatic," says Brown. "He was extremely competitive. He was extremely serious about winning games. He was the kind of guy you wanted on your side, because no matter what you think of him, he competed every night and he was there for you and he gave you everything he had every night."

## TIM KERR, SULTAN OF THE SLOT

In 1979 Tim Kerr was part of the first class of 19-year-olds eligible for the NHL draft. While the pool of players was increased, the selection process remained at six rounds, meaning a number of good players went unpicked.

One of them was Kerr, who was playing for the Kingston Canadians of the Ontario Hockey Association. Top scout Gerry Melnyk hadn't been impressed by the 6'3", 230-pounder, but eastern scout Eric Coville convinced Melnyk to allow him to offer Kerr a contract.

"There were three teams that we were negotiating with," Kerr recalls. "When I was at my training camp in Kingston for my last year of junior, Eric Coville came to the practice one day and we went out to lunch and dinner and he kind of swayed me to choose Philadelphia."

Kerr made Coville look smart by scoring 40 goals in 63 games in his final junior season, and he added another six points in a seven-game stint with the Maine Mariners, the Flyers' American Hockey League club.

The next season, Kerr made the Flyers out of training camp and scored 22 goals, but injuries limited him to just 68 games.

Aches and pains became the early story of Kerr's career. In his first three NHL seasons, he had a total of 54 goals while playing in just 153 of 240 games.

"My first two years I had good years, scoring over 20 goals," he says. "The third year is when I had a knee injury. I rehabbed it and missed six weeks. Then my first game back it went out on me and I had to have surgery on it. I worked with [trainer] Pat Croce all year long and really built up my leg strength, which had never been done before. I think that propelled me to the next year and the next level."

The next year and next level were ones of historic proportions. In 1983–1984 he showed just what he was capable of when healthy, potting a career-high 54 goals while playing 79 games. He spent the 1984–1985 campaign proving his previous season was no fluke.

"It's an easy game to be a 20-goal scorer," says Kerr. "You have to score just once every four games. When you're counted on to score, there's extra pressure."

If he felt pressure he certainly didn't show it as he again potted 54 goals. He had five hat tricks and three times scored four in a game.

His biggest frustration from the previous season was the 1984 playoffs, when he was held scoreless in a three-game loss to the Washington Capitals in the Patrick Division semifinals.

He let all those frustrations out in the 1985 postseason.

The Flyers entered Game 3 of the best-of-five Patrick Division semifinal April 13, 1985 with a 2–0 series lead on the New York Rangers, and had a chance to win a playoff series from the Broadway Blueshirts for the first time in three tries.

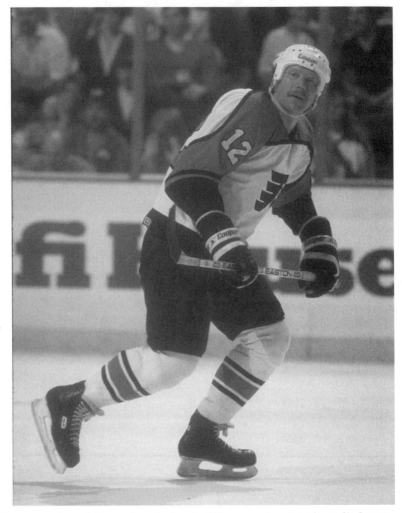

No one anchored themselves in front of the opposing team's goalie better than the burly but soft-handed Tim Kerr during his days with the Flyers.

The Flyers trailed 3–2 after Kerr's tripping penalty led to a Willie Huber goal at 9:18 of the second.

The deficit wouldn't last long, as Kerr more than atoned for his penalty. At 9:41 of the period, Mike Rogers was sent off for tripping Peter Zezel. With the Flyers on the advantage, Mark Howe rimmed a puck behind the Rangers goal to Ilkka Sinisalo along the right wall. He pushed the puck to Zezel, who set up below the goal line to the left of the Rangers goal. He threw a pass in front, where Kerr reached out and swept the puck past goalie Glen Hanlon to tie the game at 3–3 at 10:06.

Less than five minutes later, Murray Craven forced Hanlon to blindly throw the puck into the corner to his left. Kerr was there and fired a shot that went off Hanlon and the side of the net and bounced back into the slot. Rogers got a piece of it, but it pin-balled to Kerr in the right circle, and he rocketed a wrister past Hanlon to give the Flyers their first lead, at 14:58 of the period.

When Bob Brooke was penalized for dragging Rick Tocchet to the ice, the Flyers agains capitalized. On the ensuing offensive-zone faceoff, Kerr beat Larry Patey, winning the puck back to Howe at the left point. Hanlon stopped Howe's drive, but the rebound went to Zezel in the corner. He threw the puck into the slot, where Kerr shrugged off Barry Beck and backhanded the puck in for the natural hat trick.

Another penalty by Brooke, who was called for roughing when he punched Craven, gave the Flyers another power play. Zezel carried the puck across the attacking blue line, and as the Rangers closed on him, he dropped a pass to Kerr in the high slot. His one-timer found daylight under Hanlon's glove at 18:22 of the period, giving the Flyers a 6–3 lead.

The Rangers got two goals early in the third, but Pelle Lindbergh made the lead stand up, and the Flyers took the series-clinching 6–5 win.

Kerr's stunning performance set or tied four NHL records. He still owns the mark for fastest four goals in a playoff game, at 8 minutes, 16 seconds, and his three power-play goals in one period remains the NHL standard. His four goals in one period and four points in one period tied NHL marks.

"It was one of those games where the puck was finding me," he says in a drastic understatement. "When you're in the heat of the game, you don't really follow up on what's going on. It was pretty quick how it happened. Certainly it was great for the team. We were able to get through the first round that night. It was kind of magical what happened there."

He turned in another star performance a week later, assisting on the Flyers' three first-period goals in a 5–2 win over the Islanders in Game 2 of the Patrick Division Finals. But that would be Kerr's last shining playoff moment, as sprained knee ligaments suffered in Game 1 of the Wales Conference Finals against the Quebec Nordiques knocked him out for the remainder of the series. He returned against Edmonton in the Cup Finals and scored twice in the first three games, but knee pain ended his season early.

An infection he picked up during the preseason settled in the lining of his brain and kept him in the hospital and off the ice until the day before the start of the 1985–1986 season. Nothing could slow him, though, as he scored a personal-best 58 goals, including an NHL-record 34 on the power play. The glory was overshadowed, though, by Lindbergh's death.

The following season Kerr again was outstanding. Highlighted by the fifth four-goal game of his career—coincidentally, on the night of his bachelor party—he finished again with 58 goals. In NHL history, Kerr is one of just nine players to score 50 in four or more consecutive seasons, joining a list that includes Mike Bossy (nine straight), Wayne Gretzky (six), Guy Lafleur (six), Phil Esposito (five), Brett Hull (five), Marcel Dionne (five), Michel Goulet (four), and Jari Kurri (four).

Kerr kept scoring when the 1987 playoffs started. He had three goals in the Flyers' first-round win over the Rangers, and in the Patrick Division Finals against the Islanders he had a hat trick in a Game 1 win and two power-play goals and an assist in a Game 4 victory.

Those two goals, though, would be his last. Persistent shoulder problems meant that for a second straight time, the Flyers made the Stanley Cup Finals, and Kerr had to watch.

"It wasn't a pain thing, it was just the ligaments were stretched," he said. "It got to a point in that Islanders series, my arm sitting by my side, [the shoulder] would separate. I couldn't even hold a stick."

Over the summer Dr. John Gregg operated on the back of Kerr's shoulder to tighten the ligaments, and two weeks later performed the same procedure on the front of his shoulder. During the second operation, Gregg inserted a screw to help stabilize the joint, but during a check-up six weeks later, Gregg noticed the pin had shifted because it wasn't long enough. He removed it and inserted a longer screw.

When training camp started, though, Kerr felt feverish, had lost weight and still was struggling with weakness in his shoulder. "They thought I was addicted to pain killers," he says. Further examination, though, showed the screw had become infected and needed to be removed. But first the infection had to be dealt with. "I was on IV antibiotics," Kerr said. "They would change my antibiotics three times a day."

Five surgeries and months of rehab later, Kerr finally returned to the lineup in mid-March. He also got into six playoff games but was a shell of himself. The player nicknamed the Sultan of the Slot resembled a slot machine—a one-armed bandit.

Despite losing a season in the prime of his career, Kerr holds no ill-will toward Gregg.

"It was unfortunate," he says today. "I don't look back. Dr. Gregg thought he put the right length screw in. Maybe I did something to pull it out. It was unfortunate. Then the infection thing, that was crazy. It was just kind of a wash-out year."

A summer of rest reinvigorated Kerr, and he pumped in 48 goals in 1988–1989, and kept going in the postseason. He had four goals in the six-game opening-round win over Washington, and in the next round against Pittsburgh went on a scoring binge. He had a hat trick in a 4–2 win in Game 2, two assists in a 4–3 overtime loss in Game 3, a pair of power-play goals in a 4–1 win in Game 4, and two goals and two assists in a wild 10–7 loss in Game 5.

With the Flyers trailing the series 3–2, Kerr's two first-period goals—his third straight two-goal game—propelled the Flyers to a 6–2 series-tying victory, and two days later they closed out the Pens in Game 7.

But a broken thumb suffered in Game 6 left him unable to do more than grip his stick, and he was held scoreless as the Flyers lost to Montreal in the conference final. His efforts, though, did not go unrecognized, as he was awarded the Bill Masterton Trophy for perseverance and dedication to the game.

That would be Kerr's last shining moment with the Flyers. In November 1989 he had surgery to remove two bone chips, had a bone spur was decompressed, and a tear in his biceps tendon was repaired. He was limited to 40 games, though he scored 24 goals and 48 points.

The shoulder, though, didn't ache as bad as his heart on the morning of October 16, 1990. Kerr was awakened in his Pittsburgh hotel room by a call from a doctor at Pennsylvania Hospital, who told Kerr his wife Kathy, 10 days after giving birth to the couple's daughter, Kimberly, had died due to a pelvic infection that had caused what the hospital called a "sudden cardiopulmonary complication."

Kerr took two weeks off, but a broken heart was complicated by a broken knee, as torn cartilage limited him to just 10 goals and 24 points in 27 games.

He was left unprotected in the 1991 expansion draft, was chosen by the San Jose Sharks and then immediately dealt to the New York Rangers. He played one season with the Rangers and spent a final campaign with Hartford before retiring after the 1992–1993 season.

Kerr ranks third on the club's all-time list with 363 goals and sixth with 650 points, despite playing just 601 games over 11 seasons. He's also the club's all-time leader with 145 power-play goals and 17 hat tricks.

Most of those goals came from within inches of the net.

"There was no secret to where I was going to go," Kerr says. "For me it was a game within a game. That [front of the net] was my territory. People like Peter Zezel and Dave Poulin and Pelle Eklund, they knew where I was going to be and it was their job to get the puck to me and they did a great job. That's the only reason you're successful, because of the players around you."

# THE FAT LADY SINGS

## BOBBY CLARKE WINS IT IN BOSTON

There was some irony to the fact that the Flyers had so much trouble winning at Boston Garden. It was Ed Snider seeing long lines of Bruins fans outside the Garden, waiting to buy tickets to a last-place team, that inspired him to start the Flyers.

Since winning there November 12, 1967, they hadn't won at the Garden in 18 games, losing 16 of them. In the 1973–1974 season, the Flyers had lost all three trips to New England, part of the reason they finished with one fewer point than the Bruins, ceding them home-ice advantage in the 1974 Stanley Cup Finals.

The Flyers' personal Boston Massacre reached 17 losses in 19 games when the Flyers dropped Game 1 of the series.

With Bill Barber off for interference, Wayne Cashman opened the scoring for the Bruins 12:05 into the game. Fifty-six seconds later, Gregg Sheppard made it 2–0.

The Flyers battled back. Orest Kindrachuk broke through when he poked in a rebound at 7:47 of the second period. And at 5:32 of the third, Bobby Clarke jammed at a loose puck hard enough and long enough for it to finally slither under goalie Gilles Gilbert.

The momentum seemed to swing toward the Flyers, and in the game's final minute, Clarke led a three-on-two rush. He left a pass for Cowboy Flett, who faked Gilbert out of the net, but pushed his shot into the post. Orr smothered the rebound and, off the ensuing faceoff, led the charge into the Flyers' end. Ken Hodge fed a pass back to Orr at the point, and his shot went through traffic and between Bernie Parent's pads with just 22 ticks left on the clock.

Despite the final-minute loss, the Flyers were upbeat. "We'd outplayed them, and they knew it," said Clarke in *Full Spectrum*. "We were in better shape than the Bruins."

Parent was even more positive. "We were still living in the New York series in the first period," he told reporters, referring to the Flyers' semifinals win against the Rangers. "But when we went back to our system in the second period, you saw what happened. We'll beat those SOBs the next game."

It looked like empty confidence when Game 2 started. Cashman opened the scoring at 14:24 of the first period, and Phil Esposito made it 2–0 just over three minutes later.

But just like Game 1, they again took the play to the Bruins in the second period. Clarke brought the Flyers within a goal at 1:08 of the second when he tipped a Flett shot pats Gilbert, but that would be as close they would get until the game's final moments.

As the numbers on the clock began to dwindle, coach Fred Shero pulled Parent for an extra attacker. Ross Lonsberry dumped the puck into the Boston end and then rushed to harass Orr in the corner. Orr pushed the puck along the wall to Hodge, but Clarke jammed him up, and the puck slid back down to Rick MacLeish in the corner.

As MacLeish and Orr fought for the puck, the Flyers' forward heard an unlikely voice screaming for it: Moose Dupont. Without looking, MacLeish threw a perfect pass onto the Moose's stick as he reached the hash marks. A stunned Gilbert didn't have time to square himself up, and Dupont was into his Moose Shuffle as the red light came on.

There was just 52 seconds left on the clock.

Both goalies reverted to their impregnable selves in the extra session. Gilbert made in-close saves on MacLeish, Simon Nolet, and Terry Crisp. John Bucyk, sent in alone by a Sheppard pass that bounced off referee Art Skov, went to his backhand, but Parent made a pad save.

As overtime reached its midpoint, Dave Schultz jumped over the wall for a shift with Flett and Clarke, his first ice time of the extra session.

Schultz raced after an Ed Van Impe dump-in and forced Carol Vadnais into a bad clearing attempt. Terry O'Reilly had the puck, but Clarke sealed him against the boards and forced him to push the puck back into the Bruins' end. Schultz pulled the puck off the wall and sent a pass into the high slot for Flett. The Cowboy tried getting off a backhander, but instead passed between the skates of Bruins defenseman Dallas Smith to a cutting Clarke, who had beaten Andre Savard off the half-boards. A belly-flopping Gilbert stopped Clarke's backhander, but the Flyers' captain wouldn't be denied on the rebound. With an empty net, Clarke casually flipped a forehander into the top of the net at 12:01 of overtime.

As Clarke leaped into the air to celebrate the goal, the hopes of his team and the burgeoning Flyers Nation of fans rose with him.

"I don't see how anybody could have doubts about us now," Clarke told reporters after the game. "We know we can beat them."

And that's just what they did 10 days later.

The Flyers swept a pair of games at the Spectrum to take a 3–1 series lead back to Boston for an elimination Game 5. The Flyers' Garden win streak was ended at one, though, as the home team took a 5–1 decision.

In Game 6 at the Spectrum on May 19, with Parent playing the game of his life and MacLeish's incredible hand-eye coordination providing the game's only goal, the Flyers won their first Stanley Cup.

# DAVE POULIN

Dave Poulin wasn't good enough for Canadian junior hockey. He wasn't good enough to be recruited by a major NCAA Division I hockey program. He wasn't even good enough to play for a top-level team in Europe.

But Dave Poulin was good enough to play for the Flyers. He certainly was good enough to captain a pair of teams to the

Stanley Cup Finals. And he was good enough to become one of the toughest, proudest, most dignified people to pull on a Flyers sweater.

Poulin's first introduction to the ice was as a figure skater. But when his family moved from Timmins, Ontario, to Mississauga, a suburb of Toronto, Poulin ditched his figure skates for hockey footwear.

At 165 pounds, he was considered too small for major junior hockey. Through a friend, he earned a hockey scholarship to Notre Dame, where he spent four years playing well on the ice and excelling in the classroom. He was so good, he earned a spot in the prestigious Proctor & Gamble management training program.

Before moving into the business world, he got married and spent a six-month hockey honeymoon playing for Rogle, a second-division team in Sweden.

Once the European season ended, Poulin was ready to put away his stick for good. But Ted Sator, his coach in Sweden, recommended him to Flyers coach/GM Bob McCammon, who was looking for late-season help for the Maine farm club.

It didn't take long for the Flyers to see they had stumbled into a gold mine.

Poulin had 16 points in 16 AHL games and was called up to the Flyers for the last two games of the 1982–1983 season. In his first game, in front of his hometown fans at Maple Leaf Gardens, Poulin scored on his first two shots.

His success continued with four points in the club's three-game playoff loss to the Rangers.

Days later Poulin received a letter from his boss-to-be at Proctor & Gamble. The letter included a clipping of Poulin's performance in Toronto and a note: "Obviously our paths are going different ways. I'm happy for you. Best of luck."

The next season Poulin centered a line with Brian Propp and Tim Kerr and finished with 31 goals and 76 points in 73 games.

Despite his breakout season, there was little recognition outside the Delaware Valley.

"When I got my first hockey card," he recalls, "I had a great rookie year, scored a bunch of points. On the back it said, 'Works hard.' I wanted it to say I scored 30 goals, played on a good line. It just said, 'Works hard.'"

Those two words, though, defined Poulin's career. "It's a skill that translates to whatever you're doing," he says. "Fast skater or hard shot doesn't always translate to other things, but working hard translates."

And while the hockey (or hockey-card making) world might not have noticed, others did. Poulin's road roommate was Bobby Clarke, and the pair quickly grew close. Poulin and his wife, Kim, were on vacation with Clarke and his wife, Sandy, when Clarke was named GM of the Flyers. And it was Clarke who convinced Mike Keenan to name Poulin team captain in just his second season.

"There were a lot of moving parts in that," Poulin says now. "Darryl Stitler was on the team, but after the luncheon to kick off the year, he was traded. Billy Barber was there, but he was hurt, and it was unclear where his career was with his knee injury." There were other veterans, like Mark Howe and Brad McCrimmon, who had served as alternate captains with other teams, but it didn't take long for players to learn that Poulin was the epitome of the word *warrior*. Little short of a militia could slow him down, and his willingness to play through pain became legendary.

"I think that's sort of the only reason that I could be in the league," he says. "I had to push myself to do that. That's the way I functioned."

In the 1985 playoffs Poulin suffered a slightly torn ligament in his left knee in the opening series against the Rangers and sat out the rest of that series and the next. He returned for the conference finals against the Quebec Nordiques. He scored a goal in Game 2, but suffered cracked ribs when he was sticked in the chest by Mario Marois. Poulin sat out Games 3 and 4, but returned wearing a flak jacket in Game 5, which the Flyers won to bring themselves home to the Spectrum one game from the Cup finals.

Despite the win, Poulin wasn't happy with his teammates' effort, and let them know it at a meeting before practice the next day.

"In order to win, we knew we needed everybody going, and that wasn't happening," he told reporters. "We're a confident, secure group of people, so we could talk over our problems honestly and openly."

The ultimate leader, Poulin turned up his own play in Game 6.

The Flyers took a 1–0 lead into the second period, but it immediately came under fire when Joe Patterson was sent off for a penalty in the first minute of the second period. Propp followed Patterson to the box 37 seconds later, leaving the Flyers two men down against the high-powered Nordiques.

Poulin, the Flyers' best defensive forward, lost a faceoff in his own end. The puck went back to Marois, who was working the point with Peter Stastny.

"We talked about how they kept collapsing in to the box," recalls Poulin. "Those guys had gone across the top so well, Marois and Peter Stastny. Your natural thought is to compress into a triangle and get deeper and deeper. I just stepped out."

With his simple move, he was able to get a stick on a Marois pass at the top of the circle. He gobbled up the loose disk with nothing but open ice ahead of him.

"I had such a long way to go on the breakaway," says Poulin. "From the top of the circle, it was such a race."

"It was just a reaction," he said to reporters after the game. "You rely on your reflexes out there. It hit my stick at a perfect angle, and I got the breakaway, although somebody was coming fast. I could hear the chop-chop of a skate. It was near the end of a shift, and I haven't played much in the last five weeks, so I wasn't sure I'd get there first."

He drew extra energy from a roaring Spectrum crowd.

"It shook," he recalls of the building that night. "You wonder sometimes at the peak of sound how can it get louder, and it gets louder."

Poulin said he didn't decide where he was going to put the shot until he got about five feet in front of goalie Mario Gosselin.

"I decided to put it upstairs because our scouting reports said you have to go upstairs, top of the building to beat him," said Poulin.

He didn't just beat Gosselin with the goal. The series was over the minute the red light went on.

Dave Poulin's pre-NHL background helped him become an excellent all-around player and prepared him to be captain for the Flyers.

"It was a killer for them. It demoralized them and gave us a lift," he said that night. "I think because of the potential it had for them—they were looking at scoring one, maybe two goals and going ahead...it had to be demoralizing."

Today, he believes that despite the long run-up from one end of the ice to the other, Gosselin wasn't ready for him.

"He was probably thinking he had two minutes off at that point," Poulin said. "You're up on a five-on-three in a very intense series....I'm sure human nature says there's a sigh of relief there."

Despite the joy from winning the series, it wasn't enough to cure his ailing knee or aching ribs, and the Flyers fell in five hard games in the Cup Finals to the Edmonton Oilers.

The next season put Poulin's leadership abilities to the test when it fell to him to first inform, and then help guide his teammates though the nightmare death of goalie Pelle Lindbergh.

In the 1987 Stanley Cup Finals, Poulin again suffered broken ribs, but refused to miss any time.

"I watched him every night," recalls teammate Mark Howe. "He'd be in the locker room a half an hour before everyone else, and they'd spend a half an hour freezing, doing a complete [nerve] block on his rib cage just so he can play games. The needles were so long, I thought they were going to come out the other side. That's the dedication."

To Poulin, though, it was just the nature of the game.

"You're in the locker room and you've grown with these guys," he says. "You were going to play if you could. As soon as you got medical clearance that you were going to be fine, you played."

By the 1989–1990 season, with Paul Holmgren as head coach and the Flyers close to missing the playoffs, Poulin lost first his captaincy, then his spot with the club. He was dealt to the Boston Bruins in a deal Clarke ranks among the worst and most painful of his career.

"Crushing," is how Poulin recalls feeling on that March day in 1990 when he was moved out. "But it was the best thing that happened. You needed a change at that time, even though you didn't know it. Afterward, you learn that's the harsh reality of the business. I had a lot going on in my life. It was a whole lot of things. I came very close to retiring at that time. I had a business going on. I had worked in the offseason and had a good business situation I was in: stock brokerage."

Instead, Poulin stayed in the game, helping the Bruins, along with the expatriated Brian Propp, to the 1991 Cup Finals, where they lost to Mario Lemieux and the Pittsburgh Penguins. He also played for the Washington Capitals before retiring in 1995.

## THE GAME THAT WOULD NEVER END

Game 4 of the 2000 Eastern Conference semifinals wasn't exactly a must-win for the Flyers, but it was pretty close.

After losing the first two games of the series in Philadelphia, the Flyers needed overtime in Pittsburgh to win Game 3 on Andy Delmore's goal 11 minutes into the extra session.

With just one day to recover, the Flyers hit the ice for Game 4 on May 4, 2000, in Pittsburgh.

Alexei Kovalev gave the Penguins a 1–0 lead with a wicked low slap shot just 2:22 into the game, and Pens goalie Ron Tugnutt nearly made that lead stand up. Finally, though, the Flyers answered 4:47 into the third period. Four seconds into a Flyers power play, Daymond Langkow beat Jan Hrdina on an offensive-zone faceoff, pushing the puck back to Eric Desjardins. Desjardins's slap shot through traffic deflected off a scrum in front, and after a replay review to make sure it wasn't knocked in by a John LeClair high stick, the goal counted. The game was tied and headed for overtime.

LeClair then nearly won it on the first shift of the extra session, stealing the puck from Tugnutt behind the Pens' goal, wheeling in front and sending a pass into the slot to Langkow, but he rang his one-timer off the crossbar 31 seconds into overtime.

There would be other scoring opportunities, but Tugnutt and the Flyers' Brian Boucher stood tall, and the game wore on and on.

Three overtimes. Four overtimes. Five overtimes.

The contest became less of a game and more of a war of attrition. Players sounded more like Civil War soldiers from a Ken Burns documentary, writing home about dwindling supplies as food and beverage stocks disappeared.

"After the second overtime, third overtime period, we're out of power gels, power bars, Gatorade," recalls Keith Primeau. "We

Keith Primeau recalls teammates scrounging for something to eat between periods during the incredible five-overtime win against the Penguins in Game 4 of the 2000 Eastern Conference semifinals.

were looking for food. We were literally looking for food to come into the locker room because you needed to get something into your system."

"Guys were coming in and saying, 'Somebody just end it, please,'" recalls Boucher. "Guys went through the pizza we ordered for after the game."

Were it not for that team's closeness, the night would have been even harder.

"We had a special bond," recalls Primeau. "We weren't the most talented group. Our lineup included Craig Berube and Keith Jones and Rick Tocchet and Chris Therien. We had a really loose group of guys."

With concessions stands closed in Mellon Arena, Tocchet tried having pizza delivered to the building, but no pizzeria would believe a professional athlete was calling.

"Ran out of everything," remembers LeClair. "Food was a big issue for some guys. There were some guys who were really struggling with it."

Some, like Jones, were struggling more than others.

"Between the second and third [overtimes]," remembers Primeau, "Jonesy wasn't playing very much at all, but you thought he was about to die of starvation."

"I got in a groove where I was changing for him for a while," says LeClair. "He'd go about 10 feet and come back to the bench and say, 'That's all I've got.' He was cutting it short. It was funny."

Jones didn't dispute that comment on the Flyers' 40th anniversary DVD, when he said, "I can remember going on for a shift, standing at center ice right in front of our bench, looking one way, looking the other way, and saying, 'Change.'"

The players skated so hard for so long, they passed the point of exhaustion and entered the realm of the bizarre.

"I remember it being comical at times," says LeClair. "I went to the bench at times, and you get past the point of being tired. It almost got to the point, halfway through [each overtime] period, 'Let's just get through this and get back to the locker room.' I was taking IVs to keep from cramping. Jonesy was hysterical. I'm laughing at him, and he's cracking jokes. He complained about everything."

After the game, *Courier Post* reporter Chuck Gormley recalls, "I remember Keith Jones saying, 'I'm like a bear, I'm living off my fat.'"

It wasn't just the players getting desperate, either. Food was scarce for everyone.

"They ran out of any food in the press box," remembers Gormley. "I think there were PR guys from the Pens running downstairs and getting water bottles for us. It was comical."

"After a while," said Gary Dornhoefer, who was working the telecast for Comcast SportsNet, "You don't even know what time it is, you don't know how many periods you played."

His play-by-play partner, Jim Jackson, recalled one of his funnier moments was watching Dornhoefer munch on a slice of pizza when the announce crew was told they were going back live on the air sooner than expected. As Jackson was speaking, he noticed pizza sauce dripping out of the corner of Dornhoefer's mouth.

Steve Levy, doing the TV broadcast for ESPN, read a prewritten promo early in the fourth overtime for the next show after the game. He then laughingly said, "Yeah, sure, SportsCenter is next. Whenever next is."

Next didn't come for another period and a half.

It wasn't until Primeau jumped on the ice midway through the fifth overtime that the game came to a merciful conclusion.

Said Primeau on the Flyers' 40th anniversary DVD, "Two other times earlier in the game I had gone wide on [Penguins defenseman] Darius Kasparaitis, only to get cut off at the net, so I faked like I was going to go outside on him again. And once he crossed his feet over, I was able to pull the puck back on my forehand and get a shot off."

Boucher said he had watched from a distance as Primeau tried the same move earlier in the night: "I think Preems tried that same move maybe four or five times that night, and each time the puck rolled off his stick. He was able to pull it off, and it ended up being a great shot and a great goal."

The puck rocketed over Tugnutt's glove and into the middle of the net, ending the game at 2:35 AM, after 92 minutes, 1 second of overtime. At a total time of 152:01, it was the longest game in the modern era of the NHL (only a pair of six-overtime games in the 1930s went longer).

Boucher didn't need to see the winning goal; he heard it clearly from 200 feet away.

"There's a different sound when it hits the front bar and the back bar," he said. "The front bar, it's more like a ping, and the back bar is more like a clunk, and you can hear it go clunk, and you could hear it clear as day."

Today, says Primeau of his historic goal, "I think it was a combination of [relief and joy]. At the time I just looked at it as we had given ourselves an opportunity to get back in the series. I told people that until I retire...I don't think I'll understand the magnitude of the game until my playing career is over, and I'll look back at it as a memorable moment in my career.

"It's was one of those nights you remember vividly. I remember [Langkow] hitting the post on the first shift of the first overtime. He scores there, none of this happens. Then it goes five periods. It's

# JOHN LECLAIR SCORES SIX-HOLE

John LeClair scored a lot of goals for the Flyers, but only one led to a change in the NHL rulebook.

On April 14, 2000, at 4:53 of the second period, LeClair one-timed a Dan McGillis shot on Buffalo goalie Dominik Hasek. The red light went on, and the Flyers went on to win the game 2–1.

One problem: LeClair didn't score. The puck found a hole in the netting outside the right post—call it the six-hole—but was ruled a goal because the league didn't have access to the ESPN camera angle that clearly showed the puck not passing between the posts. After that, referees were instructed to check the netting on the goals before each game.

amazing, especially against a team as skilled as that team. For Brian to hold them from scoring for five periods was really a feat in itself."

Boucher says it's a good thing Primeau scored when he did. He finished with 57 saves on 58 shots, but when the fifth overtime began, the rookie netminder had no idea how much he had left in him.

"I know, for me, that eighth period was enough. I can remember scraping my crease at the start of the period and my hips cramping up."

The win made for a fun trip back across Pennsylvania. There wasn't much celebrating, though, as Primeau remembers. "The flight home," he says, "all I can remember is hearing Eric Desjardins dry-heaving in the bathroom."

Boucher said the most celebrating he did was on his way down the ice to join his teammates: "I remember skating down, and I tapped [referee] Rob Shick on the head, like I was celebrating with him. It was an awesome feeling."

Of the unique evening, Gormley recalls, "It was comical but intense. It wasn't like watching the Devils. It wasn't like nobody had any chances. There were end-to-end rushes, there were incredible saves, missed nets. And it was great. It was great action. That game was incredible."

# THE FLYERS FAMILY

## BOBBY CLARKE

No story can be told about the Philadelphia Flyers without a sizable chunk being devoted to the club's all-time greatest player, Bob Clarke.

From second-round draft pick to Hall of Fame player to championship team builder, Clarke's face is prominently carved into the Flyers' version of Mount Rushmore.

"We have been [joined at the hip]," says team chairman Ed Snider. "And I'm proud of it."

For those who don't know Clarke, he can give off an aloof, almost intimidating aura, a degree of inapproachability. He was all fire and brimstone on the ice, and almost the same as a manager.

"He's revered," said Rod Brind'Amour. "He's a godlike figure. I was always nervous around him."

"I think he speaks his mind," says Keith Primeau. "I think he does it in a style that's very small-town Canadian. What you see is what you get. If what I say offends you, it's your problem, not mine."

Adds agent Rick Curran, who went toe-to-toe with Clarke many times in contract negotiations, "I really like Clarkie. There's a person that's not always right, but you know one thing, whatever he says and does comes from his heart."

Getting to know Clarke, what you find today is a grandfather who loves his family and hockey—especially Flyers hockey—in equal parts. He only listens to oldies music and programs the same radio station into all his car stereo presets—when he can get the buttons to work.

"He actually returned a car because he couldn't make the buttons work," says his daughter, Jody, who works at the Flyers' practice site in Voorhees.

She adds, "He only listens to the same three CDs over and over. Patsy Cline, Roy Orbison, and his all-time favorite is Gordon Lightfoot. I have to keep the CD in my house for when my dad comes over."

Despite his outstanding numbers in junior hockey, Clarke slipped to the second round of the 1969 draft due to his diabetes. Snider pushed for his selection anyway, but it nearly blew up in his face. Snider arrived that fall at training camp, and on his first day watching Clarke, the player fainted. Clarke had overslept and skipped breakfast in his haste to get to the rink on time. It was the only time in his career he had such an occurrence.

"As long as I looked after myself, the diabetes wouldn't affect my game," Clarke said. "I was playing in Flin Flon [Manitoba], and I guarantee you the travel and the hockey life up there was a lot tougher than the hockey life in Philadelphia. And the travel was a lot easier [in the NHL] than it was in Flin Flon. So if I could play junior in Flin Flon, and if I was good enough to play in the NHL, it was a lot easier to play in the NHL than it was up there."

And he certainly was good enough for the NHL.

No player defined the Broad Street Bullies era more than Clarke. He captained the team to three straight Stanley Cup Finals and two championships. He had the finesse to score 358 goals and dish out a Flyers record 852 assists for a team-best 1,210 points.

"Bob Clarke was a great, great hockey player," says Snider. "They talk about [Wayne] Gretzky seeing the ice, Clarke was the same way. When he went into the corner with somebody, he either came out with [the puck] or nobody did. He never lost a battle in the corners."

He also ran up 1,453 penalty minutes, fourth all-time on the franchise list, and many who watched him or played against him called him one of the dirtiest players in the game.

# CLARKE CONTRACT

Despite leading the Flyers in scoring in the 1969 preseason, Bobby Clarke went into the final exhibition game without a contract.

He had rejected the club's first offer, a two-way deal that would have paid him one amount if he played in the NHL and a lesser amount if he was in the minors. Clarke's objection to the deal wasn't the NHL salary. It was the minor-league end.

"I was working in the mines [at home in the summer], and I was making $10,000, and you're offering me $7,500 to play? That's not fair. Why should I take a pay cut?" he said.

The morning of the final game, in Hershey, Pennsylvania, Keith Allen made another proposal, in the parking lot outside the arena: $14,000 for the season if he was in the NHL, $10,000 if was in the minors, and a $5,000 signing bonus.

Clarke signed the deal while leaning on the trunk of Allen's car.

"If I hadn't learned to lay on a two-hander once in a while, I'd never have left Flin Flon," he once told a Canadian writer.

The people who didn't like Clarke never played with him. Those who did call him an inspiration, a captain who motivated the players around him to lift their games.

"Just a tireless worker," said Bob Kelly. "In practice and in games. Played through a lot of pain, took a lot of hits."

"No one worked harder on the ice than Clarke," added Gary Dornhoefer. "He led by example, and that's what you want a captain to do. He never gave up. The fights for the puck, the aggressiveness in the corner, he did whatever he had to do to win a hockey game. His attitude and how he played rubbed off on everyone else."

Clarke understands his place among the game's greats, but it's a chore to get him to talk about himself.

"I've tried to understand what they call leadership when it relates to me, and I really can't," Clarke told Jim Jackson in *Walking Together Forever*. "When I played, I just played."

He played to a Hall of Fame level for 15 seasons, winning a pair of Stanley Cups; three Hart Trophies as league MVP (1973, 1975, 1976); a Lester B. Pearson Award for being the league's best player, as voted by fellow players (1973); a Bill Masterton Trophy for commitment to hockey (1972); and the Frank J. Selke Trophy as the league's best defensive forward (1983).

With Clarke at the forefront, the Flyers became the most successful of the original six expansion franchises, a draw at home or on the road. You can turn on an NHL game being played anywhere in the U.S. or Canada, and there's a better-than-average chance you'll see a fan in a Flyers sweater. While some complain the Broad Street Bullies were the worst thing that ever happened to the glorious history of hockey, there's no question fans on both sides of the border loved their brawling style.

"I thought it was exciting," recalls Dave Brown, who grew up a Flyers fan in Saskatoon, Saskatchewan. "I remember where I was the first year they won the Cup. I would have been 11, 12 years old. I was at my uncle's, we were up at the lake and listening to it on the radio. I remember when they won it. We identified with them because we liked that style."

"Growing up, it was kind of neat," said Windsor, Ontario native Tim Kerr. "You'd turn on Hockey Night in Canada and you'd see some fights and some aggressive play."

Another Ontario native extolled Clarke's virtues to his son, who ended up playing for Clarke's Flyers in the 1990s. The man's name was Carl Lindros.

Clarke was 34 when the 1984 playoffs ended, but the Flyers were going through a transitional phase, and coach/GM Bob McCammon had been fired, leaving a hole in the team's front office. Team president Jay Snider had a list of one to fill the position—Clarke.

"I still intended to play," Clarke says now. "I think I was I still one of the better players when Washington beat us [in the playoffs]. In those days 34, 35 was getting a lot older for a player, but defensively I was still a really capable player, capable of helping this team."

**Bobby Clarke is unquestionably the Flyers all-time greatest player.**

But the offer was made, and Clarke knew it wouldn't last forever.

"Had I kept playing, which I could have done, I don't know, maybe I would have stayed in hockey—scouting, coaching. I had no vision of what I was going to do. Jay Snider offered me this position, and I knew I could play for a few more years, but I knew the end was coming. If that's what the Flyers thought was right for me, then okay."

As he said the day he was introduced in his new role, "Brighter minds than mine thought I was capable of doing this, so I jumped at it."

Clarke took the job as seriously as he took his playing career. The wild, shaggy hair was tamed and trimmed to a professional length; the false front teeth that seemed to have a homing beacon on teammates' beer mugs stayed in their owner's mouth; and the hockey sweater and skates were replaced by a suit, tie, and dress shoes. And Bobby was shortened to the more corporate-sounding Bob.

The love of the game and the loyalty to the organization, though, never wavered. His first stint as GM ran from 1984 to 1990. In that time, the team went to Stanley Cup Finals in 1985 and 1987, and earned five playoff appearances in six seasons.

In his first major decision, he hired Mike Keenan to coach the team. He drafted key players like Scott Mellanby, Kerry Huffman, and Dominic Roussel, and made trades for Murray Craven, Kjell Samuelsson, Chico Resch, and J.J. Daigneault.

There also were misses, including bad trades that sent away stalwarts like Lindsay Carson, Doug Crossman, Brad McCrimmon, Peter Zezel, Dave Brown, and two months apart in 1990, Dave Poulin and Brian Propp.

Clarke got little in return in those deals, and more often than not, his drafts were failures. With the final pick in the first round of the 1985 draft, Clarke took center Glen Seabrooke, who played in 19 NHL games, passing on Joe Nieuwendyk and Mike Richter. In 1986 he went for Huffman at number 20 overall rather than Adam Graves, who went two picks later. He chose Darren Rumble in the first round in 1987, and he made Claude Boivin the 14th overall choice in 1988. The top choices in 1989, second-round picks Greg Johnson and Patrik Juhlin, played a total of 56 games with the Flyers—all by Juhlin.

It all culminated in a 30–39–11 record in the 1989–1990 season. The 71 points were the fewest for the club since the 1971–1972 season, and the Flyers missed the playoffs for the first time since 1972.

"Through most of it, we were always competitive, we were always good, we were always trying to do the right things to try and win the Cup," says Clarke. "We made mistakes, I made mistakes along the way, but some of the things I did were right, too."

But with fans chanting "Bob Must Go," Jay Snider knew something had to be done.

On April 16, 1990, Jay Snider called Clarke in for a short meeting, where the club president told the face of the franchise it was time for a facelift. He asked Clarke to stay on in a yet-to-be created position, but Clarke refused and asked for the move to be announced as a firing.

When Jay Snider fired Clarke, Ed Snider was at his home in California with his new wife and daughter. Despite being 3,000 miles away from the battle lines, the owner knew there was dissension in the ranks.

"It was like having two sons that were squabbling," he says. "I tired to patch things up, and I couldn't."

When pushed, Ed backed his birth son over his adopted favorite, and just like that, the unthinkable had become reality.

In hindsight, Clarke says getting fired wasn't as awful a thing as he thought at the time.

"Getting fired was the worst and the best," he says now. "It's an awful feeling to get fired, but I was still young, and I was basically just getting going in this job. In hindsight, if I was going to continue in this job, I had to go somewhere else, get with other people. I was so committed to the Philadelphia Flyers that losing a game tore me apart and I couldn't do nothing about it and I didn't know how. I didn't know how to handle the job as the GM...and all of a sudden, I couldn't do anything. You try but you don't really know.

"After I got fired and went to Minnesota, I regrouped, reorganized in my own life. I didn't have to go to Minnesota; I could have decided I'll go somewhere else in my life. But once you make the decision that you're going to try and stay in the management end of the sport, I knew I had to change the way I lived, the way I treated it. I couldn't go on the way I was because it was killing me. I wasn't handling it the way you have to handle it if you're going to live in this world....There was no fun from a win, but there was hell from a loss, and you have to have a way better balance. You got to learn to find a way to get some pleasure from the good, and you're responsible for the bad, but you can't let the bad eat you up or you'll never survive. I'm not the only one who found that happening to them."

Clarke built a winner in Minnesota, as the North Stars reached the Stanley Cup Finals in his first season, and after a short return to Philadelphia, he spent 15 months building the expansion Florida Panthers.

He always stayed close to Ed Snider, though, and when the club missed the playoffs for a fifth straight season, in 1994, the owner decided changes were needed.

"He said, "Do you want to be the manager? I'm going to take over the club,'" Clarke recalls. "'We've struggled for a while, but I think you and I have been able to work together in the past, and I think we can again.'"

Clarke was comfortable in South Florida, but, "This is still Mr. Snider and still home."

On June 15, 1994, Ed Snider welcomed Bob Clarke back to the Philadelphia Flyers, naming him team president and general

## LICENSE PLATE

There are Flyers fans who go a little too far in their worship.

Jodi Clarke, Bob's daughter, recalls working at the Jersey Shore one summer as a teenager when she met an older man who worked in the same building. When he found out who her famous father was, he made a confession.

"He told me that when they won the Stanley Cup, he stole the license plates off my mom and dad's Corvettes," she said. "I went home and said, 'Mom, do you remember anyone stealing your license plates?' She said, 'Do I remember? They didn't just steal them once, they stole them three times.' Same guy. He said I found out where you lived and I kept stealing their license plates.

"I said [to my mom], 'You gotta come meet this guy who works in the building with me, he's the one who stole your license plates.' She couldn't understand why someone would keep stealing them. They weren't vanity plates, they were normal license plates."

## FARWELL SQUEEZED OUT

Bob Clarke was viewed as the savior when he replaced Russ Farwell as GM in 1994 and promptly got the team back to the playoffs in his first season.

A lot of the chips Clarke cashed, though, were won by Farwell.

Players Farwell acquired included Mark Recchi, Rod Brind'Amour, Mikael Renberg, Peter Forsberg and, of course, Eric Lindos.

"There were a lot of things building-wise that I'm not ashamed of, but we had four years out of the playoffs, and Jay's dad was most comfortable with Bob," Farwell says.

manager; he sweetened the deal by giving Clarke a small ownership stake.

"I'm hoping he once again leads us to the Promised Land," Snider said at a press conference.

As good as he was, Clarke was no Moses, and never led the Flyers to that hoped-for third Stanley Cup. But in his second, 12-year run as Flyers GM, there were a number of accomplishments and memorable moments.

He traded for John LeClair and Eric Desjardins, creating a core group that got the Flyers to the 1997 Stanley Cup Finals. He dealt for Keith Primeau, and watched Primeau nearly carry the team single-handedly to the 2004 Cup Finals. He signed stud free agents like Joel Otto, Jeremy Roenick, and Peter Forsberg.

His drafts, criticized in his first tenure with the Flyers, started becoming more productive as the team landed players like Brian Boucher, Dainius Zubrus, Simon Gagne, Antero Niittymaki, Justin Williams, Joni Pitkanen, Jeff Carter, and Mike Richards.

There were misses, like the misguided free-agent signing of Chris Gratton in 1997, the way he badly misread the change in the game coming out of the 2004–2005 lockout, and his bargain-basement shopping spree in the summer of 2006, which helped send the Flyers into the abyss of 2006–2007.

There was the coaching carousel—he went through Terry Murray, Wayne Cashman, Roger Neilson, Craig Ramsay, Bill Barber, and Ken Hitchcock in 12 seasons, with only Murray and Hitchcock last more than two full seasons—as well as the franchise-engulfing Eric Lindros soap opera.

But when his 12-year run ended October 22, 2006, the good far outweighed the bad. There were five division titles, four trips to the conference final, and the 1997 Eastern Conference title.

"I don't think Bob Clarke has done a perfect job, but I don't know any general manager who has," said Ed Snider. "I'm sure Bob would like to take back some of the decisions he made. Maybe he wasn't the greatest at picking coaches. But we were always competitive. We were always in the top level of the league under his stewardship."

In 17 full seasons (not counting the 2004–2005 lockout, or his aborted stint in 2006–2007), his Flyers teams went to the playoffs 16 times, played for the conference title seven times, and made three Stanley Cup Finals.

But there was just one thing missing.

"I deeply regret not bringing a Stanley Cup here," Clarke said the day he retired from the GM post. "We got there a few times, but we couldn't close."

## FAMILY BONDS

Traditionally, the shelf life of an NHL player is not a long one. Most players come into the league in their early twenties, and by their mid- to late thirties, it's time to start looking for another occupation. When that time comes, some organizations will thank a player for his service, wish him luck, and tell not to let the door him in the back on the way out.

And then there are the Flyers.

"I have a special affection for most players," says team chairman Ed Snider. "Hockey is a rough sport. If I have the opportunity to give back, then I will."

And Snider has spent more than 40 years giving back to his players.

# BOB THE BUILDER

Can he build it? Yes he can.

Bob Clarke's legacy as a team-builder is borne out not just by his success with the Flyers, but by his record with other organizations.

After being fired by the Flyers in 1990, he took the GM post for the Minnesota North Stars; in his first season, the team went to the 1991 Stanley Cup Finals.

In 1993 he signed on to run the expansion Florida Panthers, and though he stayed just 15 months before returning to the Flyers, the team recorded the best-ever debut season for an expansion team and played for the Stanley Cup in 1996, featuring a number of players he had acquired.

"They've always said the Flyers are like family," said current head coach and former player John Stevens. "Some places try to say that, but here it truly is."

Stevens isn't alone as a former Flyer working in the organization. The club's front-office depth-chart reads like an all-time roster—general manager Paul Holmgren; senior vice president Bob Clarke; director of player personnel Dave Brown; assistant coaches Jack McIlhargey and Craig Berube; goaltending coach Reggie Lemelin; player development coach Eric Dessardins; Phantoms coaches John Paddock, Kjell Samuelsson, and Neil Little; amateur scouts Dennis Patterson, Ilkka Sinisalo, Mark Greig, and Simon Nolet, who was one of the original Flyers; and pro scouts Al Hill and Ross Fitzpatrick. That list doesn't include Ron Hextall and Bill Barber, who got their front office starts in Philadelphia before moving elsewhere.

But former players aren't just given those traditional post-playing jobs or hired for glamorous broadcasting posts like Keith Jones, Chris Therien, or Brian Propp. Bob Kelly works in community relations, as do Bernie Parent and Gary Dornhoefer. And Joe Watson is a senior account executive, selling tickets not just for the Flyers, but for all events at the Wachovia Center.

"I could get my foot in the door where a lot of salesman couldn't because of who I was," Watson said in *Walking Together Forever*.

"It worked out very well because people wanted to talk hockey and talk sports, and that was one thing I was always good at."

"These guys earn their living," says Snider. "They do a good job, they work hard. There's not one guy that we've given a job to that we don't feel has done the job."

"It's a loyalty," says former Flyers captain Keith Primeau. "That's why historically [the Flyers] are recognized as such a great organization. Mr. Snider doesn't have to do that. He could say you served your purpose, now go out in the real world and find something else to pay your bills. He doesn't. He recognizes and appreciates the effort these guys have put in for him in the past and is willing to say, 'Whatever the cost it is to me, it's such a menial cost for what [the players] have brought.' And that's why he's such a great man and why he's so well respected by his players."

"Organization-wise, the way the Sniders run the Flyers, it's absolutely first-class," adds Tim Kerr. "The loyalty has always gone both ways. You're always treated first-class, [and] players give that back. It's got to be one of the greatest organizations in sports. They were always there for the players and their families. I don't think there's a better organization to play for than the Flyers."

Those outside the team recognize it, also.

Says Howard Eskin, the WIP radio host who has covered Philadelphia sports since the 1970s, says, "[Ed] Snider is as loyal a person as you'll ever see and meet."

Agents, those trying to reach deep into Snider's pockets, also respect the man.

"The general impression of Mr. Snider is someone who has presence, someone who you can't help but respect," says Rick Curran, an agent based in the Philadelphia suburb of Devon, Pennsylvania, who has represented a number of Flyers players over the years. "You don't always agree with him, but he always has the right intentions with his organization and fan base."

Loyalty is a hallmark of the Flyers organization, and the Flyers' family is a very real concept. It's not just former players working for the team; Jody Clarke, Bob's daughter, works as a receptionist at the Flyers' practice site in Voorhees. A son, Luke, works as an equipment manager, while another, Wade, is a scout;

Lauren Hart, daughter of the late Gene Hart, the team's legendary broadcaster, has sung the National Anthem before every home game since 1997; Mary Ann Saleski, wife of former Flyer Don Saleski, is the senior vice president of the Comcast-Spectacor Foundation and the Flyers charities.

"I don't think I know what it's like not to feel like that," JodyClarke said of the warm embrace of the Flyers family. "It's all I've ever known. They've treated us like family, and in return my dad has treated other alumni like family. I guess the difference being when my dad did work for Minnesota and Florida, it wasn't true. They didn't have that atmosphere. Not for their players, not for their staff, not for their alumni."

"It's still a business," said Brian Hart, Gene's son, who remains in contact with the team, "and in the end people are let go and guys are traded, but it just operates differently. People are connected to each other, differently than other Philadelphia teams, different than other hockey teams. People know it's a good organization to work for. You're treated well and treated with respect. They try to accommodate players as much as they can. And not just the players—everybody."

"I've always considered, and will continue to consider the Philadelphia Flyers as one of those teams you can't help but have the utmost respect for, in terms of the organization, in terms of the people, in terms of the way they handle things," says Curran. "They're not beyond making mistakes, but more often than not, it's a mistake through a genuine effort to be better as a hockey club, a genuine effort to give the people of Philadelphia a winning team."

Ed Snider may be the patriarch of the Flyers' family, but few have done more to foster the organization-wide family feeling than Bob Clarke.

From the outside, Clarke may seem like an iron-fisted dictator, but players knew he cared about them as people, not as cattle easily herded in and out of uniforms.

Clarke's loyalty to his players knew few bounds. After suffering his third concussion in 20 months in October 2005, Clarke helped Keith Primeau find the best doctors during his attempted recovery, and never once forced him to make a decision on continuing his career. He paid for Peter Forsberg to go through more than 50 pairs of skates during the 2005–2006 season in his quest to find a pair that felt comfortable on his chronically sore feet, and when that didn't work, he had the club foot the bill for extensive, risky foot surgery.

While those are examples with two very prominent players, Clarke's loyalty extended to every member of the Flyers family.

"I'm grateful for what he did for me," says Kjell Samuelson. The defenseman was a member of the 1987 Stanley Cup team, and had two different stints with the Flyers covering nine seasons in black and orange. "He traded for me from New York [Rangers], and that's the best thing that happened to me in my hockey career. I went to Pittsburgh for three years, and he signed me again as a free agent. Then he brought me back to work in the organization as a coach."

Dave Brown spent 11 of his 14 NHL seasons in Philadelphia. Clarke hired Brown as an assistant coach in 1996, and hired him again as director of player personnel in 2006.

"I've been lucky in that the Flyers have been good to me," he says. "They do have a lot of people from the past in the organization, but I like the idea that you have some type of history with the organization. I think that's important. You have to grasp onto what was built there before you. The early days for me, when I came in, it was like I had to carry on what was there before me."

That list also includes Stevens. Before coaching, he was playing for the Philadelphia Phantoms in December 1998 when he was hit in the right eye by a puck. Bones were crushed, his retina became detached, and his vision was permanently impaired. Just like that, his career was over, just 25 games into his 15th pro season.

"When I got hurt, it was a pretty traumatic thing," he says. "I was dealing with a pretty serious injury that can affect you long after your playing days are over. He [Clarke] just called right away and said, 'We'd like to maintain you as an assistant coach and get you involved in that end of it and make the transition.'

"When something like that [the injury] happens, you always wonder what's next. For him to take the time to put everything at ease, to know that you can continue in a new aspect of the game and not have this big transition thing with what you're going to do, is very helpful for my wife and very exciting for me. It certainly helped me get over what I was going through."

Stevens served as an assistant coach with the Phantoms under Barber for one season, and moved up a spot when Barber shifted to the Flyers. Dealing with Clarke on a more direct basis, Stevens saw just how few bounds Clarke's loyalty knew.

"We've had older players in the minors that had severe injuries in the last years of their contracts, and he's extended them based on character, maybe knowing they might have a tough time getting another job right away," he says. "But because their service was strong here, I think he puts a lot of onus on the character and loyalty of the players, and he rewards that.

"Guys are on the road, guys' wives are having babies. Joey Hope called me at 2:00 in the morning, his wife was having a baby. We got him on a plane the next morning, got him home so he could witness the birth of his child. I'm not sure that stuff goes on everywhere, but they certainly make it happen here. They think beyond the hockey. They treat people like people here, players like people. I think that's why they're so well-respected and that's why people love playing here."

And Stevens says his eye injury wasn't the first time Clarke and the organization helped him. A 1984 Flyers draft pick, Stevens spent six seasons with the Hartford Whalers organization, but gladly returned to Philadelphia in 1996. He wasn't back long when tragedy struck.

"My mom had a heart attack when I played for the Phantoms," he says. "They flew me and my family home at 6:00 AM the next morning. This was my first year back, 1996–1997. They didn't even bat an eyelash."

Bob Kelly, who was drafted the same year as Clarke and was a major part of the two Cup winners, was another player who witnessed Flyers loyalty first-hand. Kelly spent 10 years with the club before he was traded to the Washington Capitals in August

**After playing the majority of his career in Philadelphia, Bob Kelly returned there to retire and became a team ambassador in 2003.**

1980. He spent of two seasons in Washington before retiring. He could have gone anywhere, lived anyplace he wanted. But there was only one kennel the Hound could call home.

"When I got traded away at the end, I never sold my home," he says. "This is my roots. I've been to all the different cities throughout North America; everybody has a different hockey atmosphere. But here, we're so close to everything. Had we not won two Cups, maybe I'd be just another guy, but because we won the two Cups, it was 2 million people bonding here. Going home to Canada was not an option. It's awesome down here."

After ups and downs in a few different business ventures, Kelly returned to the Flyers in 2003 as a team ambassador. It's far from a ceremonial position. Kelly meets more people than a fleet of Wal-Mart greeters. He's all over the Wachovia Center before and during most home games, talking to fans, shaking hands, and posing for pictures. And when there are no games, Kelly takes his show on the road throughout the Delaware Valley, heading the club's "Hooked on Hockey" scholastic program. He leads youth hockey clinics at ice rinks throughout the area, and he makes appearances at hospitals, golf outings, and all sorts of other public events.

"Dave Coskey [former president of Comcast-Spectacor marketing] asked me to come back and be the white World B. Free," Kelly says, equating himself to the former Philadelphia 76ers player who holds a similar position with the city's basketball team. "I'm not allergic to work."

"In my mind, I represent the Flyers and Comcast-Spectacor," Kelly said in *Walking Together Forever*. "It's certainly not a job where I shuffle papers. I am expected to be out and about. I'm getting a chance to do things with kids, go to hospitals, to do clinics, whether it be roller hockey or street hockey, or I can do meet-and-greets. I'm thankful to have a job with this organization and do my best for them."

The Flyers family won't hesitate to wrap its arms around a person. And in return, those people have shown the same loyalty in return.

"This is a first-rate organization," says Primeau, who has made Voorhees the permanent residence for his family. "It's run first-class. They treat their players as good as, or better than, any other organization, not just in professional hockey, but in professional sports."

"They [the Flyers] are very demanding," says Stevens, "but they're very fair and they treat you with great respect and they take care of you while you're here. I think that's all anybody can ask for. I think you get treated better here than anywhere else."